TRANS-METRO-POLITAN:

THE NEW SCUM

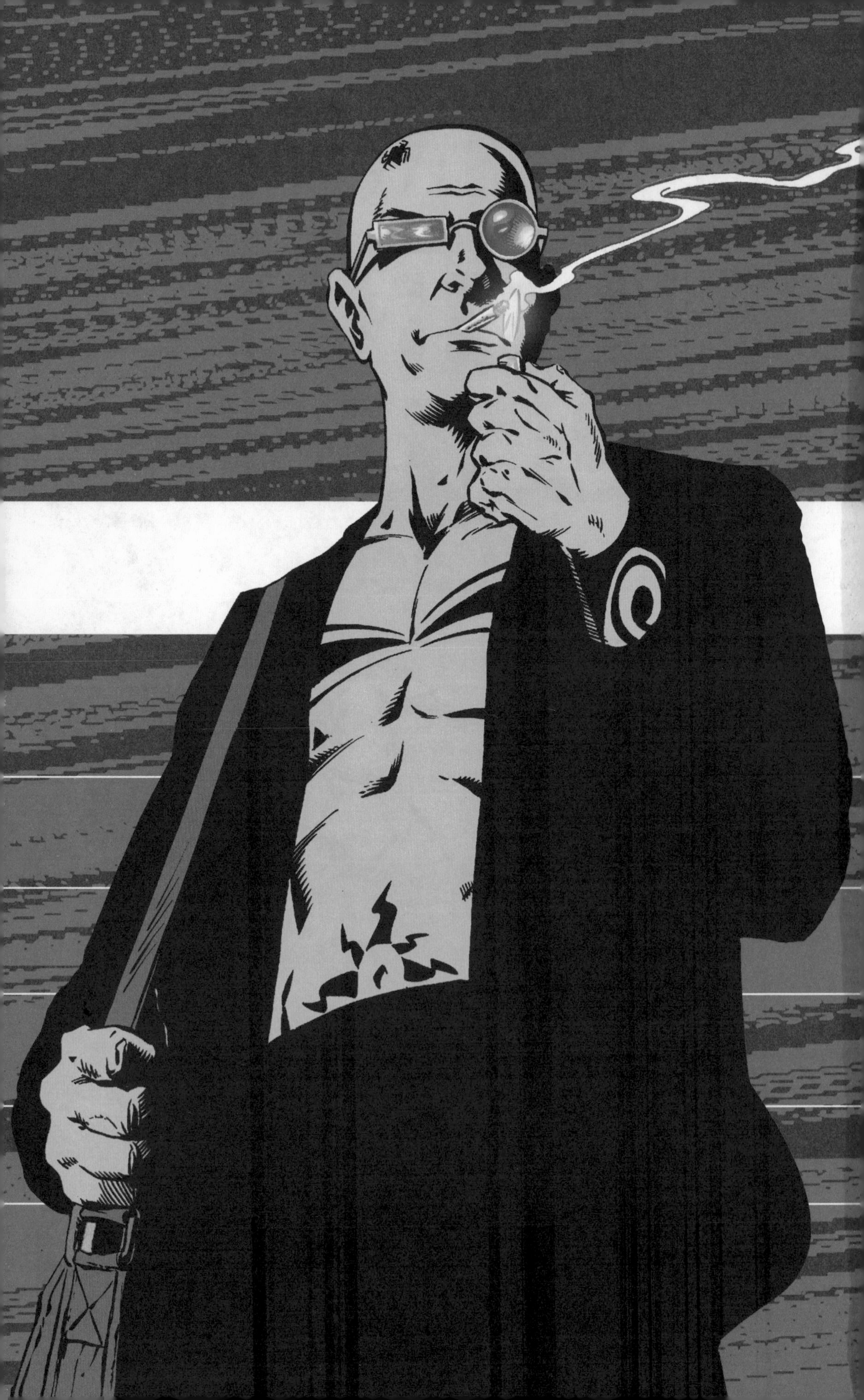

TRANS-METRO-POLITAN:

THE NEW SCUM

Warren_Ellis
Writer

Darick_Robertson
Penciller

Rodney_Ramos
Keith_Aiken
Inkers

Nathan_Eyring
Colorist

Clem_Robins
Letterer

Darick_Robertson (#19-21)
Geof _Darrow (#22-24)
Original Series Covers

TRANSMETROPOLITAN created by
Warren_Ellis and Darick_Robertson

Karen Berger SVP – Executive Editor Stuart Moore Shelly Roeberg Editors – Original Series Cliff Chiang Jennifer Lee Assistant
Editors – Original Series Georg Brewer VP – Design & DC Direct Creative Bob Harras Group Editor – Collected Editions
Scott Nybakken Editor Robbin Brosterman Design Director – Books Curtis King Senior Art Director

DC COMICS

Paul Levitz President & Publisher Richard Bruning SVP – Creative Director Patrick Caldon EVP – Finance & Operations
Amy Genkins SVP – Business & Legal Affairs Jim Lee Editorial Director – WildStorm Gregory Noveck SVP – Creative Affairs
Steve Rotterdam SVP – Sales & Marketing Cheryl Rubin SVP – Brand Management

Cover art by Geof Darrow.
Publication design by Ternard Solomon

TRANSMETROPOLITAN: THE NEW SCUM

Published by DC Comics. Cover and compilation Copyright © 2009 DC Comics. All Rights Reserved.

Originally published in single magazine form in TRANSMETROPOLITAN 19-24 and VERTIGO: WINTER'S EDGE 2-3. Copyright © 1999,
2000 Warren Ellis and Darick Robertson. All Rights Reserved. All characters, their distinctive likenesses and related indicia featured in
this publication are trademarks of Warren Ellis and Darick Robertson. VERTIGO is a trademark of DC Comics. The stories, characters
and incidents featured in this publication are entirely fictional. DC Comics does not read or accept unsolicited submissions of ideas,
stories or artwork.

DC Comics, 1700 Broadway, New York, NY 10019. A Warner Bros. Entertainment Company. Printed in Canada. First Printing.

ISBN: 978-1-4012-2490-5

SUSTAINABLE
FORESTRY
INITIATIVE

Certified Fiber
Sourcing
www.sfiprogram.org

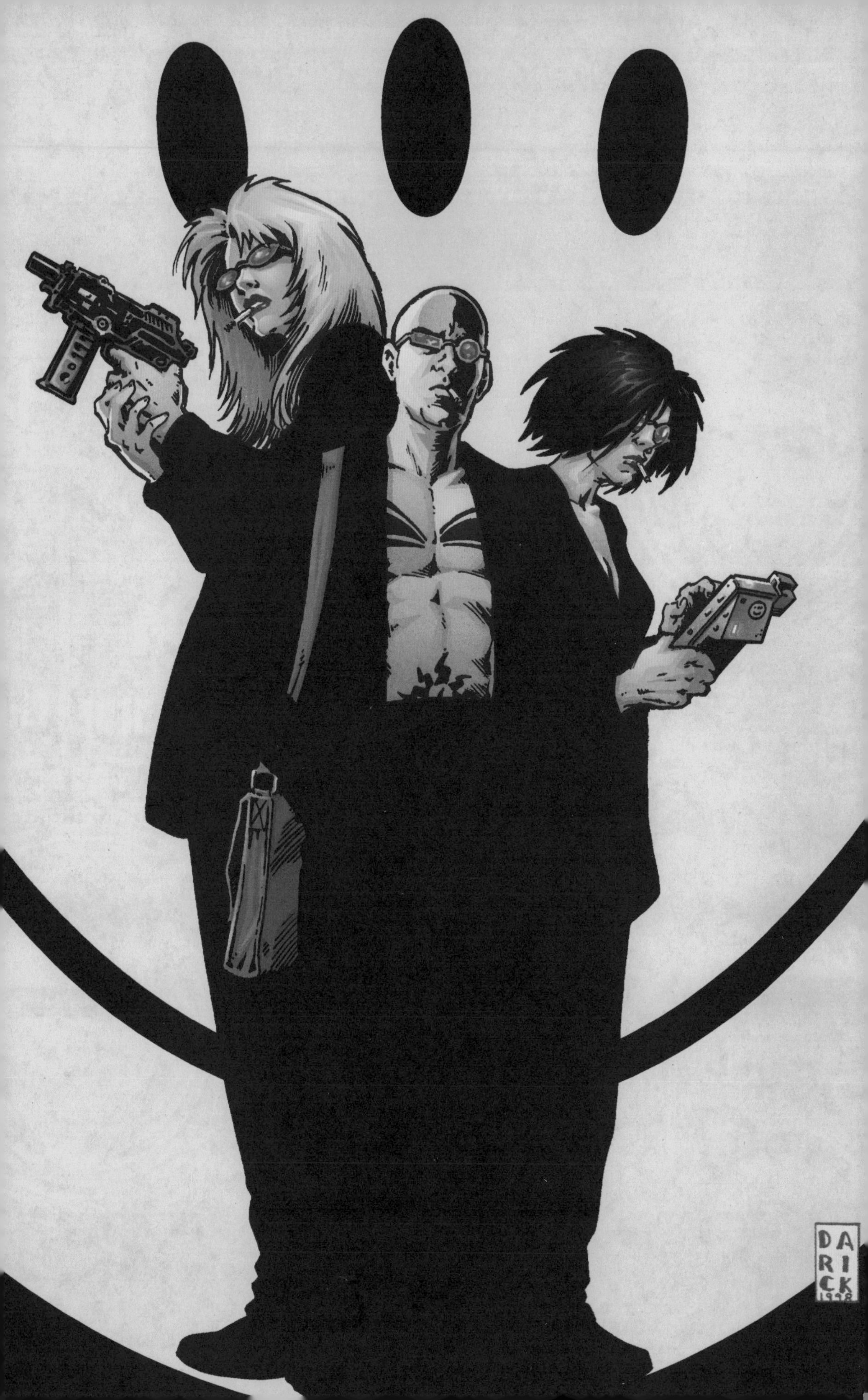
DARICK
1998

WARREN ELLIS writes and DARICK ROBERTSON pencils

THE NEW SCUM

one: NEW HOME

RODNEY RAMOS inker | NATHAN EYRING color&separations | CLEM ROBINS letterer | CLIFF CHIANG assistant editor | STUART MOORE editor

TRANSMETROPOLITAN CREATED BY WARREN ELLIS & DARICK ROBERTSON

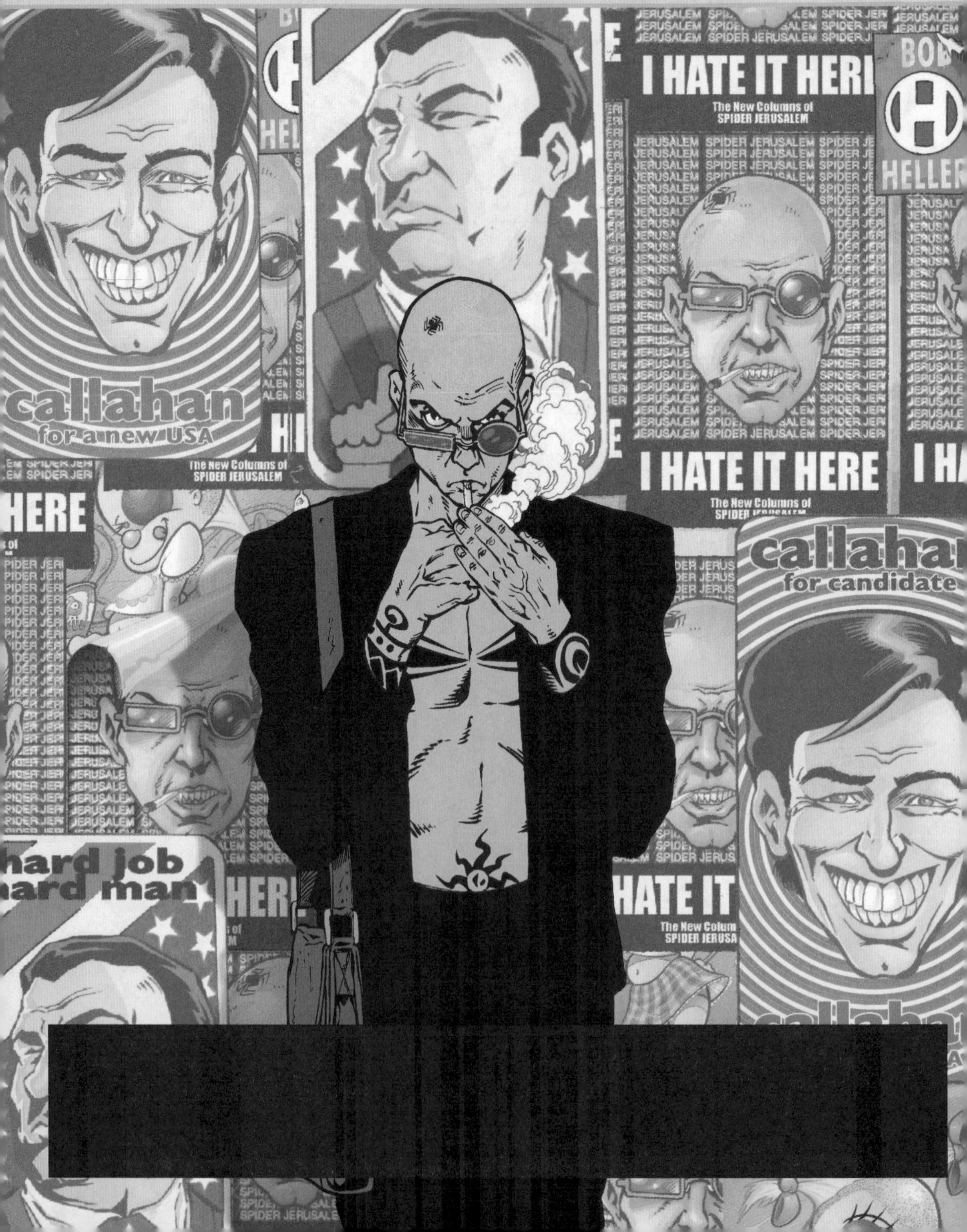

I HATE IT HERE
The New Columns of
SPIDER JERUSALEM
callahan
for a new USA
The New Columns of
SPIDER JERUSALEM
I HATE IT HERE
callahan
for candidate
hard job
hard man
HELLER

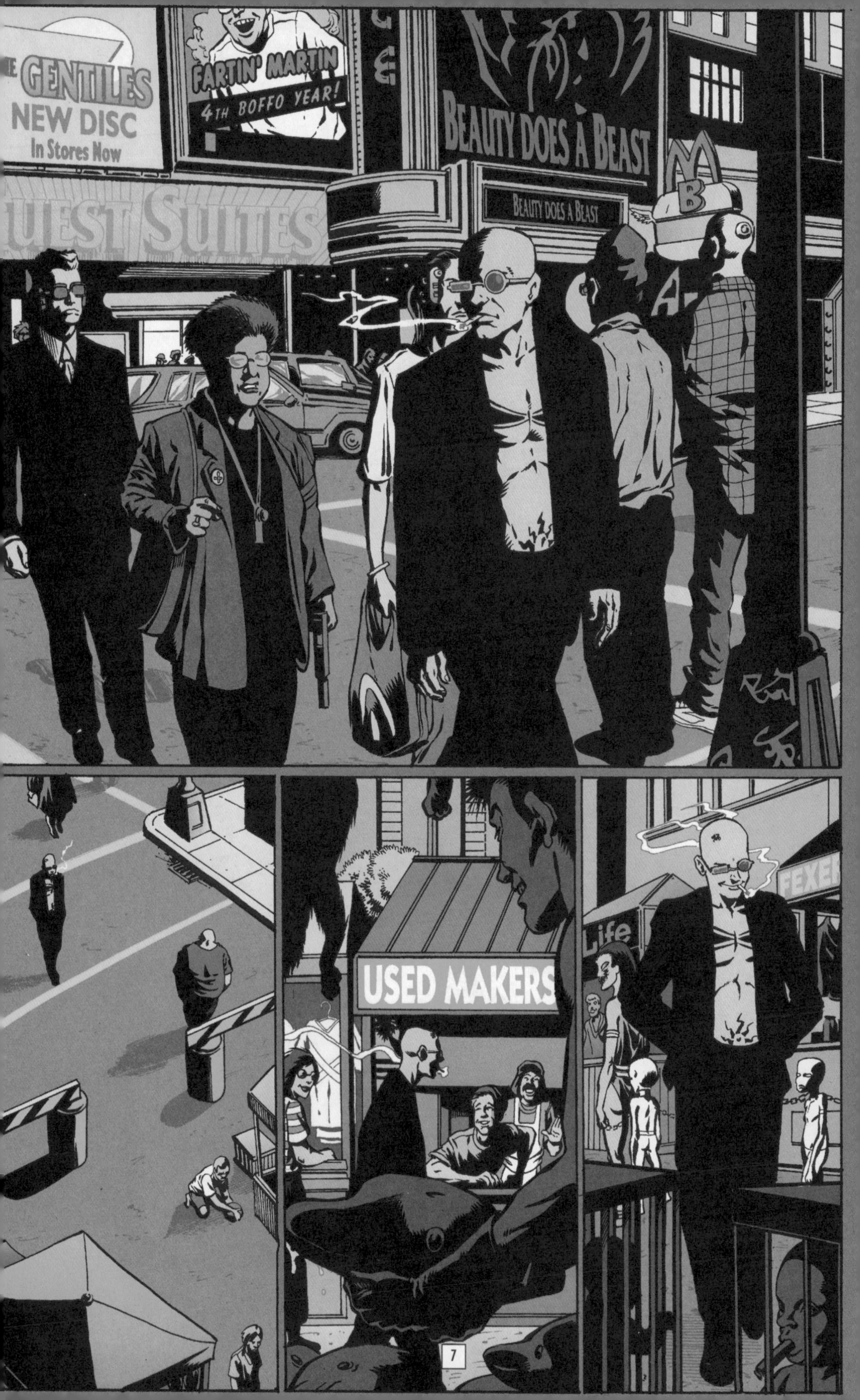
GENTILES
NEW DISC
In Stores Now
FARTIN' MARTIN
4TH BOFFO YEAR!
BEAUTY DOES A BEAST
BEAUTY DOES A BEAST
UEST SUITES
USED MAKERS
Life
FEXE

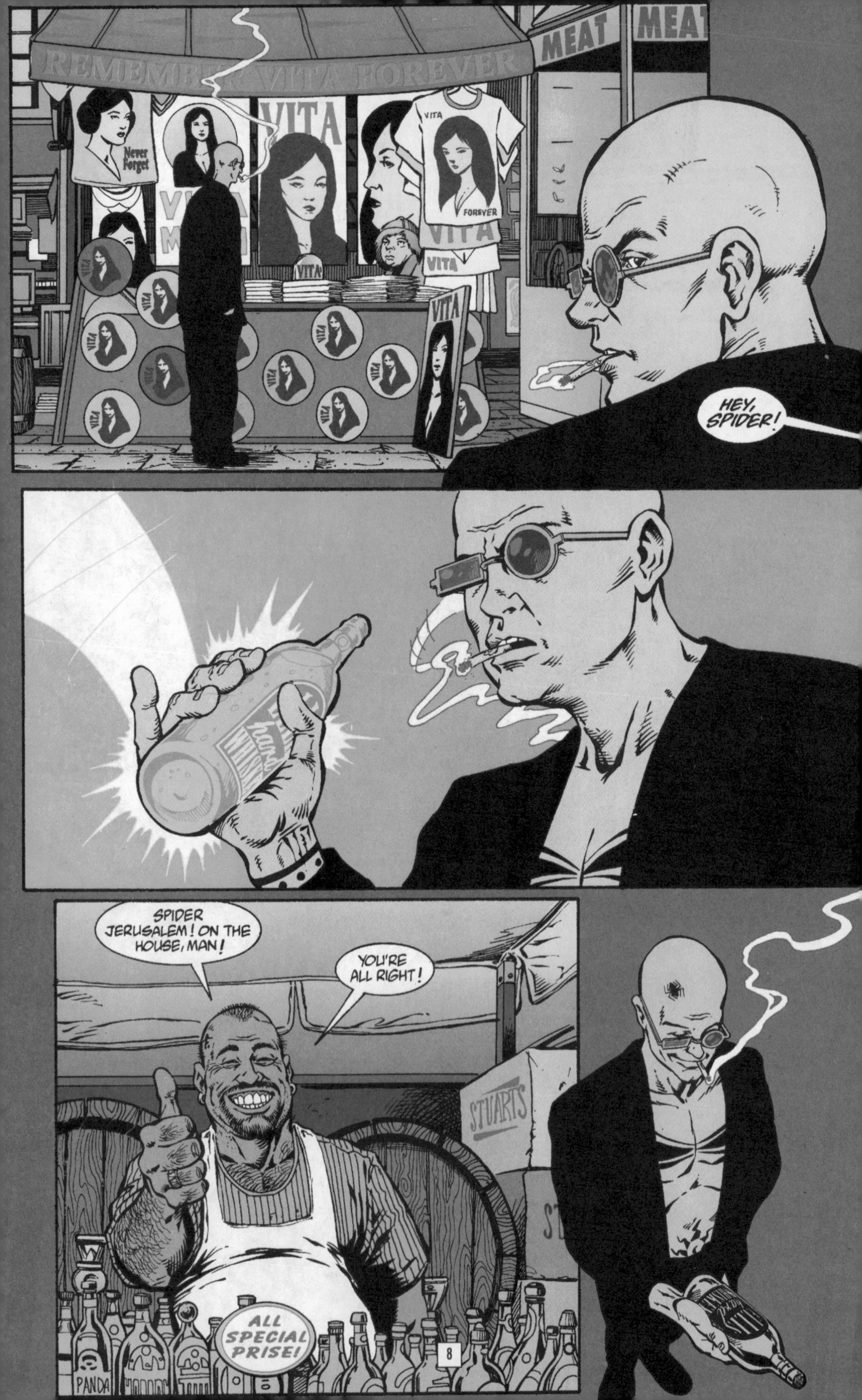
REMEMBER VITA FOREVER
MEAT
MEAT
VITA
Never Forget
VITA
FOREVER
VITA
HEY, SPIDER!
SPIDER JERUSALEM! ON THE HOUSE, MAN!
YOU'RE ALL RIGHT!
STUARTS
ALL SPECIAL PRISE!
PANDA

YOU RULE, MAN! YOU'RE GOD!
JESUS LOVE YOU AND KEEP YOU, SPIDER.
fresh
We need a voice, they say. That's all. We're sick of your hate, and we don't need your pity. We need a VOICE.

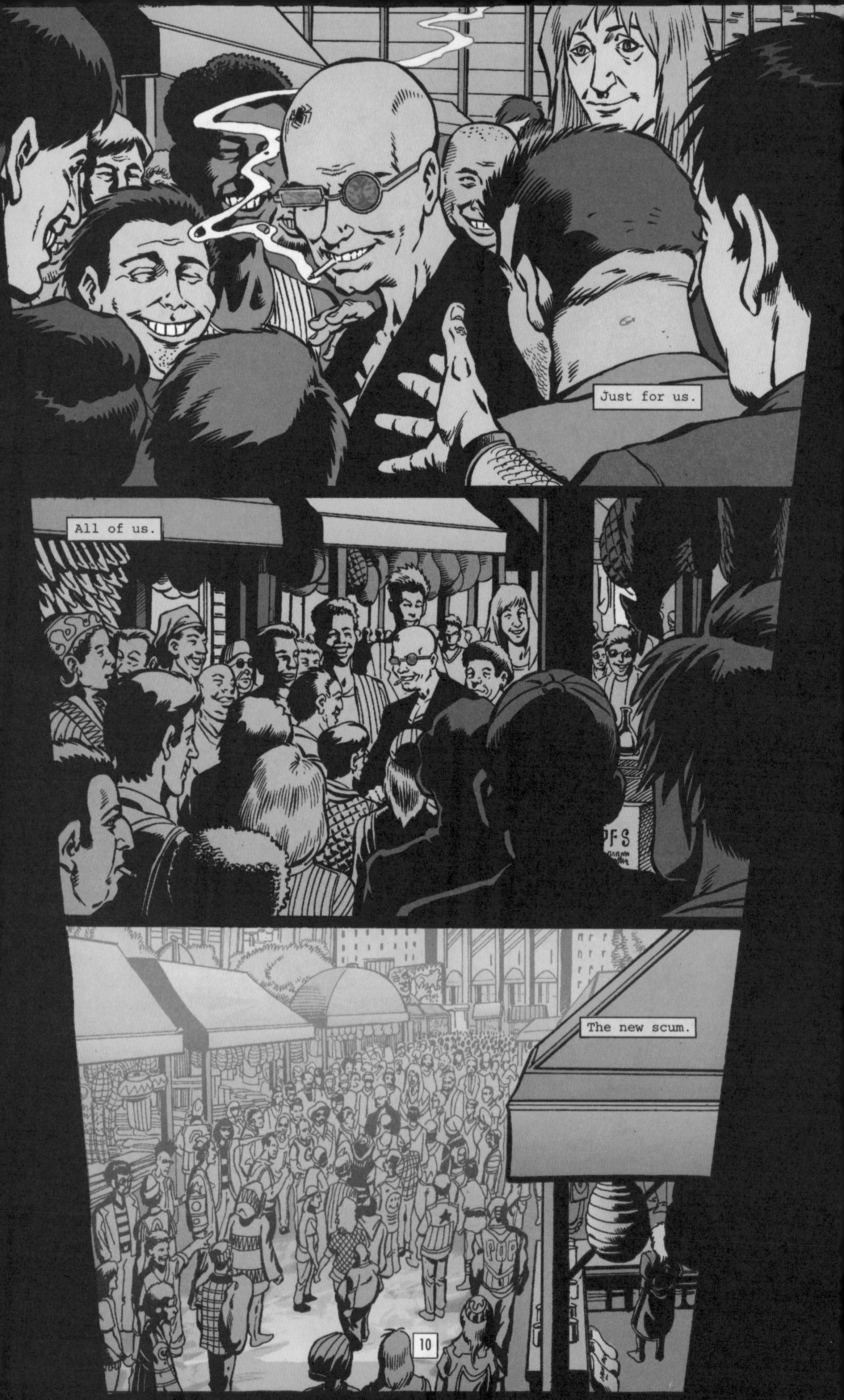
Just for us.
All of us.
The new scum.

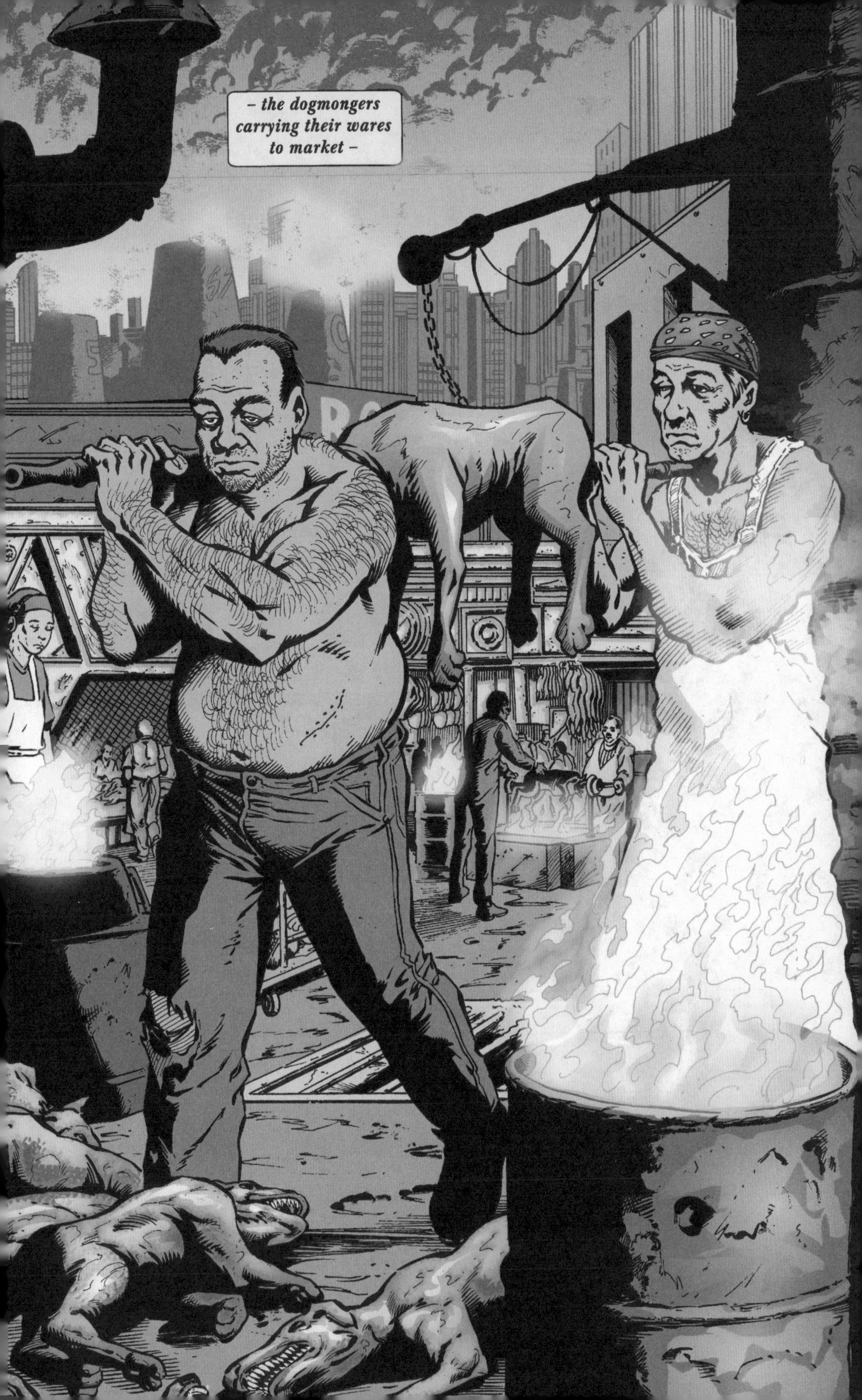
– the dogmongers carrying their wares to market –

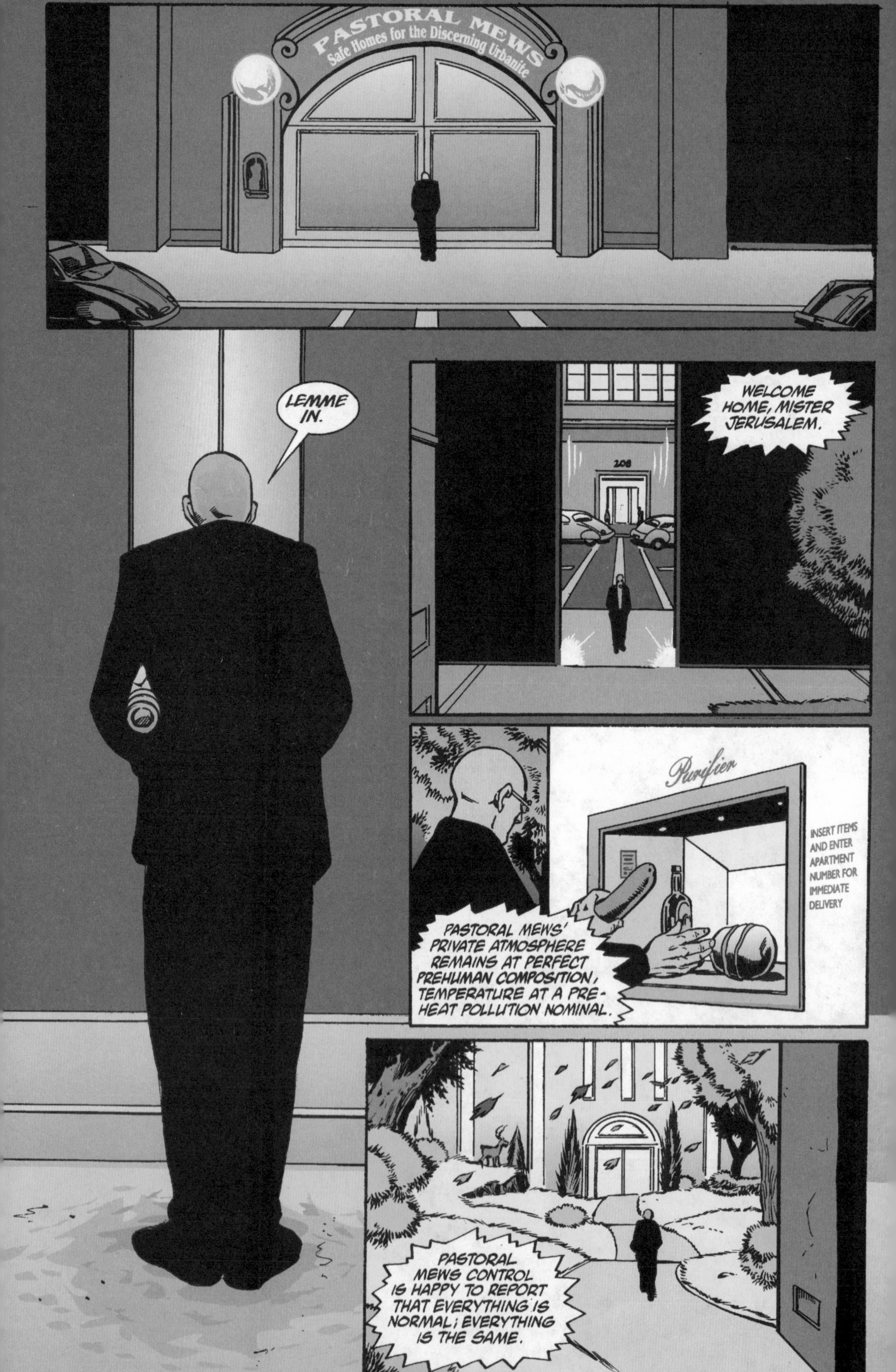
PASTORAL MEWS
Safe Homes for the Discerning Urbanite
LEMME IN.
WELCOME HOME, MISTER JERUSALEM.
206
Purifier
INSERT ITEMS AND ENTER APARTMENT NUMBER FOR IMMEDIATE DELIVERY
PASTORAL MEWS' PRIVATE ATMOSPHERE REMAINS AT PERFECT PREHUMAN COMPOSITION, TEMPERATURE AT A PRE-HEAT POLLUTION NOMINAL.
PASTORAL MEWS CONTROL IS HAPPY TO REPORT THAT EVERYTHING IS NORMAL; EVERYTHING IS THE SAME.

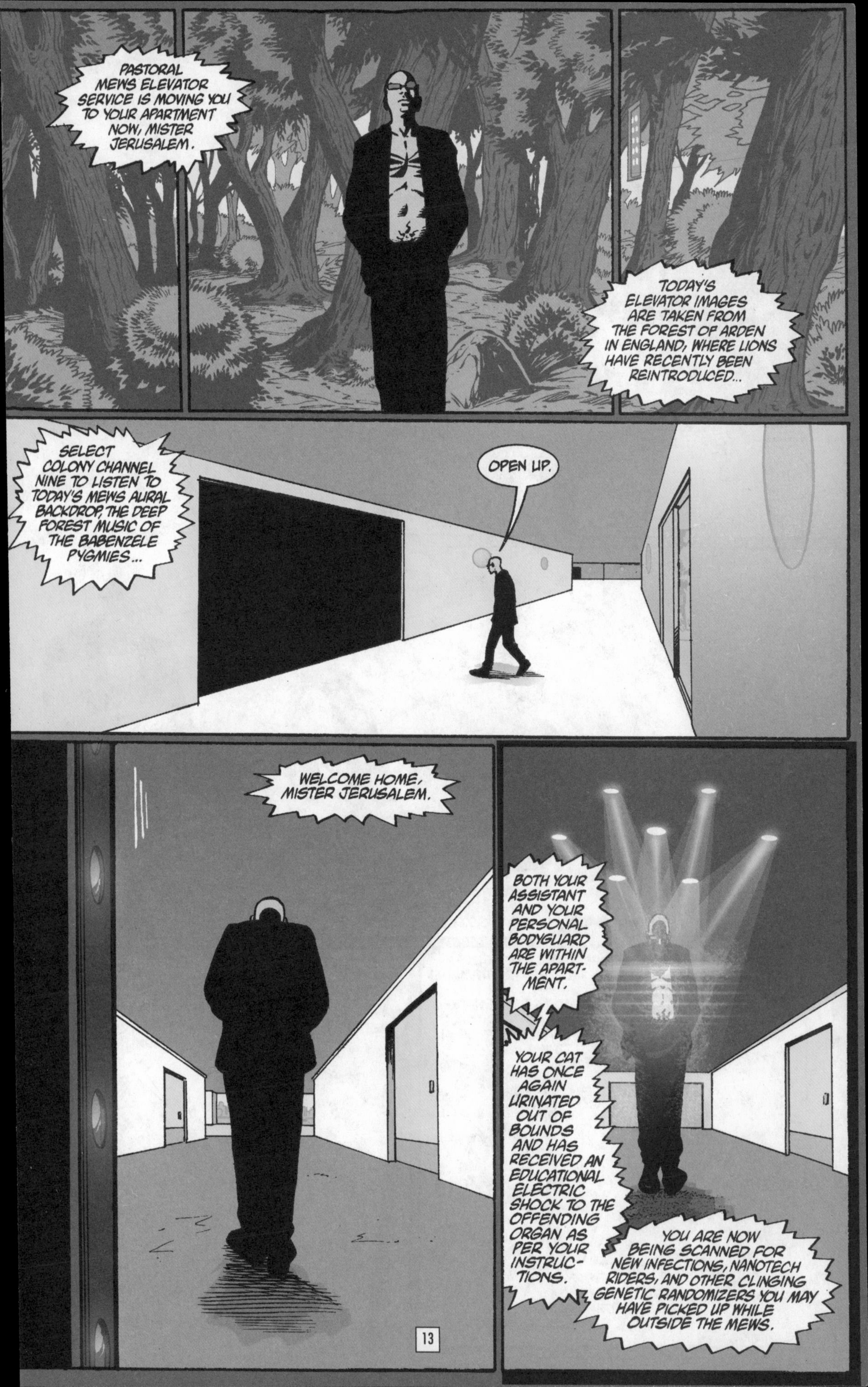
PASTORAL MEWS ELEVATOR SERVICE IS MOVING YOU TO YOUR APARTMENT NOW, MISTER JERUSALEM.
TODAY'S ELEVATOR IMAGES ARE TAKEN FROM THE FOREST OF ARDEN IN ENGLAND, WHERE LIONS HAVE RECENTLY BEEN REINTRODUCED...
SELECT COLONY CHANNEL NINE TO LISTEN TO TODAY'S MEWS AURAL BACKDROP, THE DEEP FOREST MUSIC OF THE BABENZELE PYGMIES...
OPEN UP.
WELCOME HOME, MISTER JERUSALEM.
BOTH YOUR ASSISTANT AND YOUR PERSONAL BODYGUARD ARE WITHIN THE APART-MENT.
YOUR CAT HAS ONCE AGAIN URINATED OUT OF BOUNDS AND HAS RECEIVED AN EDUCATIONAL ELECTRIC SHOCK TO THE OFFENDING ORGAN AS PER YOUR INSTRUC-TIONS.
YOU ARE NOW BEING SCANNED FOR NEW INFECTIONS, NANOTECH RIDERS, AND OTHER CLINGING GENETIC RANDOMIZERS YOU MAY HAVE PICKED UP WHILE OUTSIDE THE MEWS.

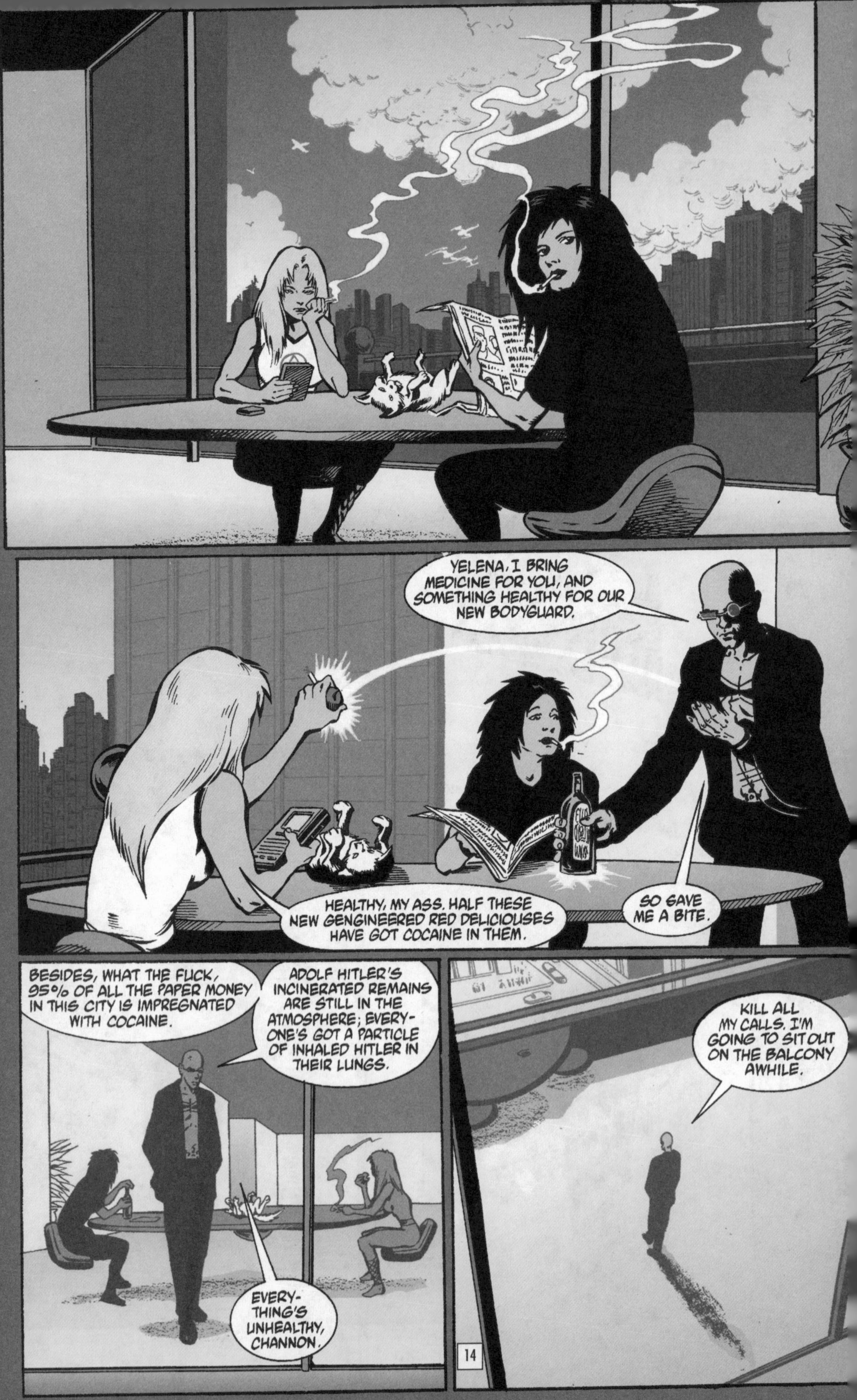
YELENA, I BRING MEDICINE FOR YOU, AND SOMETHING HEALTHY FOR OUR NEW BODYGUARD.
HEALTHY, MY ASS. HALF THESE NEW GENGINEERED RED DELICIOUSES HAVE GOT COCAINE IN THEM.
SO SAVE ME A BITE.
BESIDES, WHAT THE FUCK, 95% OF ALL THE PAPER MONEY IN THIS CITY IS IMPREGNATED WITH COCAINE.
ADOLF HITLER'S INCINERATED REMAINS ARE STILL IN THE ATMOSPHERE; EVERYONE'S GOT A PARTICLE OF INHALED HITLER IN THEIR LUNGS.
EVERYTHING'S UNHEALTHY, CHANNON.
KILL ALL MY CALLS. I'M GOING TO SIT OUT ON THE BALCONY AWHILE.

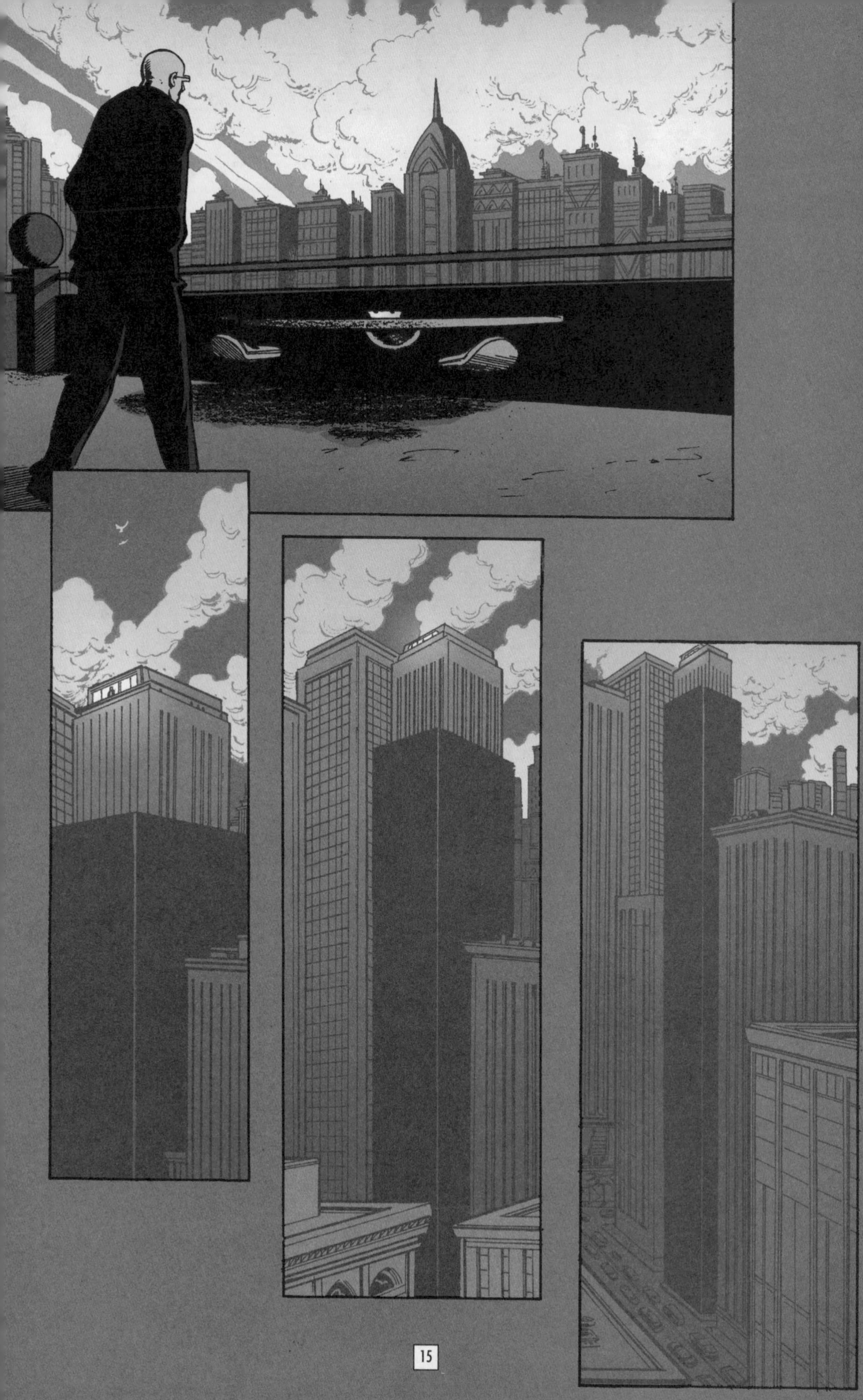

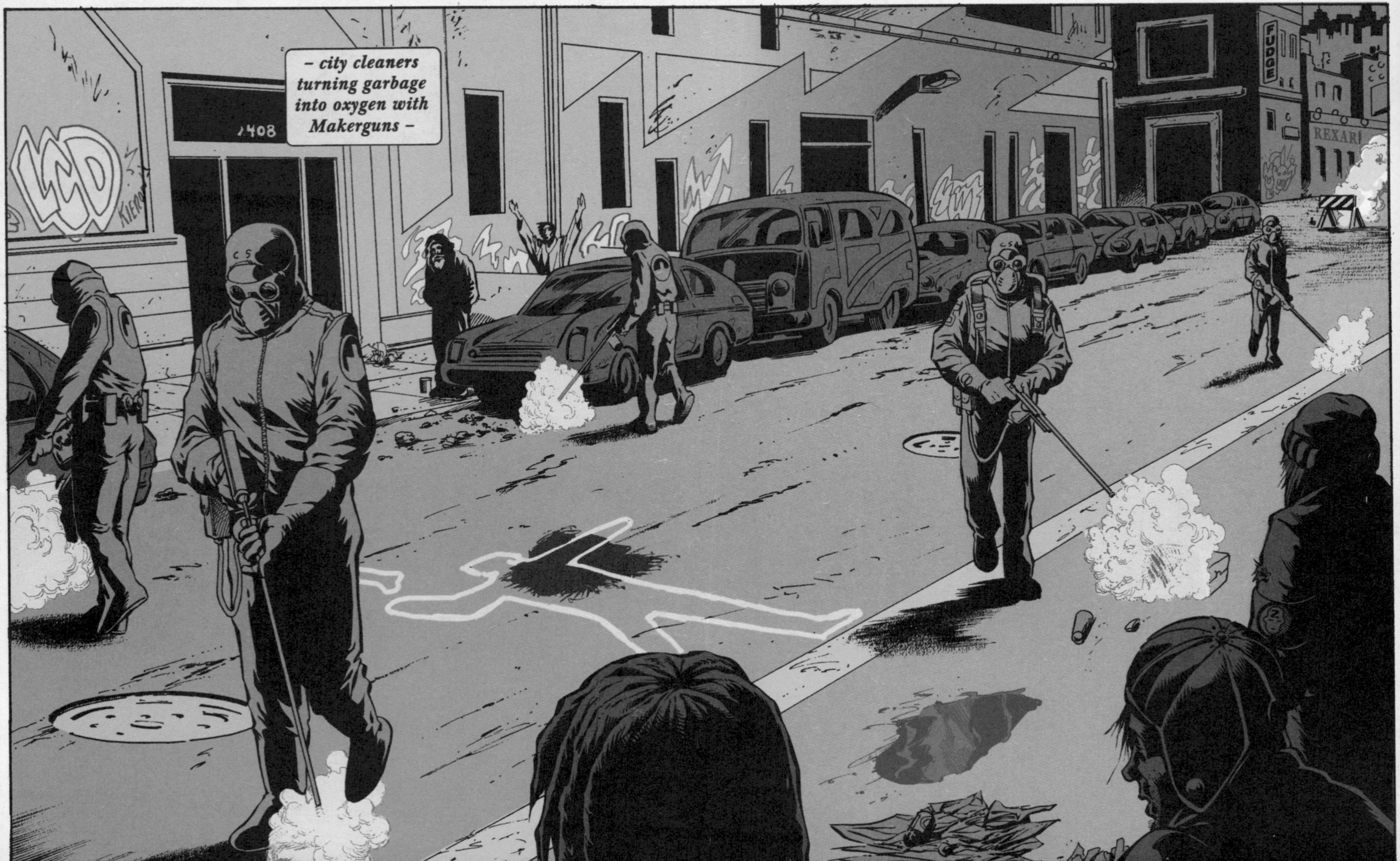
– city cleaners turning garbage into oxygen with Makerguns –
1408
LCD
FUDGE
REXAR

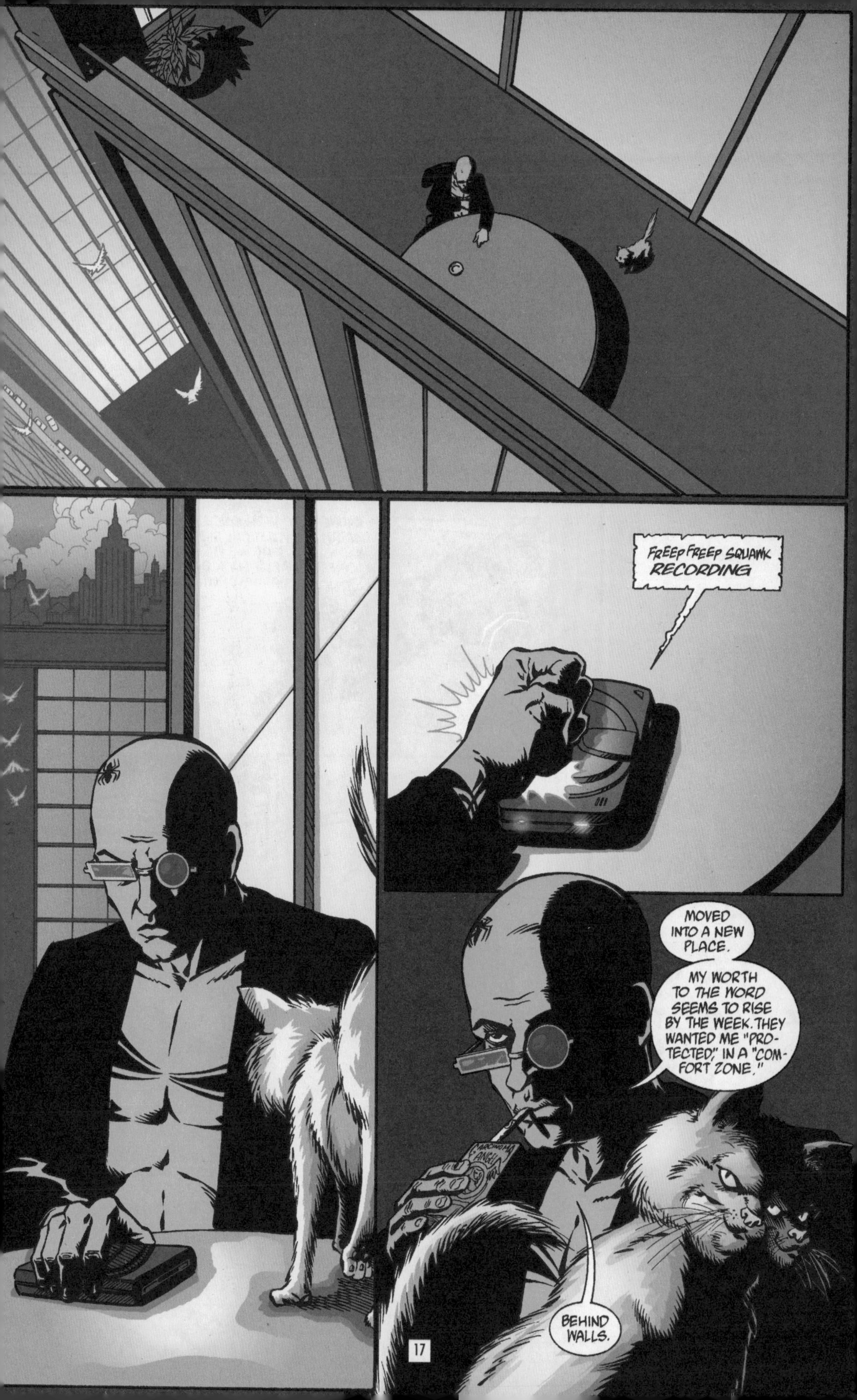
FREEP FREEP SQUAWK RECORDING
MOVED INTO A NEW PLACE.
MY WORTH TO THE WORD SEEMS TO RISE BY THE WEEK. THEY WANTED ME "PROTECTED," IN A "COMFORT ZONE."
BEHIND WALLS.

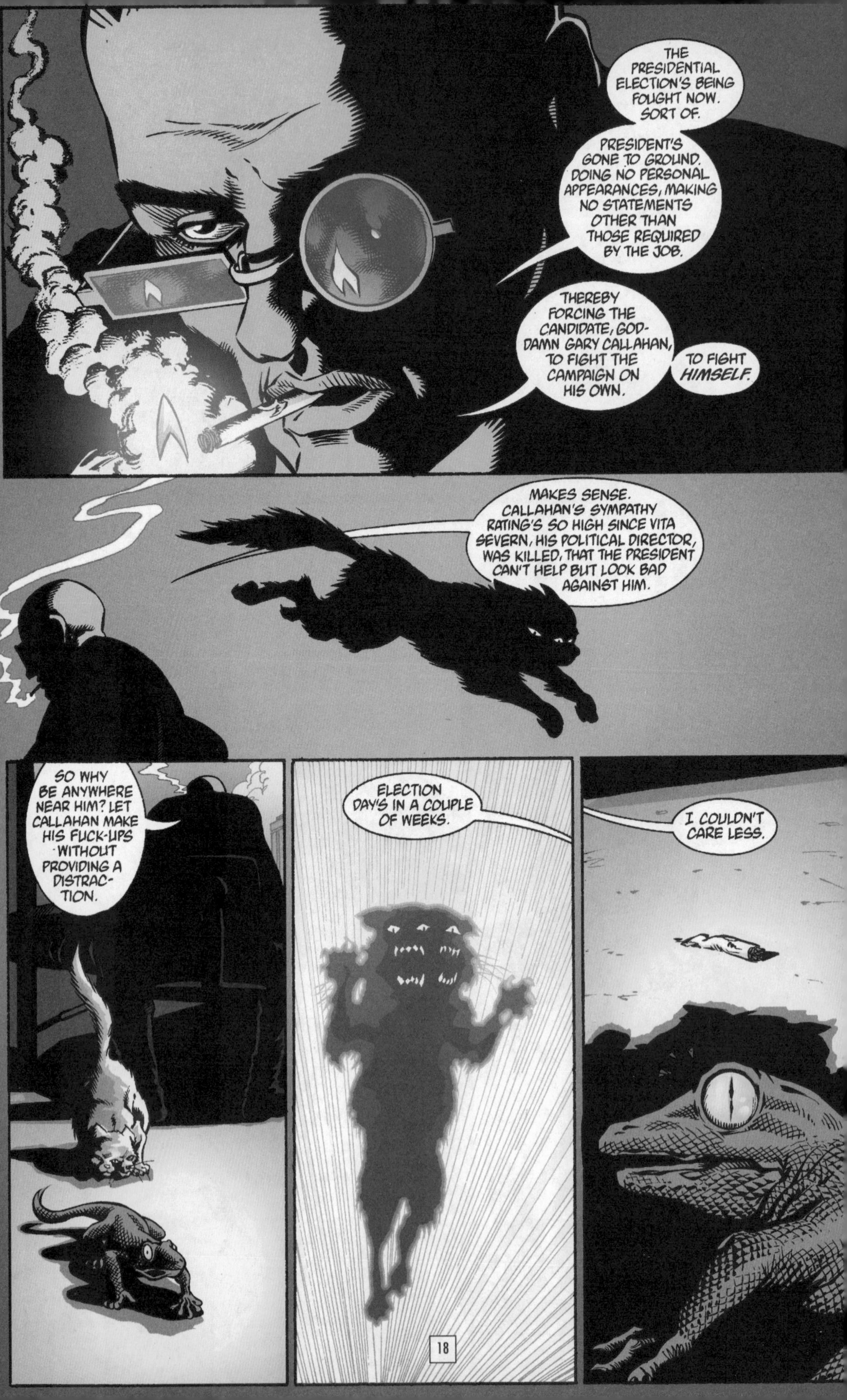
THE PRESIDENTIAL ELECTION'S BEING FOUGHT NOW. SORT OF.
PRESIDENT'S GONE TO GROUND. DOING NO PERSONAL APPEARANCES, MAKING NO STATEMENTS OTHER THAN THOSE REQUIRED BY THE JOB.
THEREBY FORCING THE CANDIDATE, GOD-DAMN GARY CALLAHAN, TO FIGHT THE CAMPAIGN ON HIS OWN.
TO FIGHT *HIMSELF*.
MAKES SENSE. CALLAHAN'S SYMPATHY RATING'S SO HIGH SINCE VITA SEVERN, HIS POLITICAL DIRECTOR, WAS KILLED, THAT THE PRESIDENT CAN'T HELP BUT LOOK BAD AGAINST HIM.
SO WHY BE ANYWHERE NEAR HIM? LET CALLAHAN MAKE HIS FUCK-UPS WITHOUT PROVIDING A DISTRACTION.
ELECTION DAY'S IN A COUPLE OF WEEKS.
I COULDN'T CARE LESS.

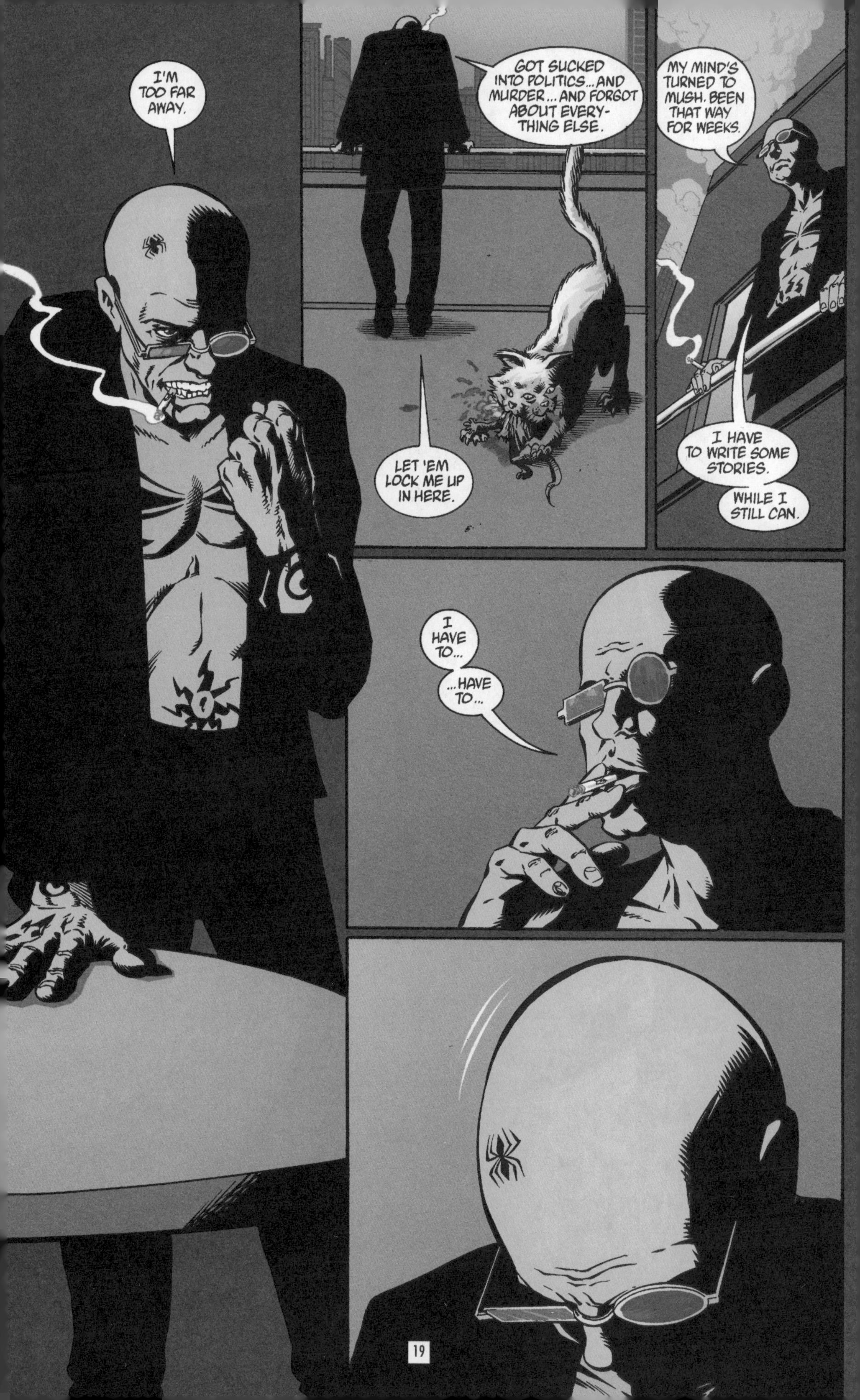
I'M TOO FAR AWAY.
GOT SUCKED INTO POLITICS... AND MURDER... AND FORGOT ABOUT EVERY-THING ELSE.
LET 'EM LOCK ME UP IN HERE.
MY MIND'S TURNED TO MUSH. BEEN THAT WAY FOR WEEKS.
I HAVE TO WRITE SOME STORIES.
WHILE I STILL CAN.
I HAVE TO...
...HAVE TO...

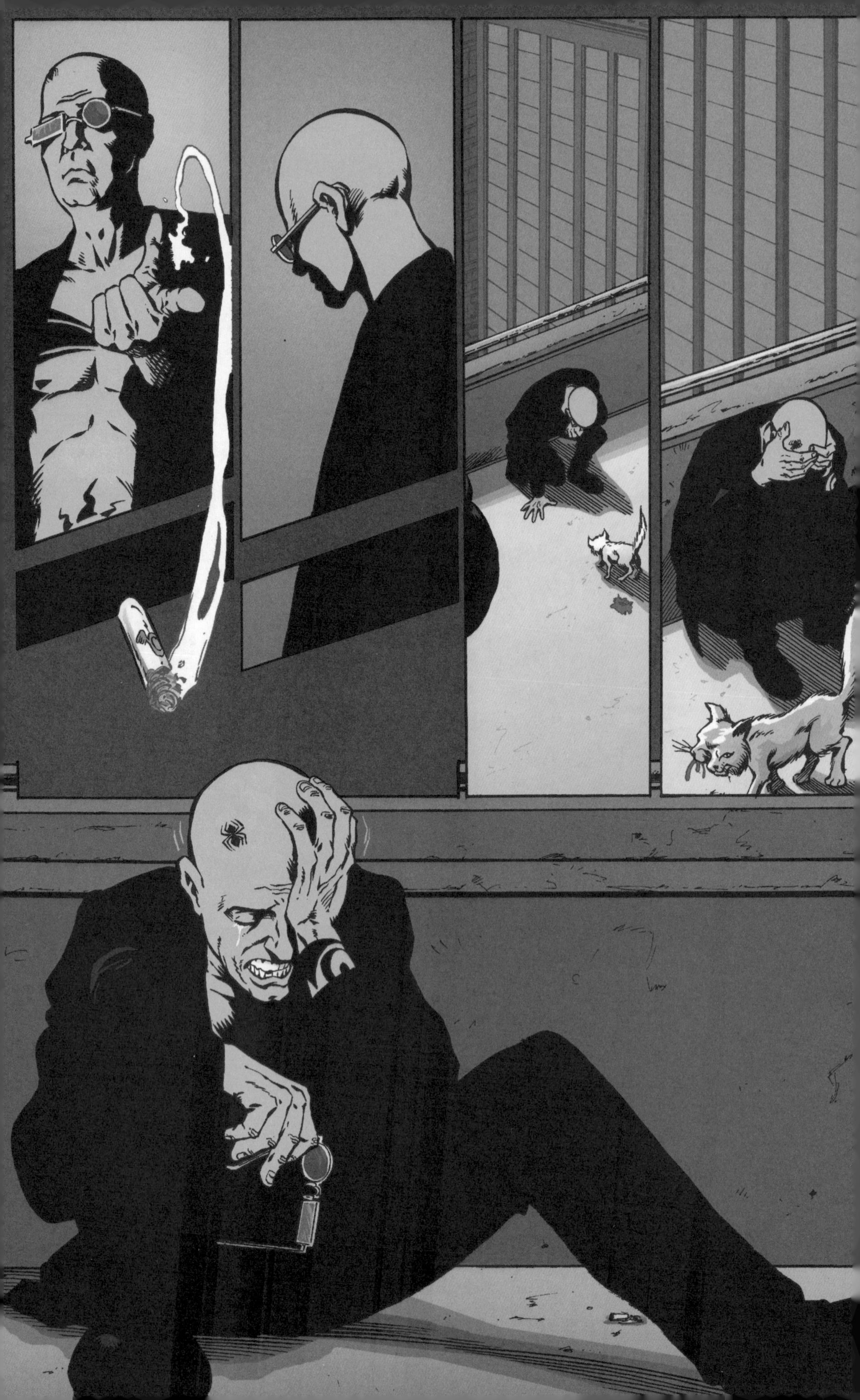

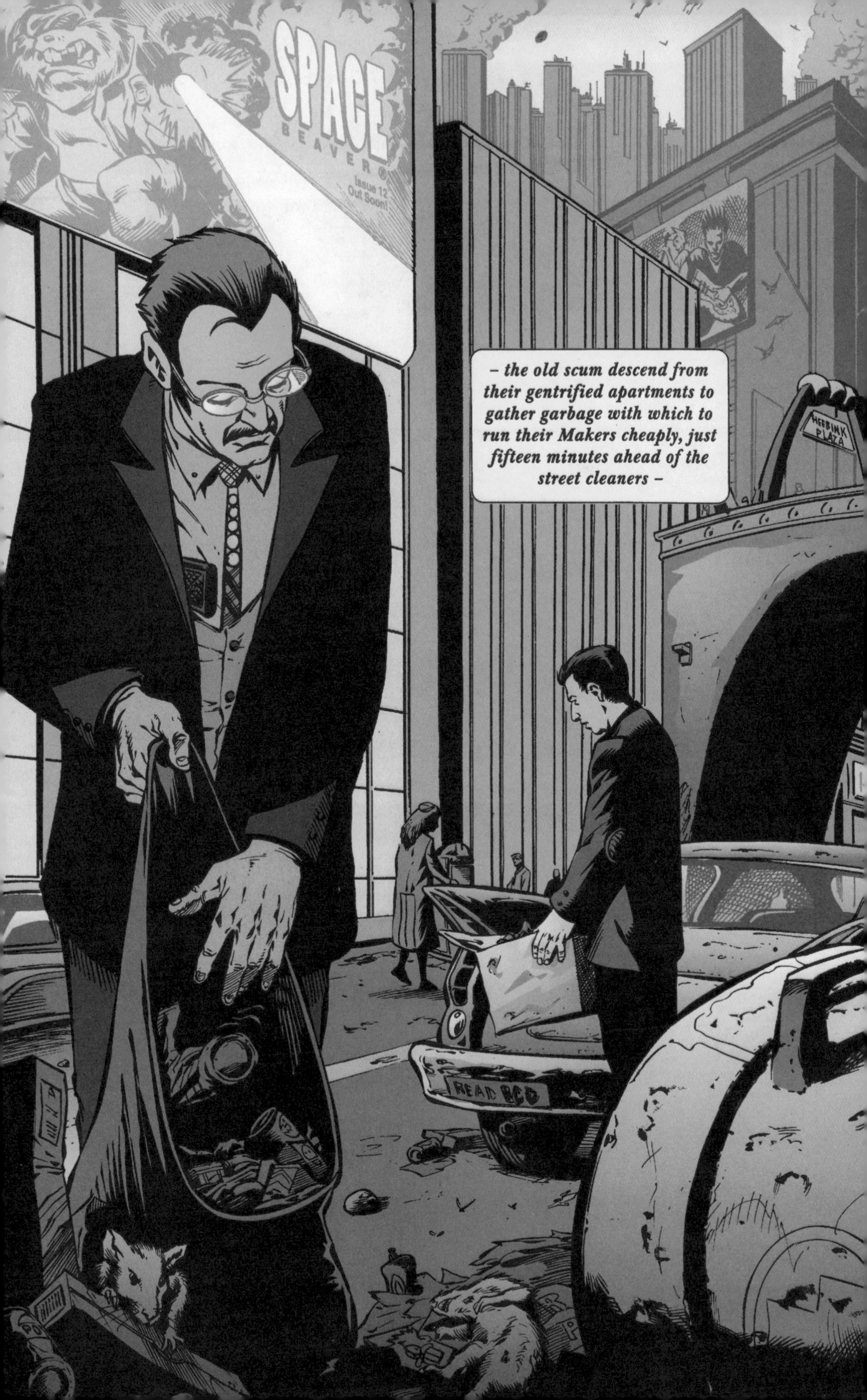
SPACE
BEAVER ®
Issue 12
Out Soon!
HEEBINK PLAZA
– the old scum descend from their gentrified apartments to gather garbage with which to run their Makers cheaply, just fifteen minutes ahead of the street cleaners –

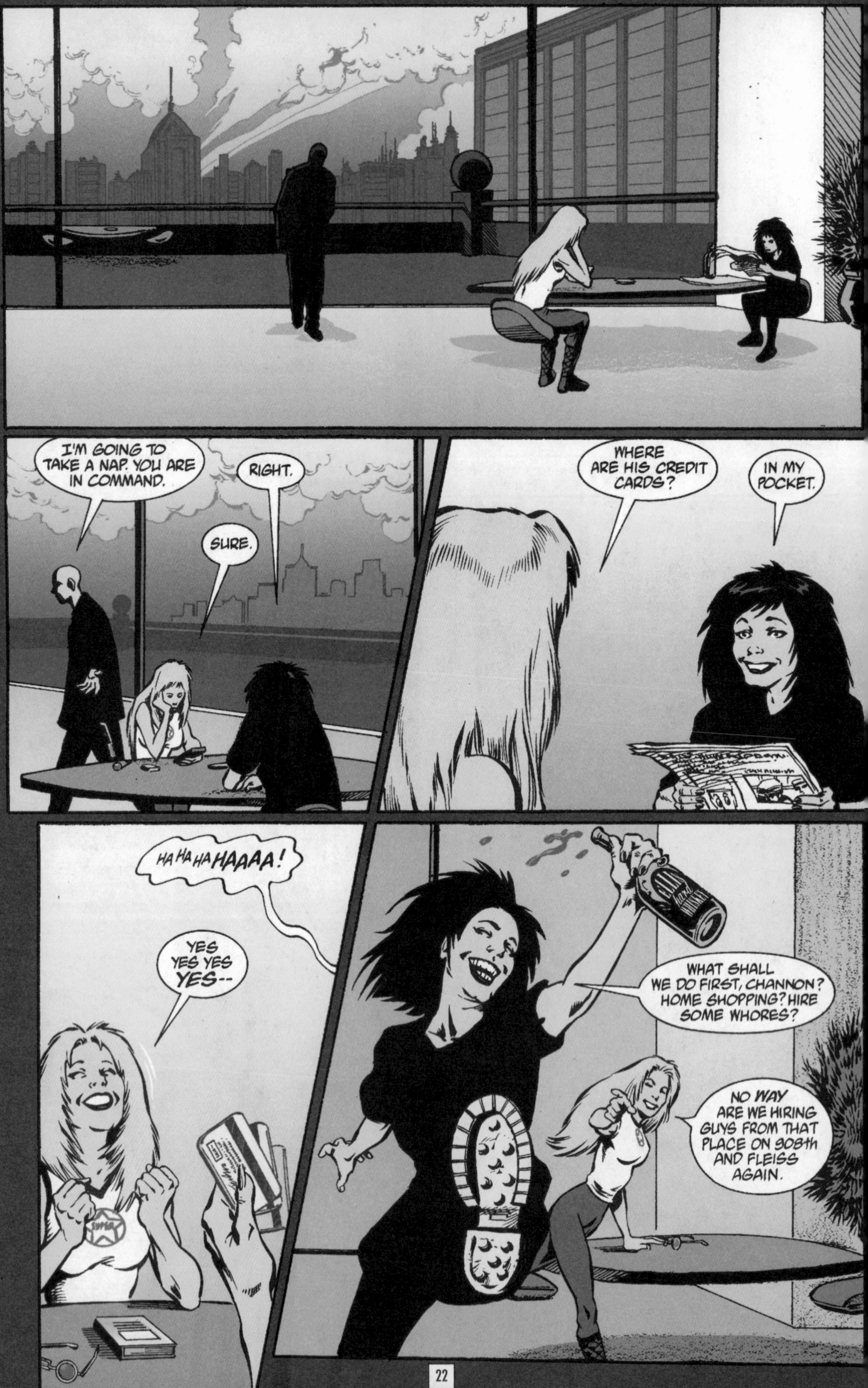
I'M GOING TO TAKE A NAP. YOU ARE IN COMMAND.
RIGHT.
SURE.
WHERE ARE HIS CREDIT CARDS?
IN MY POCKET.
HA HA HA HAAAA!
YES YES YES YES--
WHAT SHALL WE DO FIRST, CHANNON? HOME SHOPPING? HIRE SOME WHORES?
NO WAY ARE WE HIRING GUYS FROM THAT PLACE ON 908th AND FLEISS AGAIN.

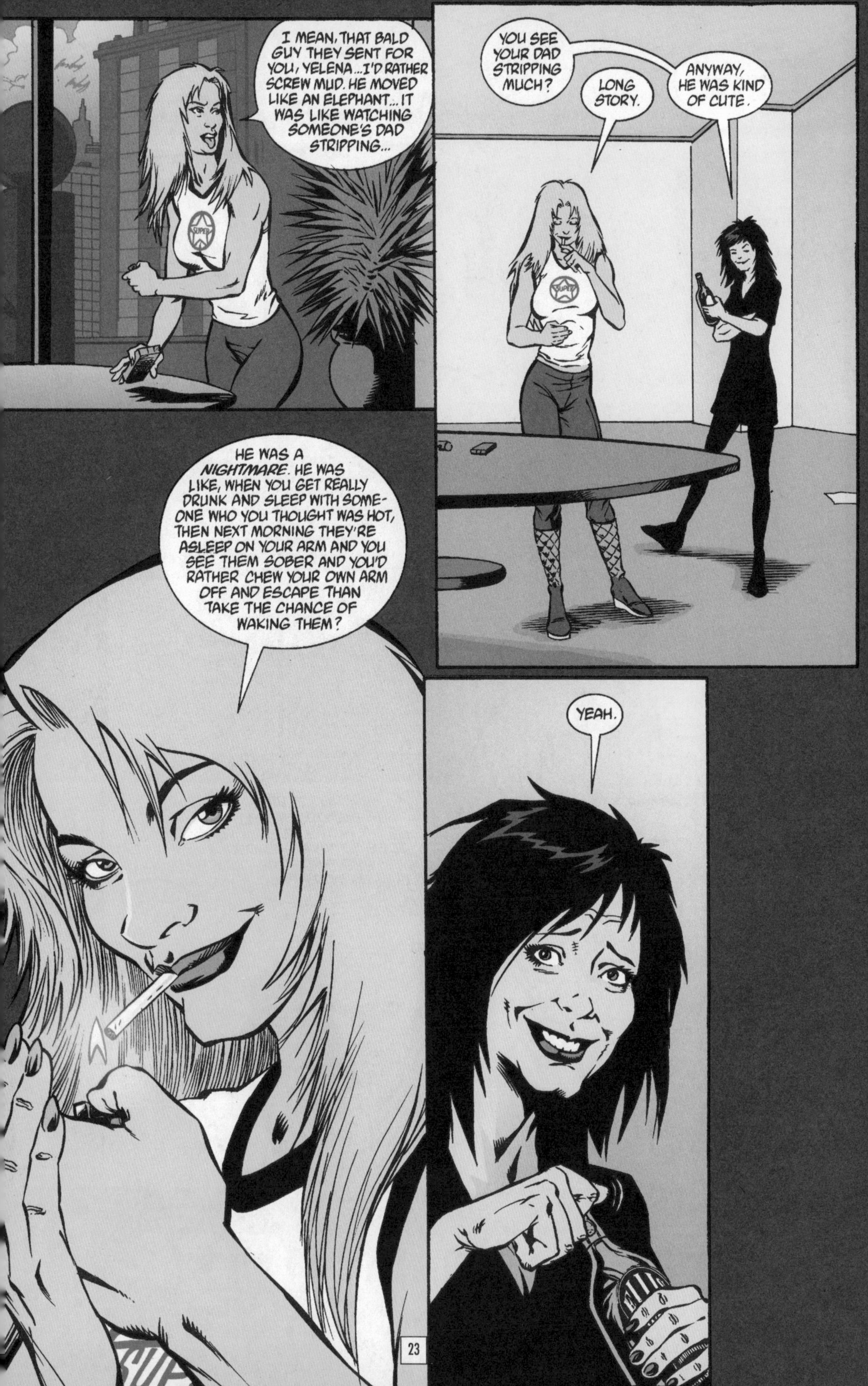
I MEAN, THAT BALD GUY THEY SENT FOR YOU, YELENA... I'D RATHER SCREW MUD. HE MOVED LIKE AN ELEPHANT... IT WAS LIKE WATCHING SOMEONE'S DAD STRIPPING...
YOU SEE YOUR DAD STRIPPING MUCH?
LONG STORY.
ANYWAY, HE WAS KIND OF CUTE.
HE WAS A *NIGHTMARE*. HE WAS LIKE, WHEN YOU GET REALLY DRUNK AND SLEEP WITH SOME-ONE WHO YOU THOUGHT WAS HOT, THEN NEXT MORNING THEY'RE ASLEEP ON YOUR ARM AND YOU SEE THEM SOBER AND YOU'D RATHER CHEW YOUR OWN ARM OFF AND ESCAPE THAN TAKE THE CHANCE OF WAKING THEM?
YEAH.

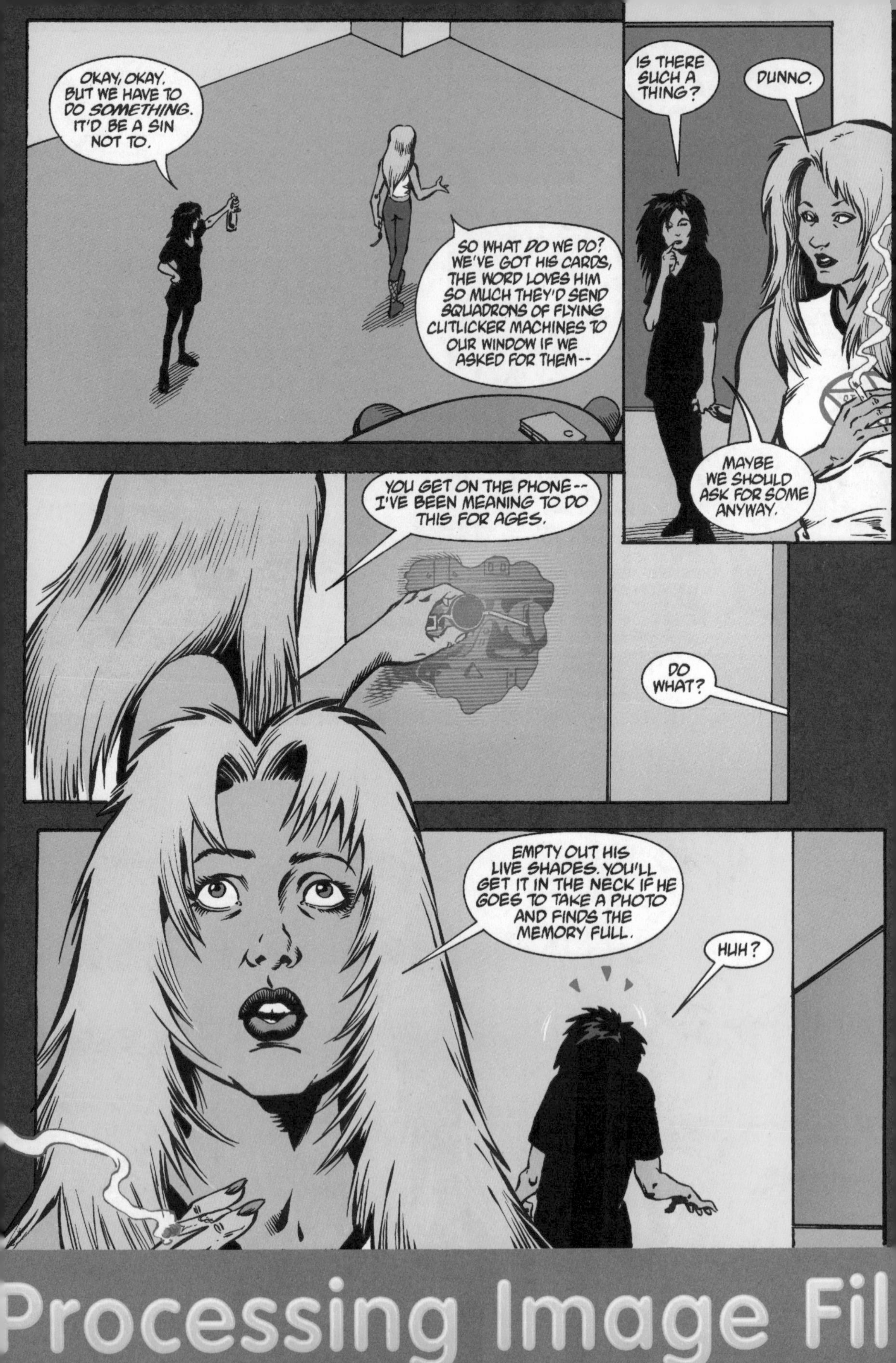
OKAY, OKAY. BUT WE HAVE TO DO SOMETHING. IT'D BE A SIN NOT TO.
SO WHAT DO WE DO? WE'VE GOT HIS CARDS, THE WORD LOVES HIM SO MUCH THEY'D SEND SQUADRONS OF FLYING CLITLICKER MACHINES TO OUR WINDOW IF WE ASKED FOR THEM--
IS THERE SUCH A THING?
DUNNO.
MAYBE WE SHOULD ASK FOR SOME ANYWAY.
YOU GET ON THE PHONE-- I'VE BEEN MEANING TO DO THIS FOR AGES.
DO WHAT?
EMPTY OUT HIS LIVE SHADES. YOU'LL GET IT IN THE NECK IF HE GOES TO TAKE A PHOTO AND FINDS THE MEMORY FULL.
HUH?

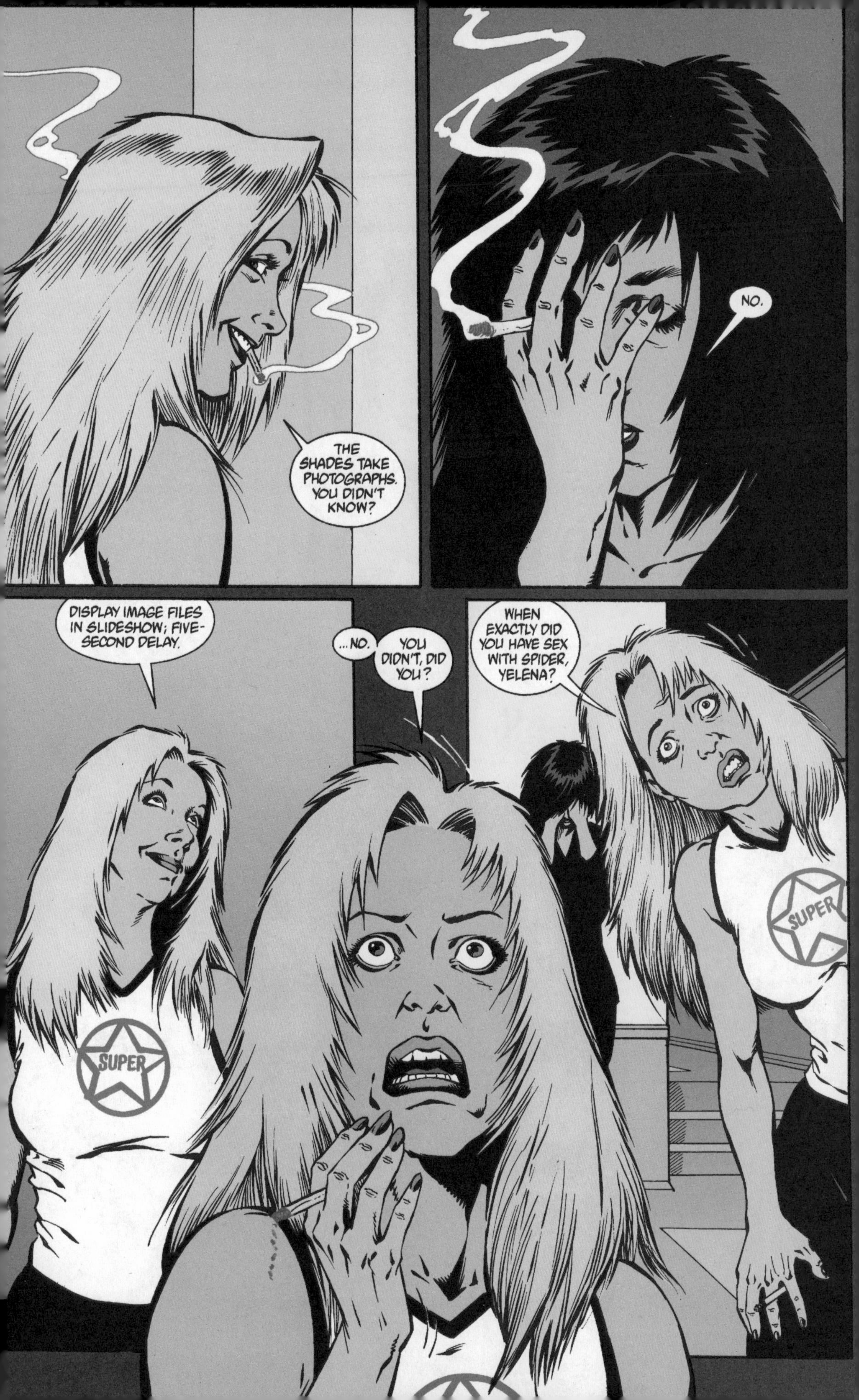
THE SHADES TAKE PHOTOGRAPHS. YOU DIDN'T KNOW?
NO.
DISPLAY IMAGE FILES IN SLIDESHOW; FIVE-SECOND DELAY.
...NO.
YOU DIDN'T, DID YOU?
WHEN EXACTLY DID YOU HAVE SEX WITH SPIDER, YELENA?

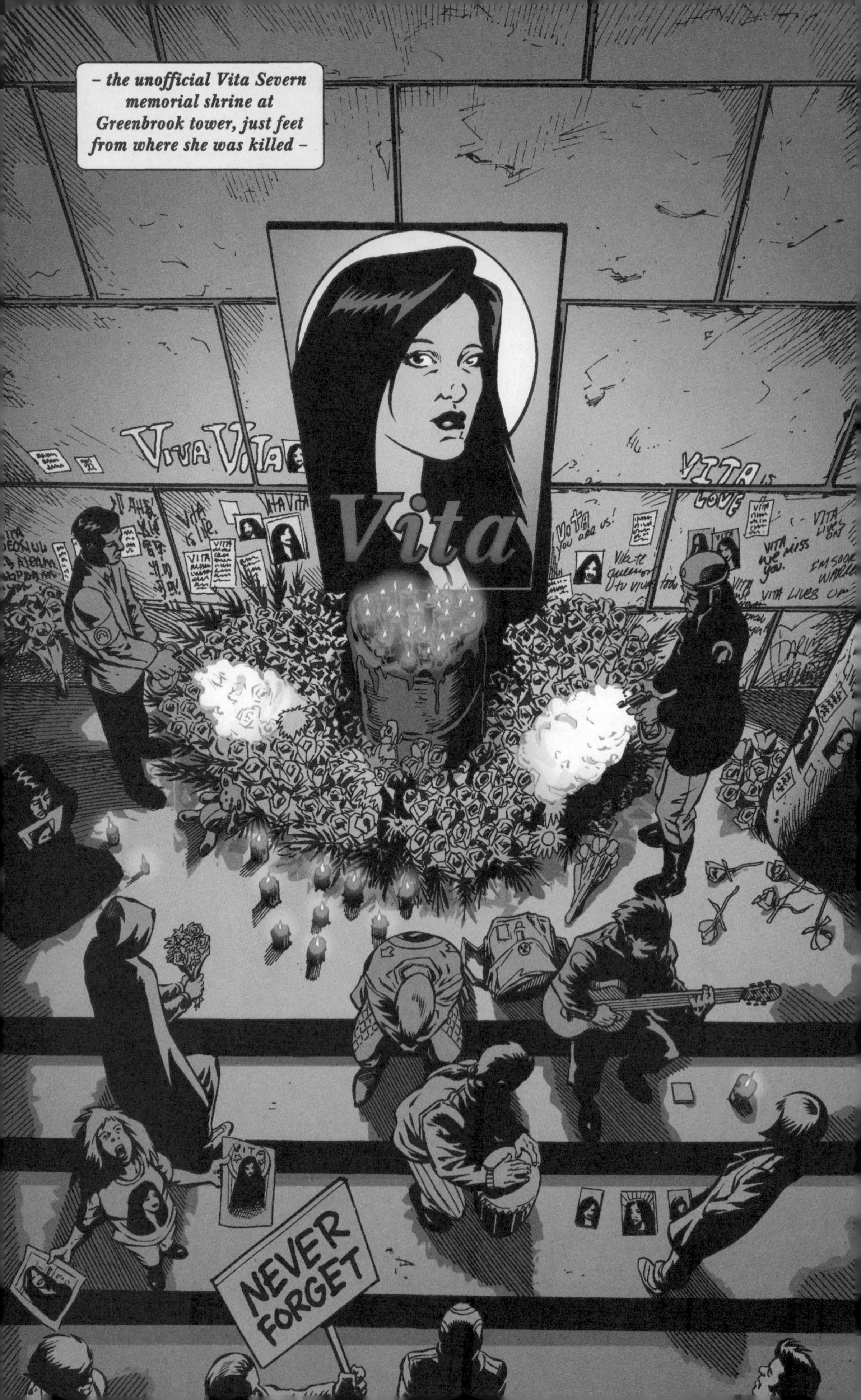
– the unofficial Vita Severn memorial shrine at Greenbrook tower, just feet from where she was killed –
VIVA VITA
Vita
VITA IS LOVE
Vita YOU ARE US!
VITA LIVES ON
VITA WE MISS YOU.
VITA LIVES ON
NEVER FORGET

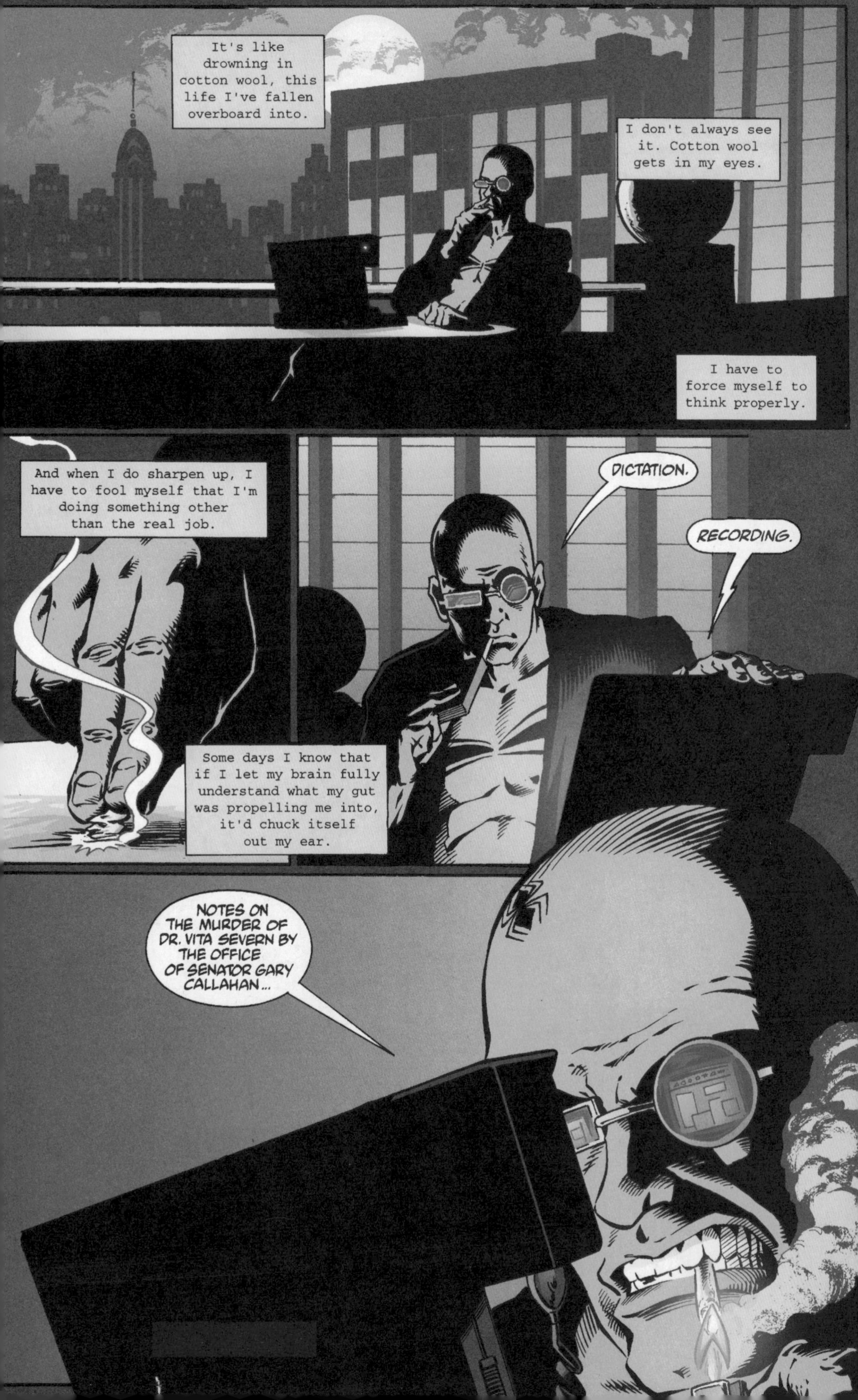
It's like drowning in cotton wool, this life I've fallen overboard into.
I don't always see it. Cotton wool gets in my eyes.
I have to force myself to think properly.
And when I do sharpen up, I have to fool myself that I'm doing something other than the real job.
DICTATION.
RECORDING.
Some days I know that if I let my brain fully understand what my gut was propelling me into, it'd chuck itself out my ear.
NOTES ON THE MURDER OF DR. VITA SEVERN BY THE OFFICE OF SENATOR GARY CALLAHAN...

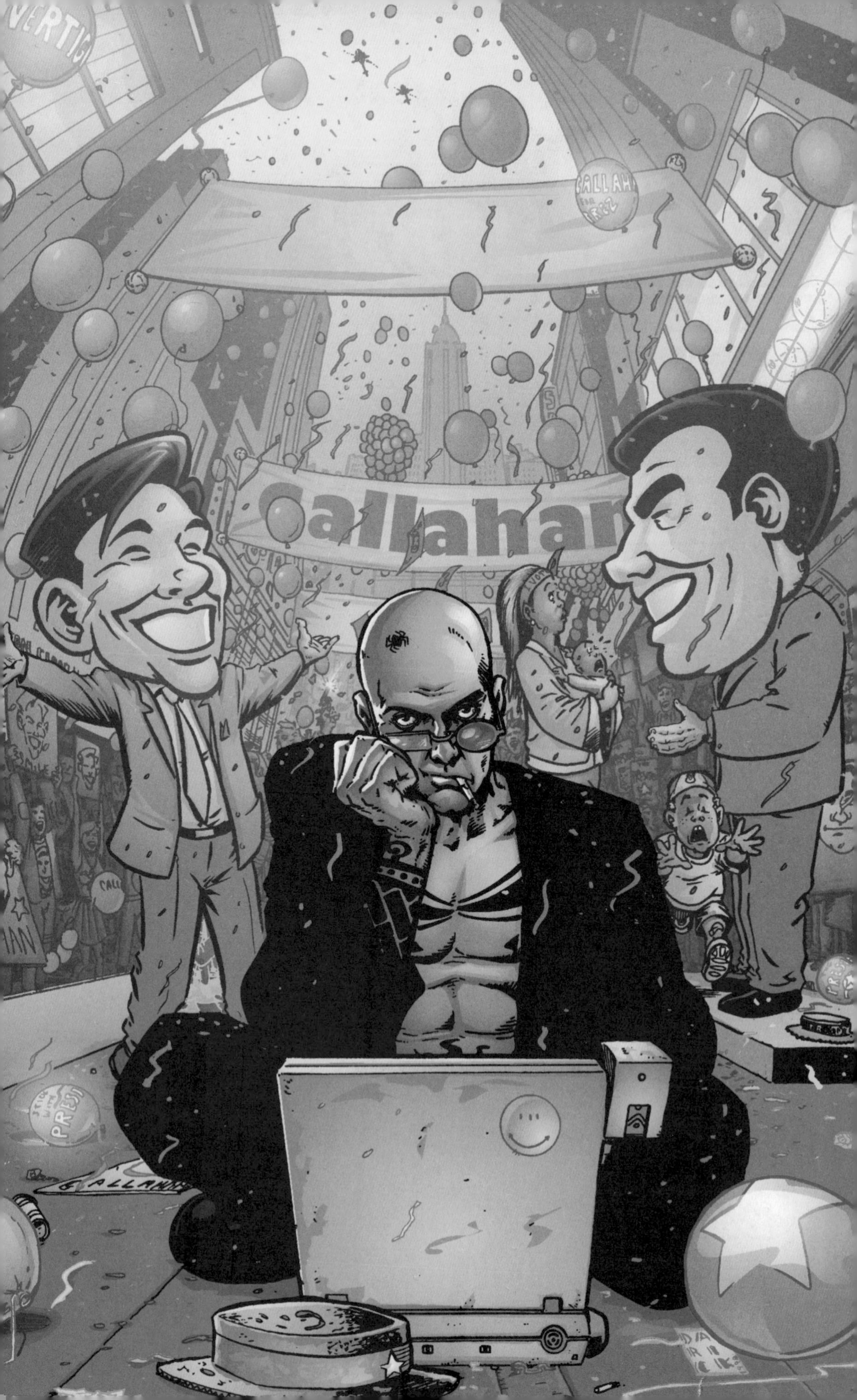
Callahan

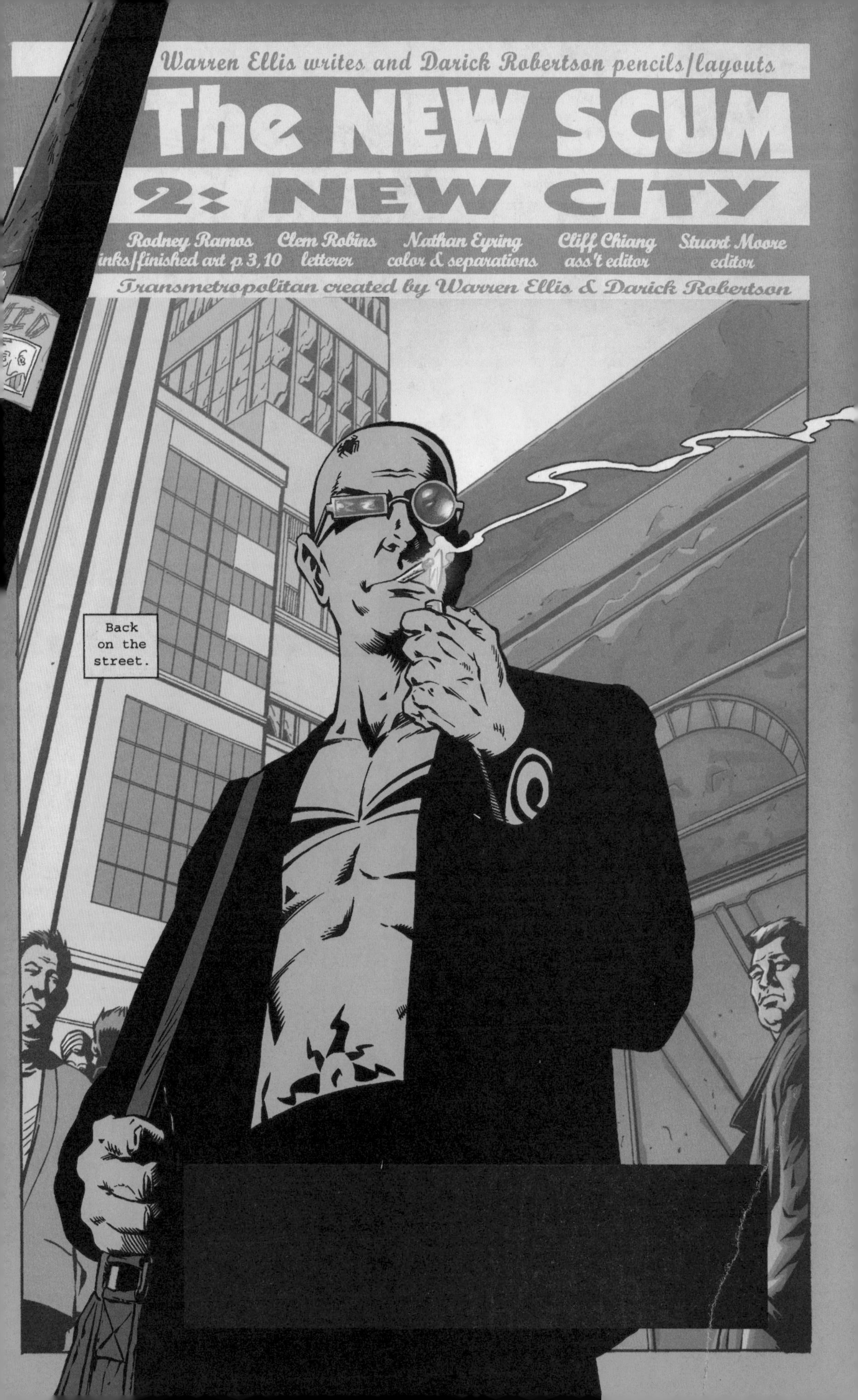
Warren Ellis writes and Darick Robertson pencils/layouts
The NEW SCUM
2: NEW CITY
Rodney Ramos inks/finished art p. 3, 10
Clem Robins letterer
Nathan Eyring color & separations
Cliff Chiang ass't editor
Stuart Moore editor
Transmetropolitan created by Warren Ellis & Darick Robertson
Back on the street.

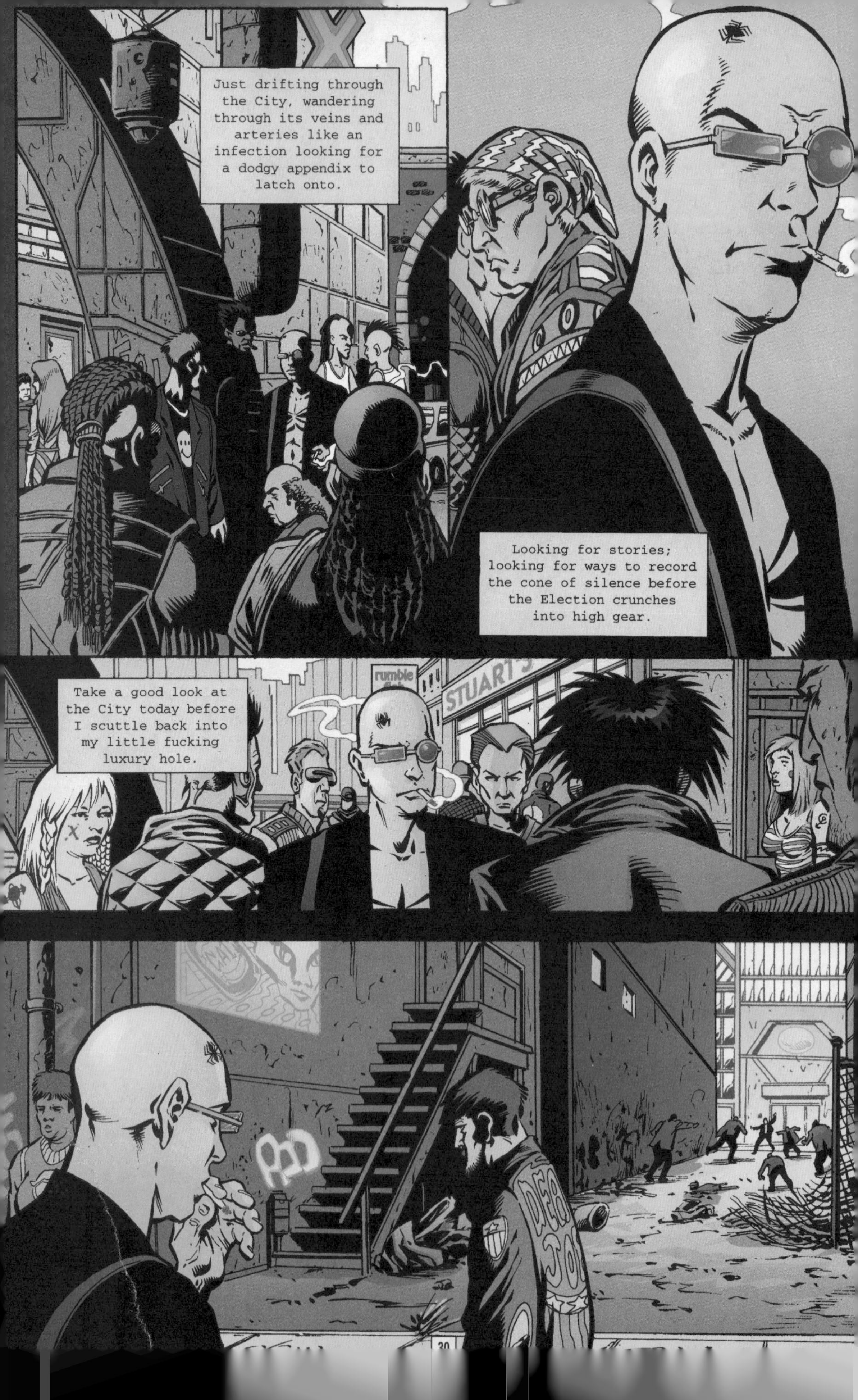
Just drifting through the City, wandering through its veins and arteries like an infection looking for a dodgy appendix to latch onto.
Looking for stories; looking for ways to record the cone of silence before the Election crunches into high gear.
rumble
STUART'S
Take a good look at the City today before I scuttle back into my little fucking luxury hole.

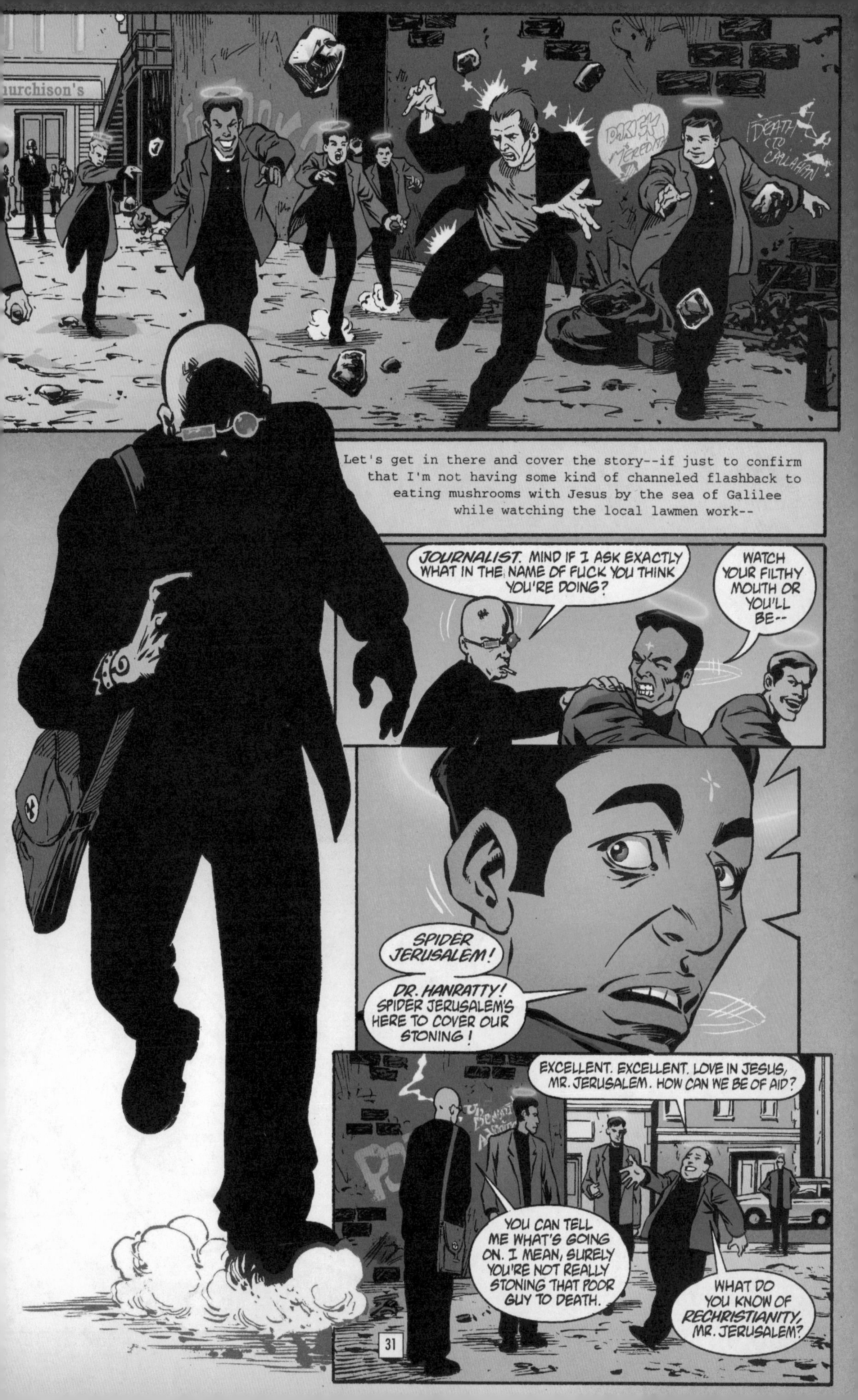

urchison's
DARICK MEREDITH
DEATH TO CALLAHAN
Let's get in there and cover the story--if just to confirm that I'm not having some kind of channeled flashback to eating mushrooms with Jesus by the sea of Galilee while watching the local lawmen work--
JOURNALIST. MIND IF I ASK EXACTLY WHAT IN THE NAME OF FUCK YOU THINK YOU'RE DOING?
WATCH YOUR FILTHY MOUTH OR YOU'LL BE--
SPIDER JERUSALEM!
DR. HANRATTY! SPIDER JERUSALEM'S HERE TO COVER OUR STONING!
EXCELLENT. EXCELLENT. LOVE IN JESUS, MR. JERUSALEM. HOW CAN WE BE OF AID?
YOU CAN TELL ME WHAT'S GOING ON. I MEAN, SURELY YOU'RE NOT REALLY STONING THAT POOR GUY TO DEATH.
WHAT DO YOU KNOW OF RECHRISTIANITY, MR. JERUSALEM?

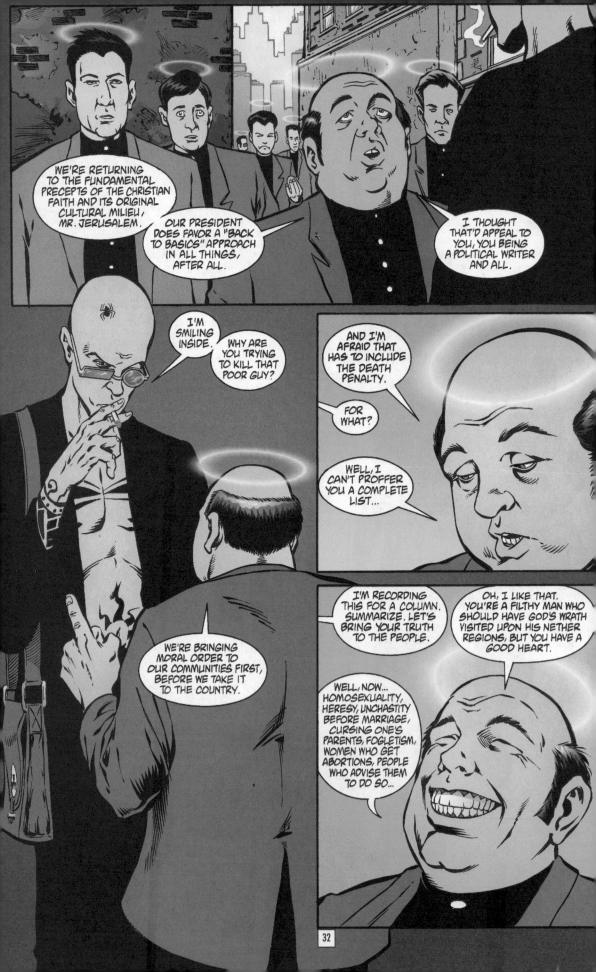

WE'RE RETURNING TO THE FUNDAMENTAL PRECEPTS OF THE CHRISTIAN FAITH AND ITS ORIGINAL CULTURAL MILIEU, MR. JERUSALEM.

OUR PRESIDENT DOES FAVOR A "BACK TO BASICS" APPROACH IN ALL THINGS, AFTER ALL.

I THOUGHT THAT'D APPEAL TO YOU, YOU BEING A POLITICAL WRITER AND ALL.

I'M SMILING INSIDE. WHY ARE YOU TRYING TO KILL THAT POOR GUY?

AND I'M AFRAID THAT HAS TO INCLUDE THE DEATH PENALTY.

FOR WHAT?

WELL, I CAN'T PROFFER YOU A COMPLETE LIST...

WE'RE BRINGING MORAL ORDER TO OUR COMMUNITIES FIRST, BEFORE WE TAKE IT TO THE COUNTRY.

I'M RECORDING THIS FOR A COLUMN, SUMMARIZE. LET'S BRING YOUR TRUTH TO THE PEOPLE.

OH, I LIKE THAT. YOU'RE A FILTHY MAN WHO SHOULD HAVE GOD'S WRATH VISITED UPON HIS NETHER REGIONS, BUT YOU HAVE A GOOD HEART.

WELL, NOW... HOMOSEXUALITY, HERESY, UNCHASTITY BEFORE MARRIAGE, CURSING ONE'S PARENTS, FOGLETISM, WOMEN WHO GET ABORTIONS, PEOPLE WHO ADVISE THEM TO DO SO...

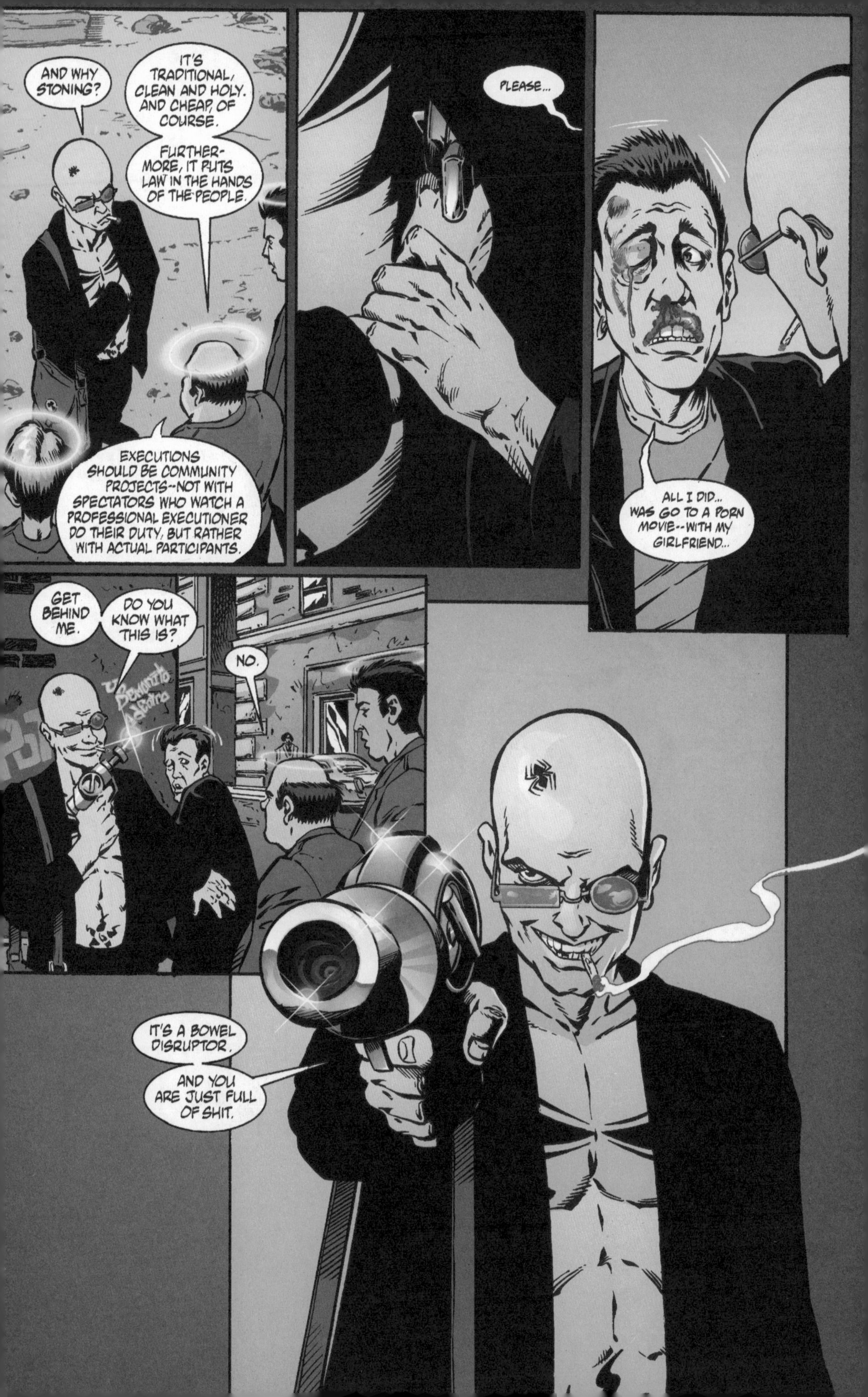
AND WHY STONING?
IT'S TRADITIONAL, CLEAN AND HOLY. AND CHEAP, OF COURSE.
FURTHER-MORE, IT PUTS LAW IN THE HANDS OF THE PEOPLE.
EXECUTIONS SHOULD BE COMMUNITY PROJECTS--NOT WITH SPECTATORS WHO WATCH A PROFESSIONAL EXECUTIONER DO THEIR DUTY, BUT RATHER WITH ACTUAL PARTICIPANTS.
PLEASE...
ALL I DID... WAS GO TO A PORN MOVIE--WITH MY GIRLFRIEND...
GET BEHIND ME.
DO YOU KNOW WHAT THIS IS?
NO.
IT'S A BOWEL DISRUPTOR.
AND YOU ARE JUST FULL OF SHIT.

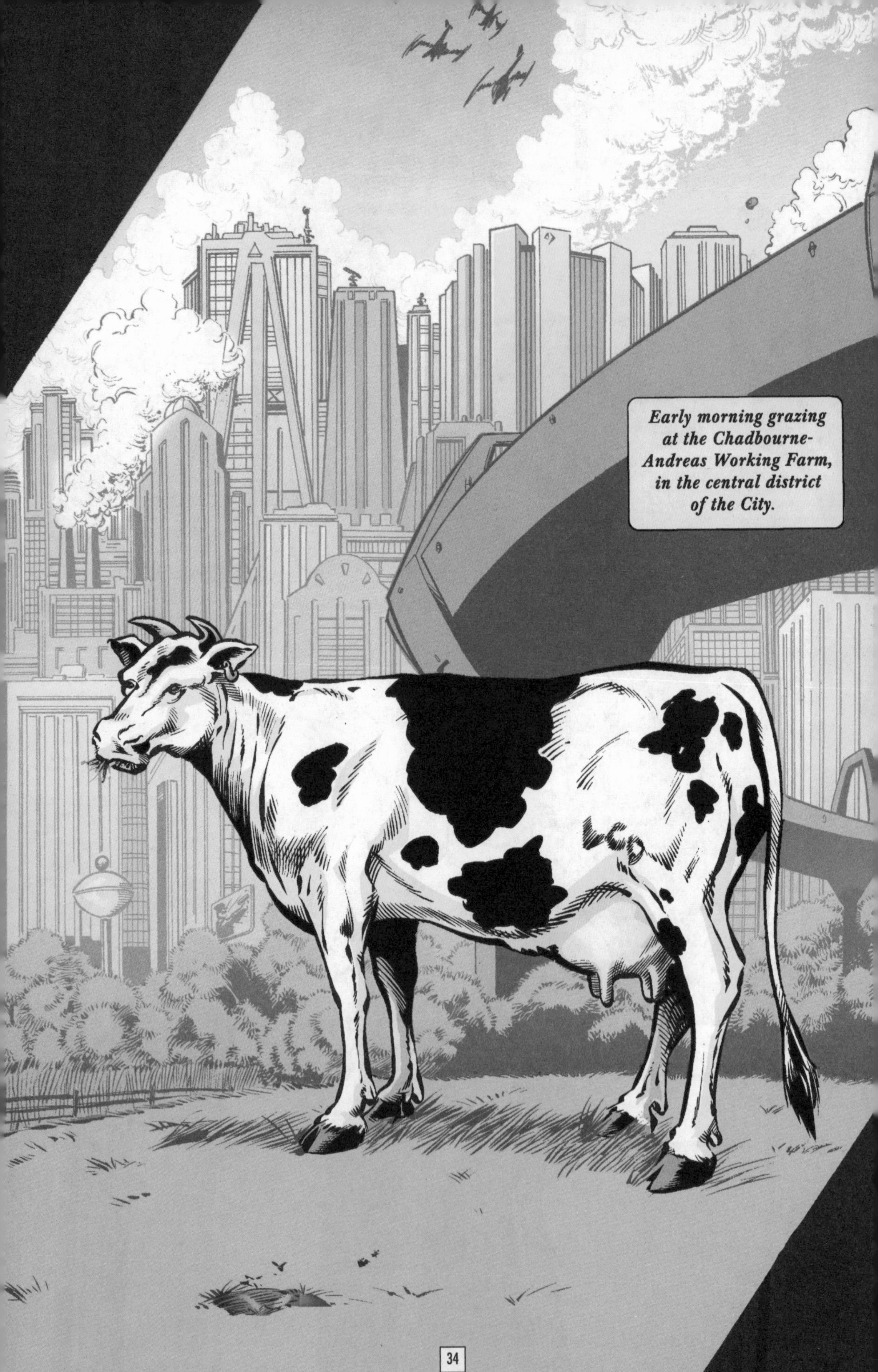
Early morning grazing at the Chadbourne-Andreas Working Farm, in the central district of the City.

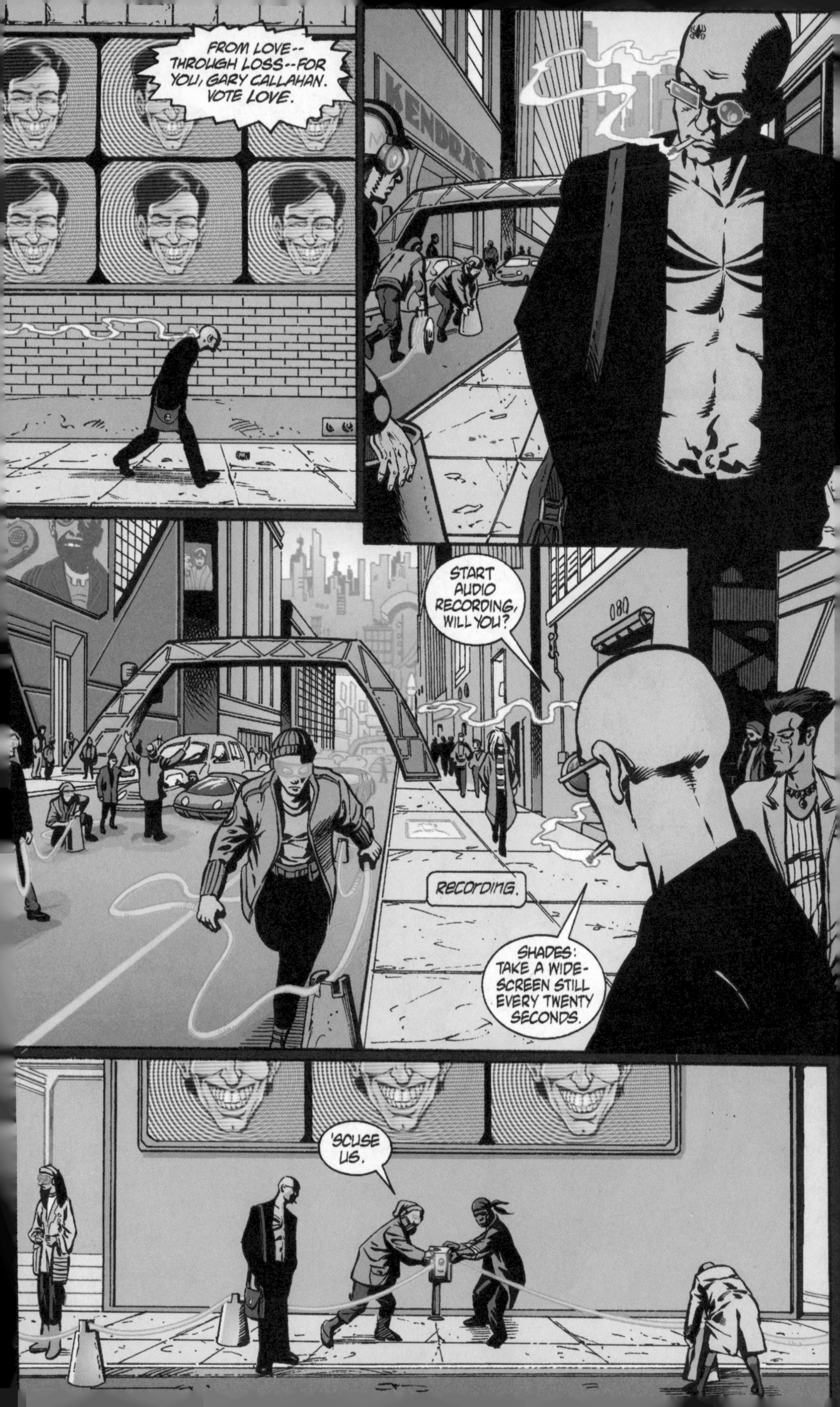
FROM LOVE-- THROUGH LOSS--FOR YOU, GARY CALLAHAN. VOTE LOVE.
KENDRA'S
START AUDIO RECORDING, WILL YOU?
080
RECORDING.
SHADES: TAKE A WIDE-SCREEN STILL EVERY TWENTY SECONDS.
'SCUSE US.

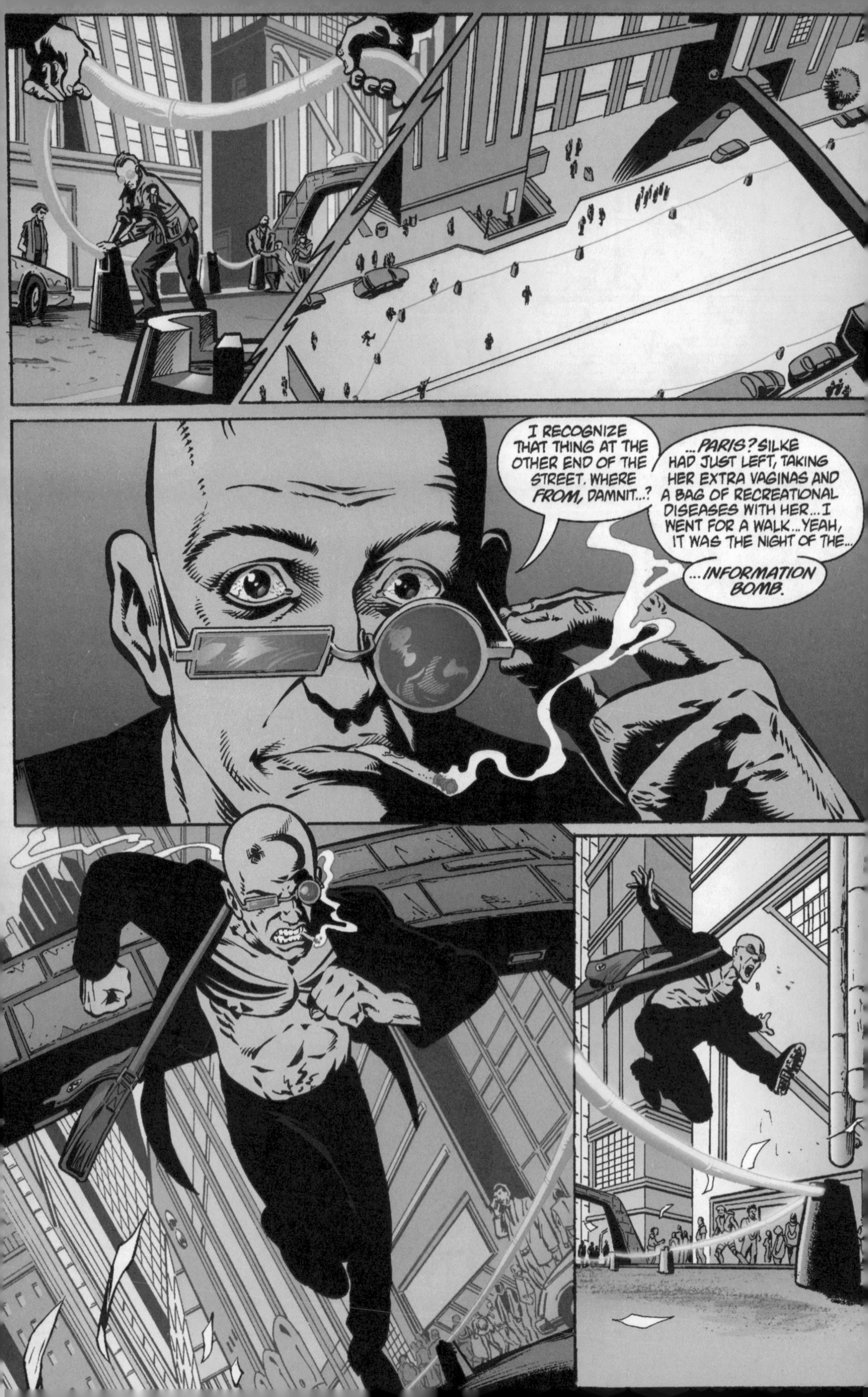
I RECOGNIZE THAT THING AT THE OTHER END OF THE STREET. WHERE *FROM,* DAMNIT...?
...*PARIS?* SILKE HAD JUST LEFT, TAKING HER EXTRA VAGINAS AND A BAG OF RECREATIONAL DISEASES WITH HER... I WENT FOR A WALK... YEAH, IT WAS THE NIGHT OF THE...
...*INFORMATION BOMB.*

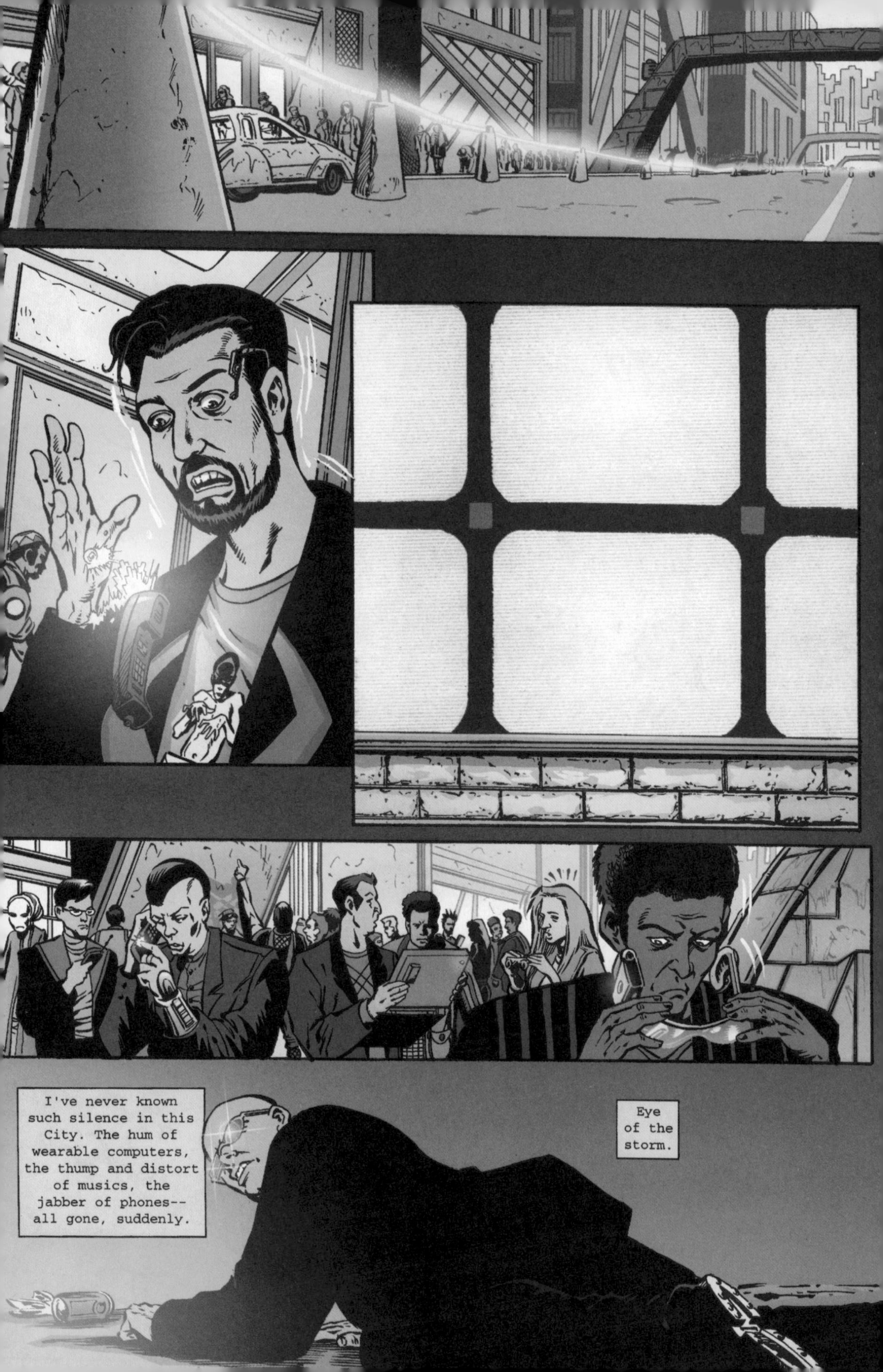
I've never known such silence in this City. The hum of wearable computers, the thump and distort of musics, the jabber of phones--all gone, suddenly.
Eye of the storm.

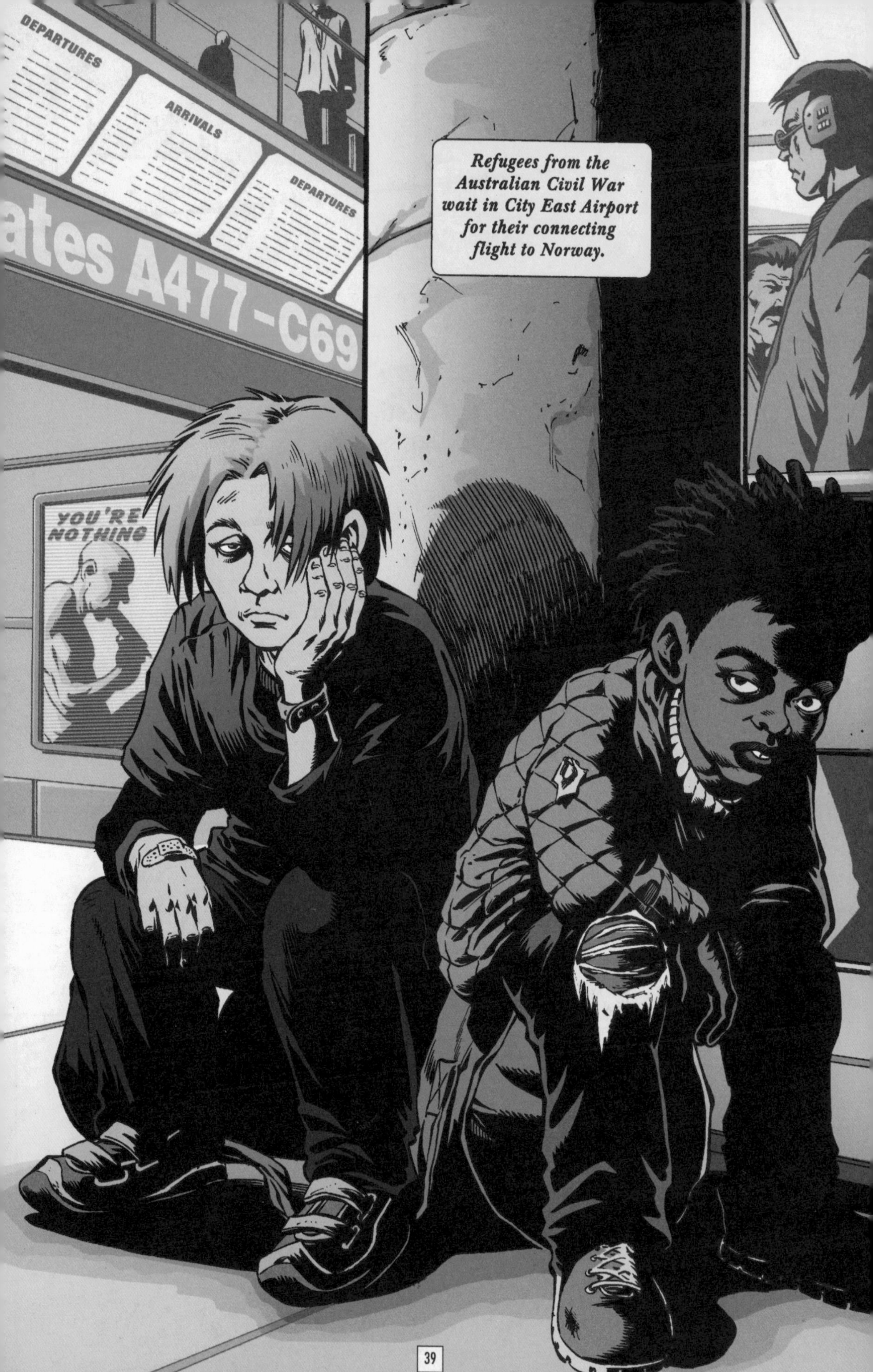
DEPARTURES
ARRIVALS
DEPARTURES
ates A477–C69
Refugees from the Australian Civil War wait in City East Airport for their connecting flight to Norway.
YOU'RE NOTHING

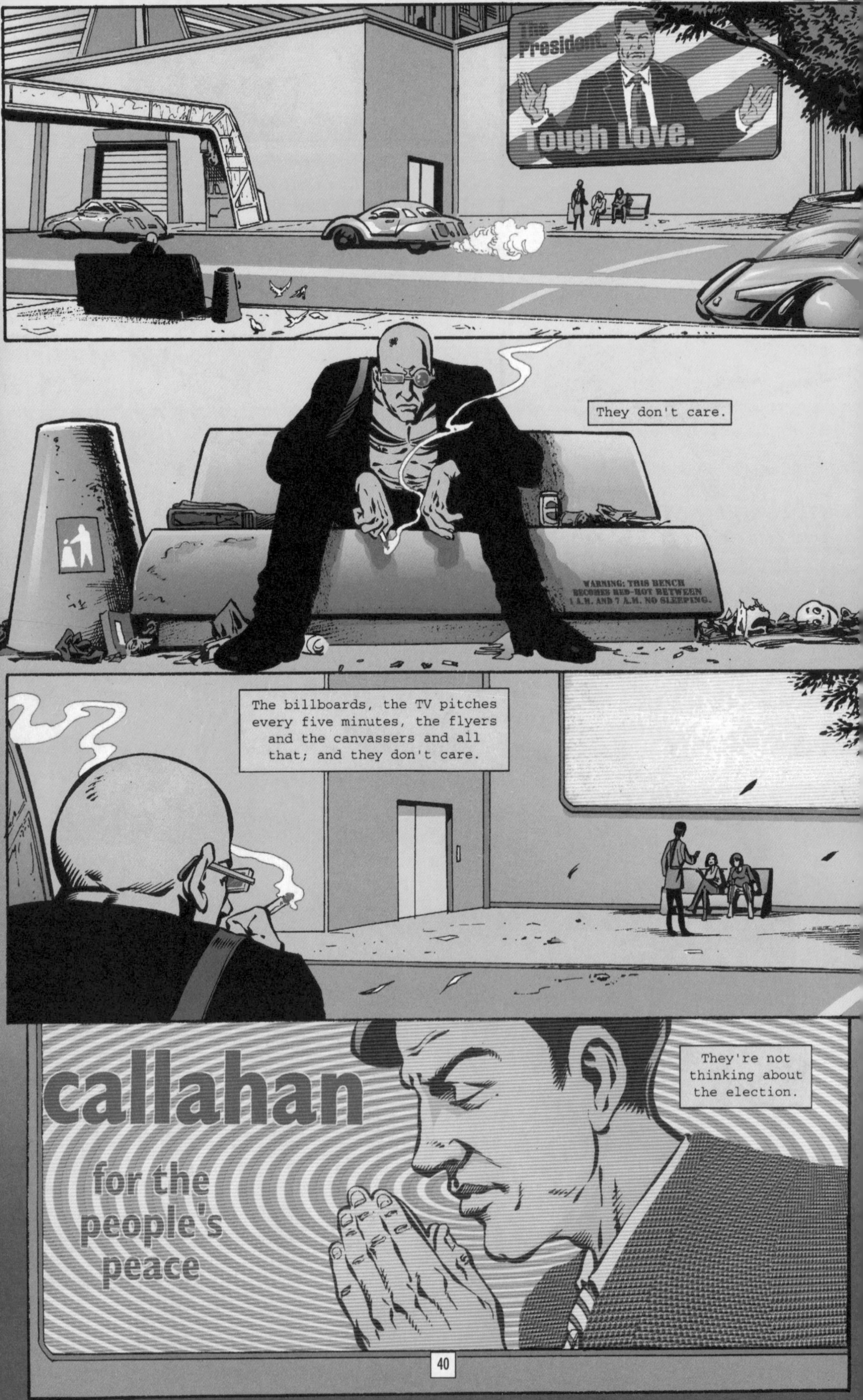
The President.
Tough Love.
They don't care.
WARNING: THIS BENCH BECOMES RED-HOT BETWEEN 1 A.M. AND 7 A.M. NO SLEEPING.
The billboards, the TV pitches every five minutes, the flyers and the canvassers and all that; and they don't care.
callahan
for the people's peace
They're not thinking about the election.

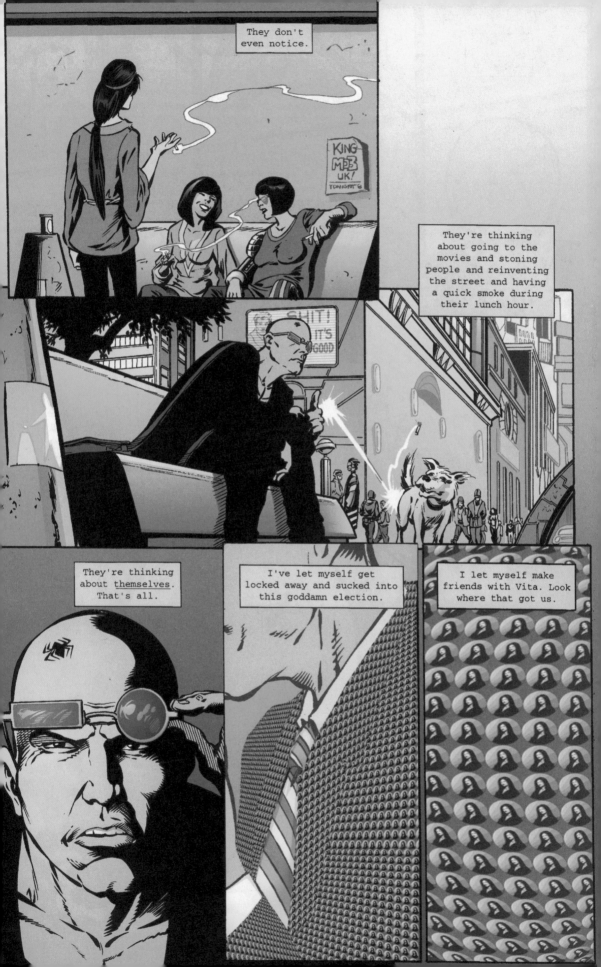

They don't even notice.

They're thinking about going to the movies and stoning people and reinventing the street and having a quick smoke during their lunch hour.

KING MB3 UK! TONIGHT 6

SHIT! IT'S GOOD

They're thinking about themselves. That's all.

I've let myself get locked away and sucked into this goddamn election.

I let myself make friends with Vita. Look where that got us.

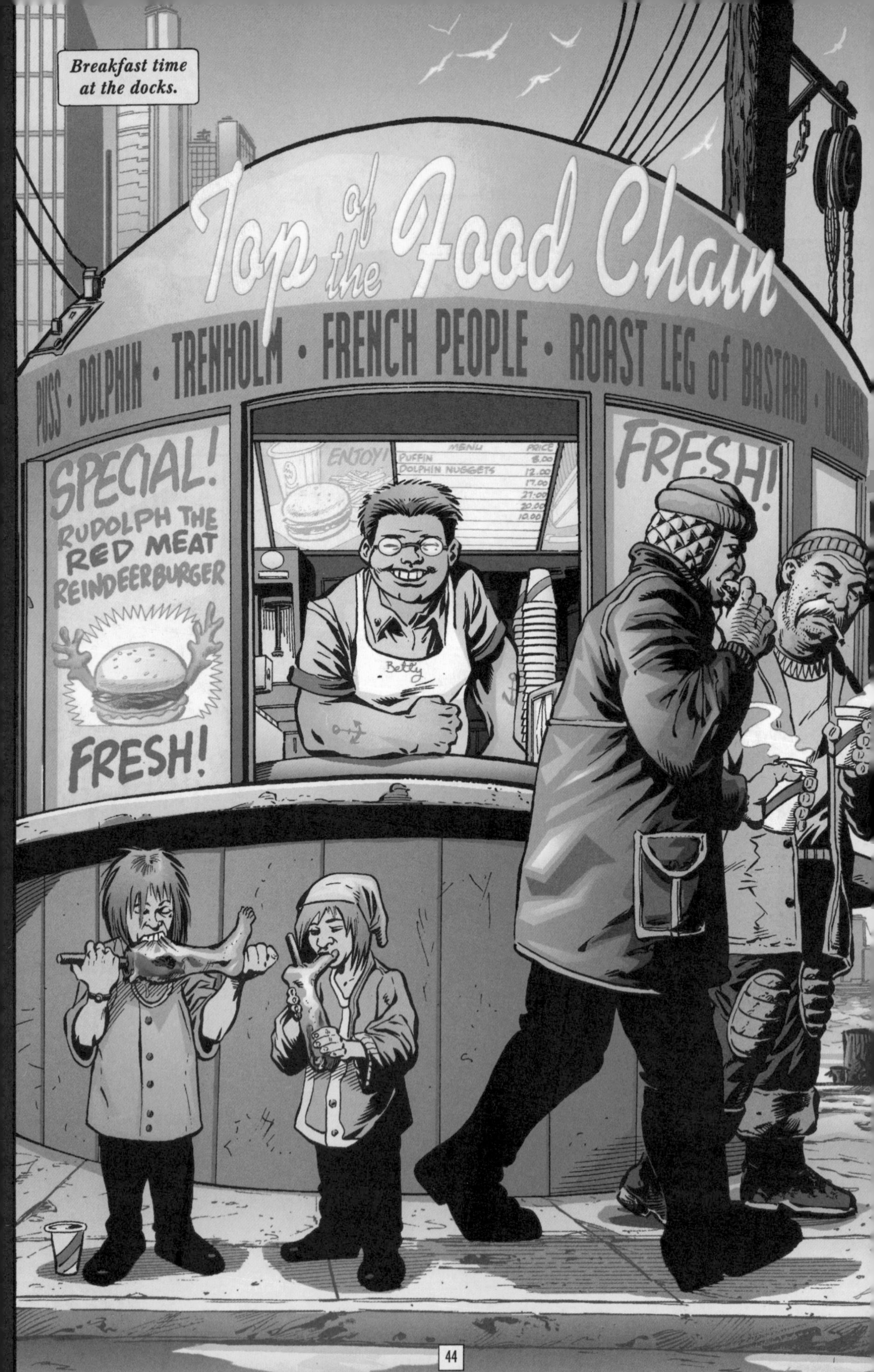

Breakfast time at the docks.
Top of the Food Chain
PUSS • DOLPHIN • TRENHOLM • FRENCH PEOPLE • ROAST LEG of BASTARD •
SPECIAL! RUDOLPH THE RED MEAT REINDEERBURGER
FRESH!
ENJOY!
MENU PRICE
PUFFIN 8.00
DOLPHIN NUGGETS 12.00
17.00
27.00
20.00
10.00
Betty
FRESH!

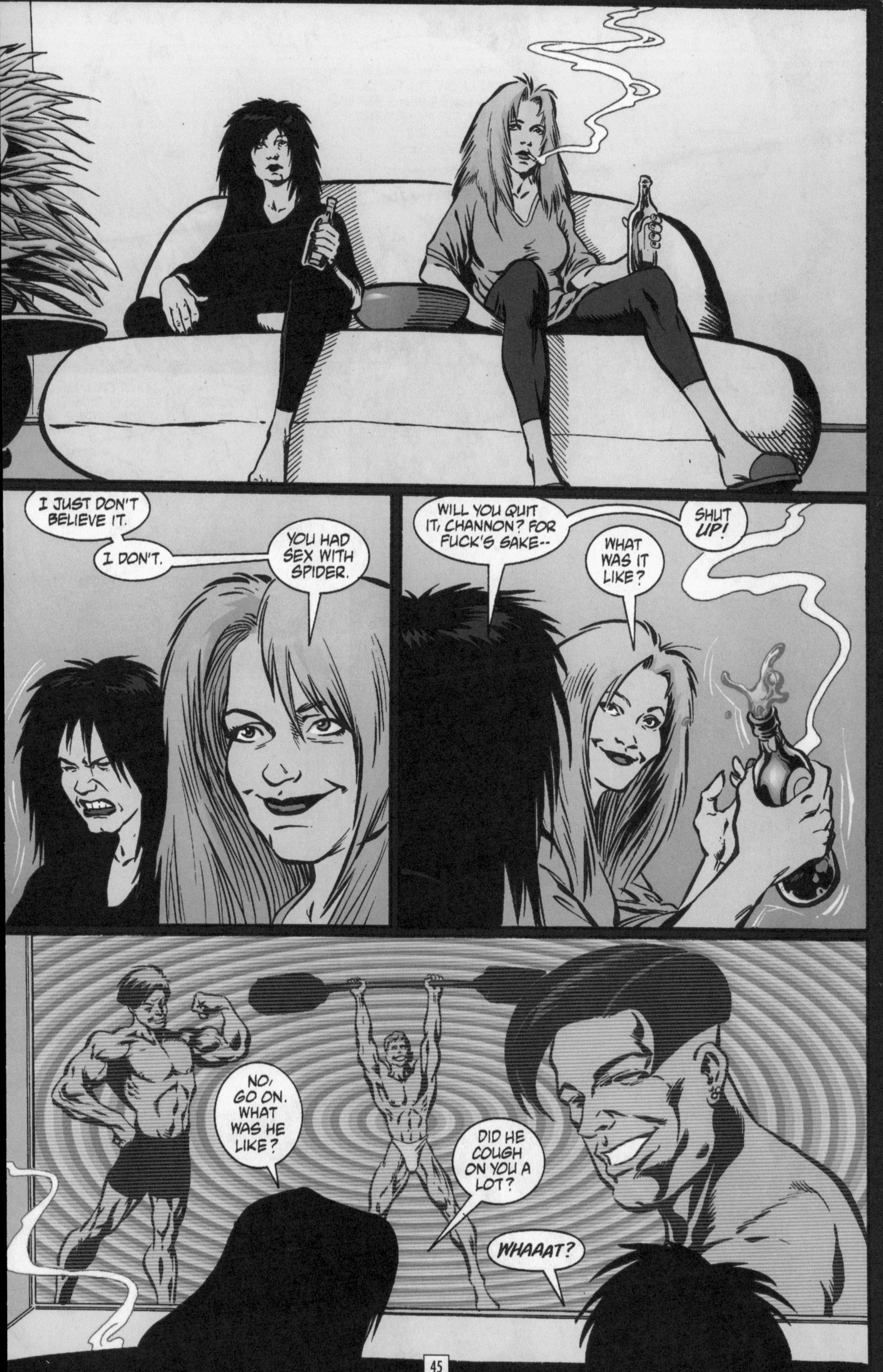
I JUST DON'T BELIEVE IT.
I DON'T.
YOU HAD SEX WITH SPIDER.
WILL YOU QUIT IT, CHANNON? FOR FUCK'S SAKE--
SHUT UP!
WHAT WAS IT LIKE?
NO, GO ON. WHAT WAS HE LIKE?
DID HE COUGH ON YOU A LOT?
WHAAAT?

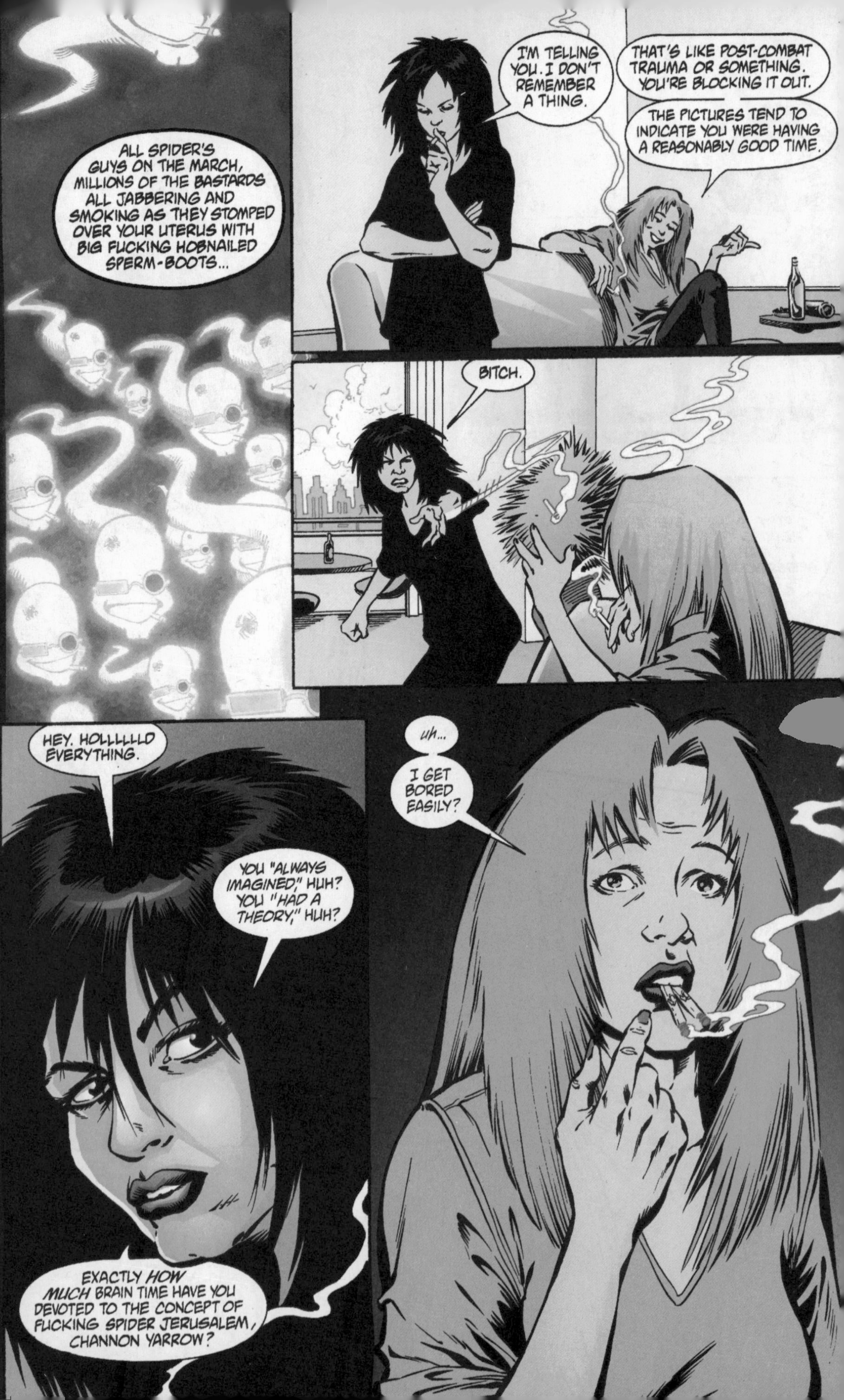
ALL SPIDER'S GUYS ON THE MARCH, MILLIONS OF THE BASTARDS ALL JABBERING AND SMOKING AS THEY STOMPED OVER YOUR UTERUS WITH BIG FUCKING HOBNAILED SPERM-BOOTS...
I'M TELLING YOU. I DON'T REMEMBER A THING.
THAT'S LIKE POST-COMBAT TRAUMA OR SOMETHING. YOU'RE BLOCKING IT OUT.
THE PICTURES TEND TO INDICATE YOU WERE HAVING A REASONABLY GOOD TIME.
BITCH.
HEY. HOLLLLLLD EVERYTHING.
YOU "ALWAYS IMAGINED," HUH? YOU "HAD A THEORY," HUH?
EXACTLY HOW MUCH BRAIN TIME HAVE YOU DEVOTED TO THE CONCEPT OF FUCKING SPIDER JERUSALEM, CHANNON YARROW?
uh...
I GET BORED EASILY?

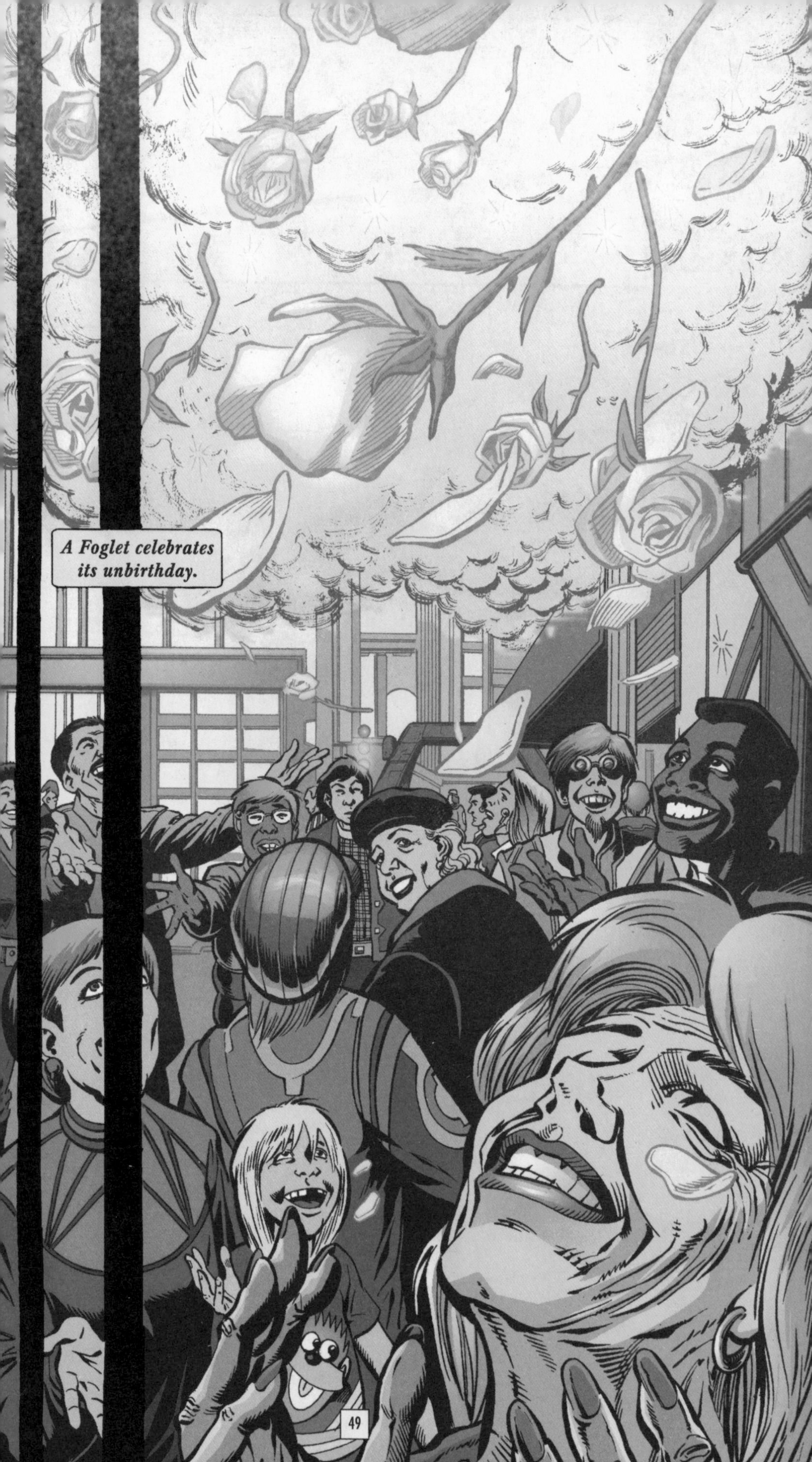
A Foglet celebrates its unbirthday.

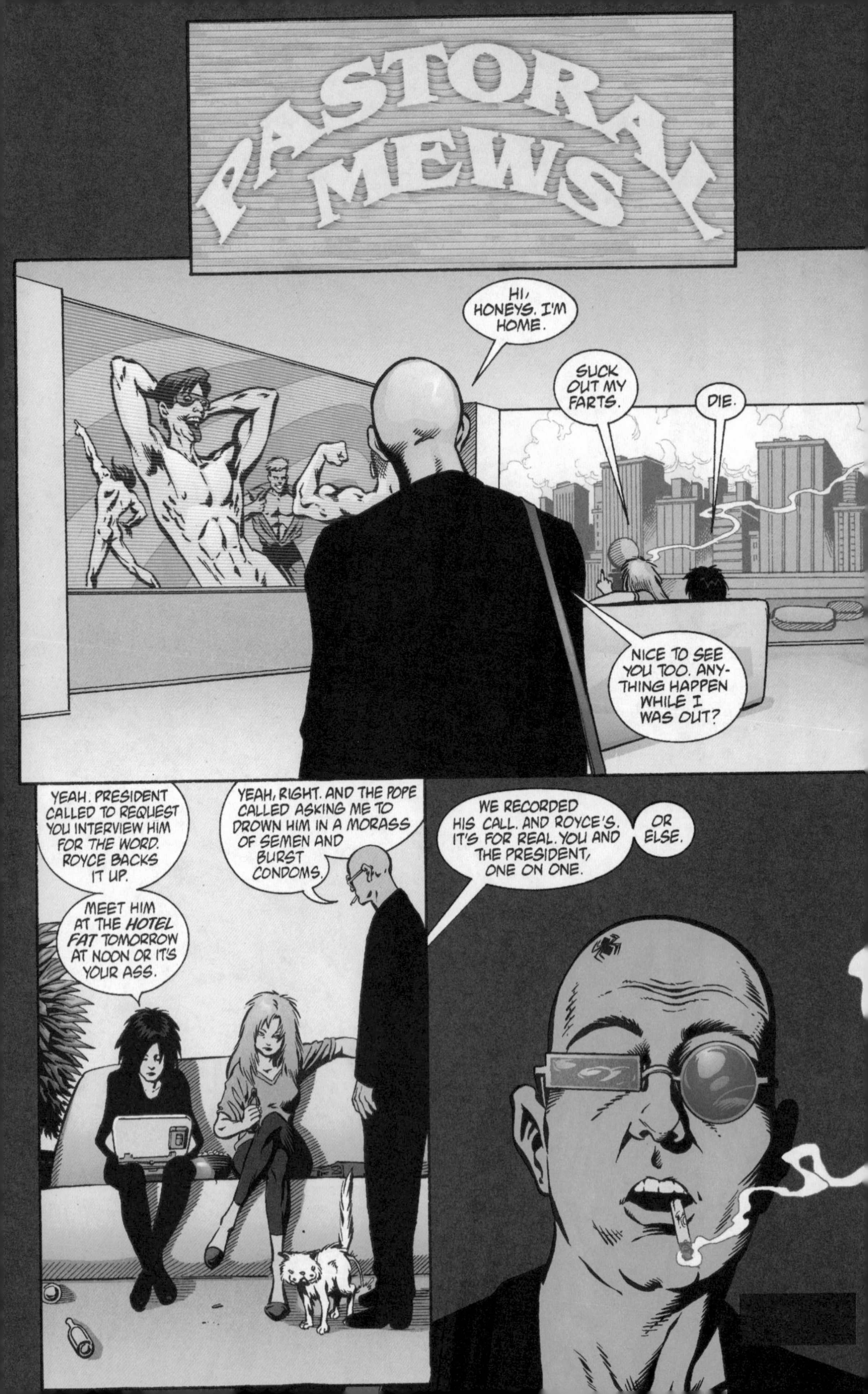
PASTORAL MEWS
HI, HONEYS. I'M HOME.
SUCK OUT MY FARTS.
DIE.
NICE TO SEE YOU TOO. ANYTHING HAPPEN WHILE I WAS OUT?
YEAH. PRESIDENT CALLED TO REQUEST YOU INTERVIEW HIM FOR THE WORD. ROYCE BACKS IT UP.
MEET HIM AT THE *HOTEL FAT* TOMORROW AT NOON OR IT'S YOUR ASS.
YEAH, RIGHT. AND THE POPE CALLED ASKING ME TO DROWN HIM IN A MORASS OF SEMEN AND BURST CONDOMS.
WE RECORDED HIS CALL. AND ROYCE'S. IT'S FOR REAL. YOU AND THE PRESIDENT, ONE ON ONE.
OR ELSE.

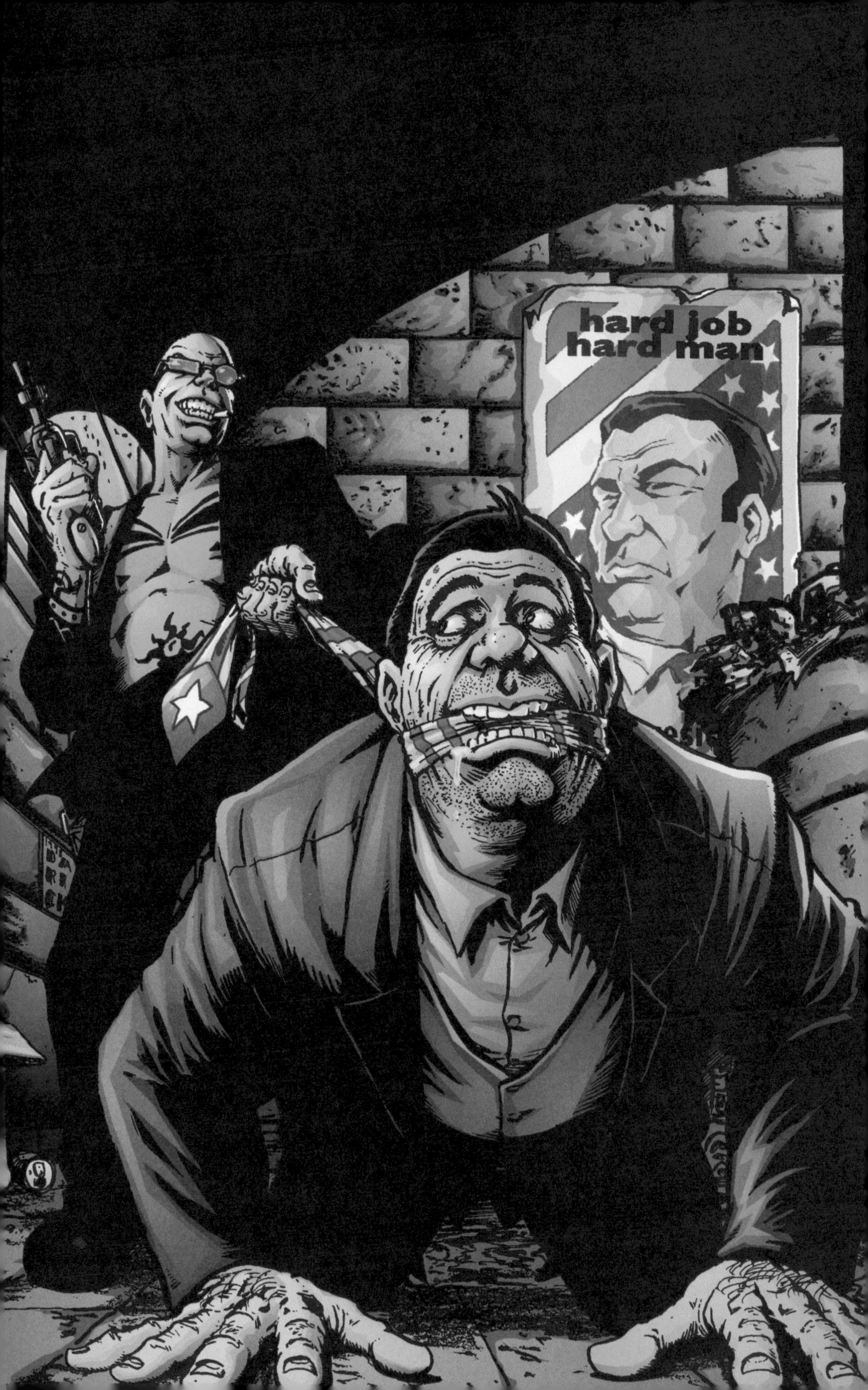
hard job
hard man

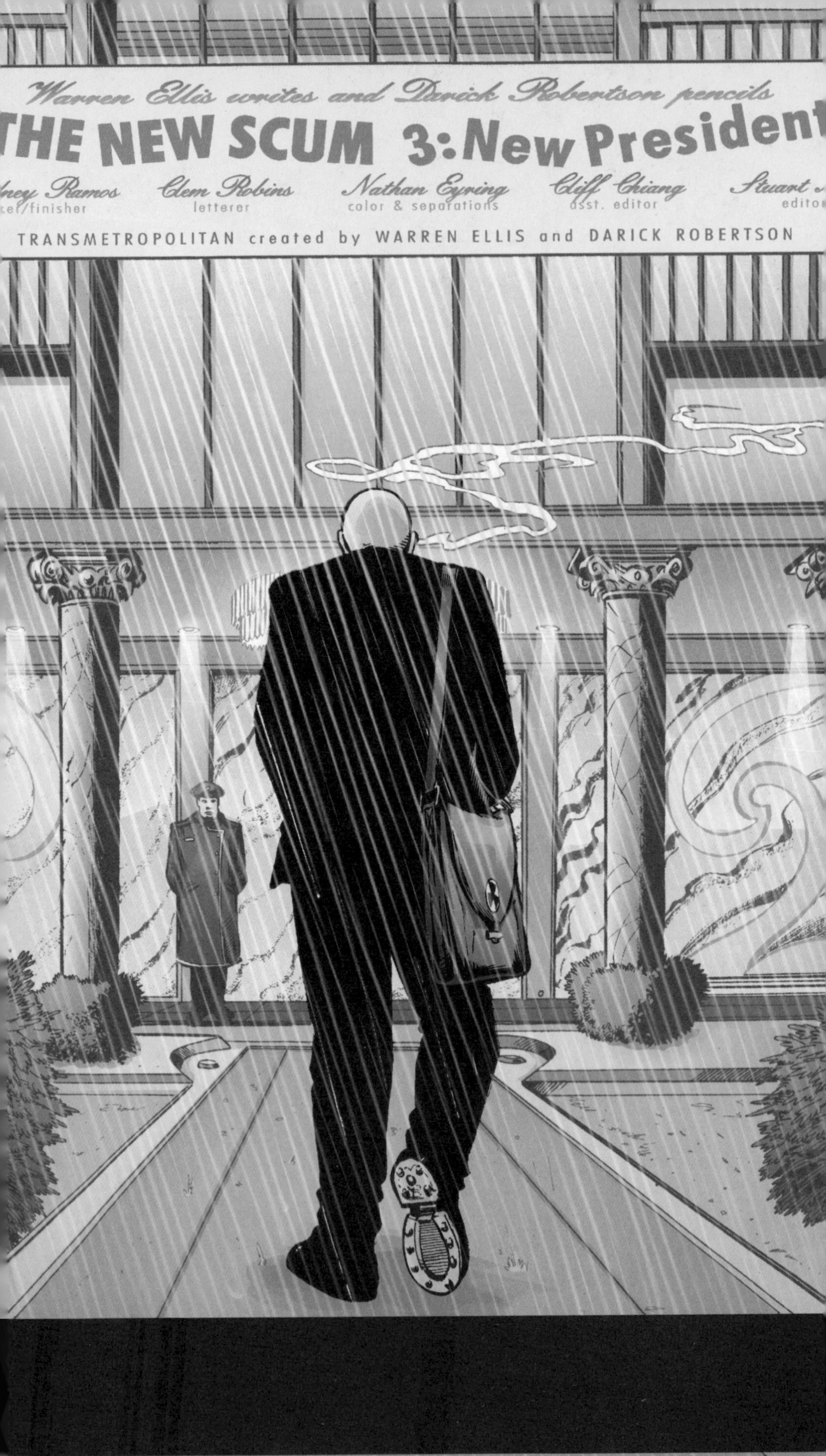
Warren Ellis writes and Darick Robertson pencils
THE NEW SCUM 3: New President
Ramos
Clem Robins
letterer
Nathan Eyring
color & separations
Cliff Chiang
asst. editor
TRANSMETROPOLITAN created by WARREN ELLIS and DARICK ROBERTSON

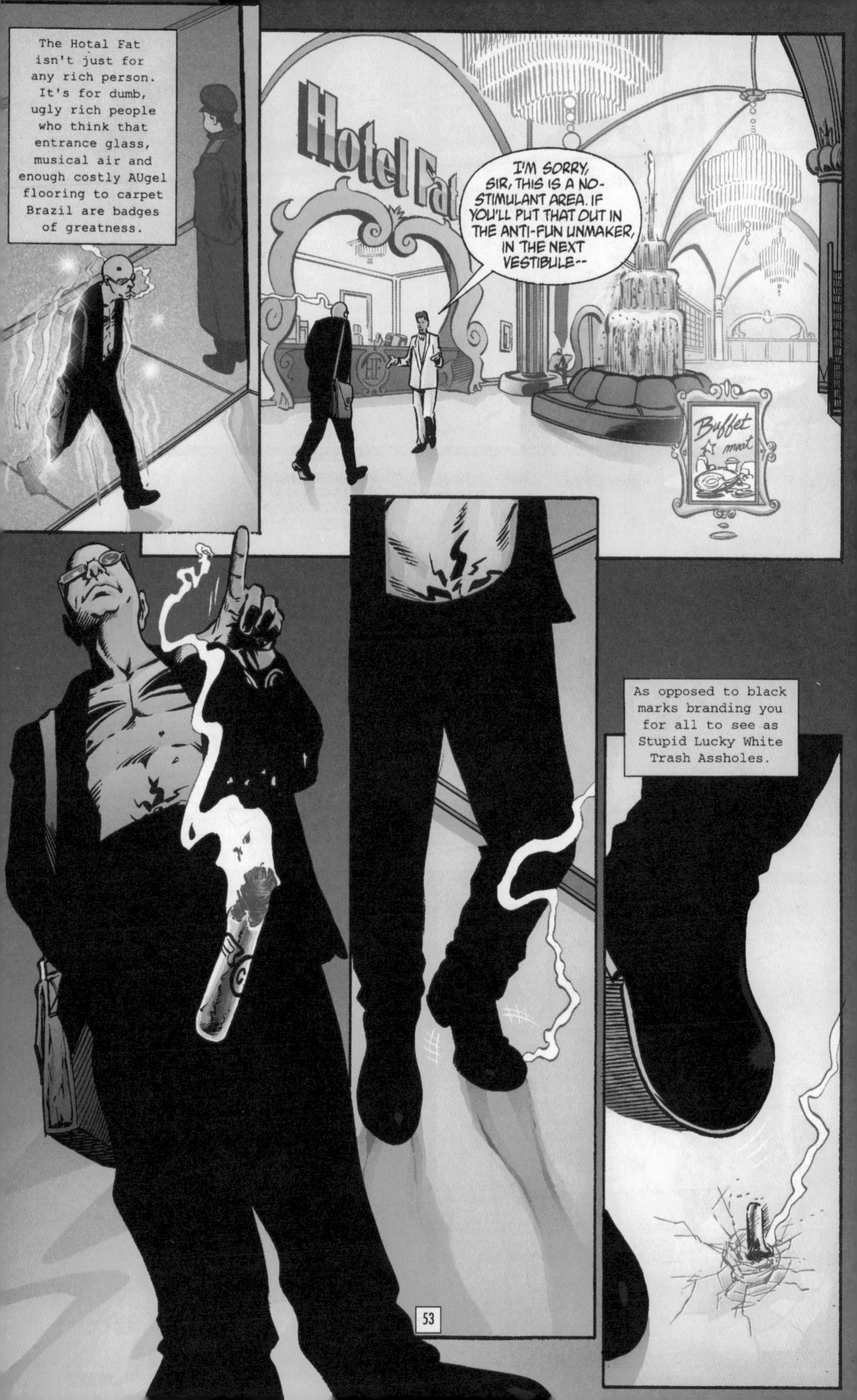

The Hotal Fat isn't just for any rich person. It's for dumb, ugly rich people who think that entrance glass, musical air and enough costly AUgel flooring to carpet Brazil are badges of greatness.
Hotel Fat
I'M SORRY, SIR, THIS IS A NO-STIMULANT AREA. IF YOU'LL PUT THAT OUT IN THE ANTI-FUN UNMAKER, IN THE NEXT VESTIBULE--
HF
Buffet
As opposed to black marks branding you for all to see as Stupid Lucky White Trash Assholes.

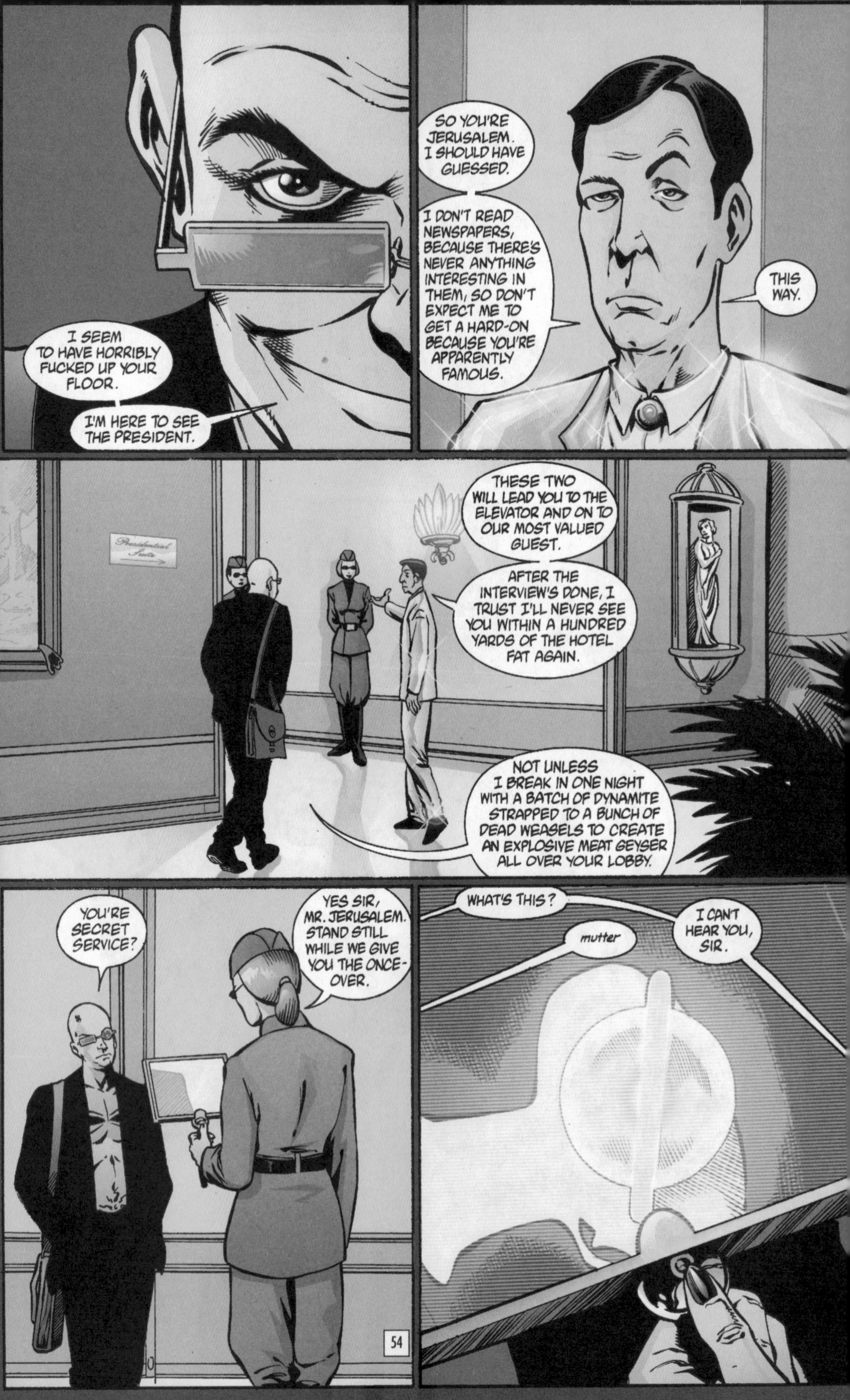
I SEEM TO HAVE HORRIBLY FUCKED UP YOUR FLOOR.
I'M HERE TO SEE THE PRESIDENT.
SO YOU'RE JERUSALEM. I SHOULD HAVE GUESSED.
I DON'T READ NEWSPAPERS, BECAUSE THERE'S NEVER ANYTHING INTERESTING IN THEM, SO DON'T EXPECT ME TO GET A HARD-ON BECAUSE YOU'RE APPARENTLY FAMOUS.
THIS WAY.
THESE TWO WILL LEAD YOU TO THE ELEVATOR AND ON TO OUR MOST VALUED GUEST.
AFTER THE INTERVIEW'S DONE, I TRUST I'LL NEVER SEE YOU WITHIN A HUNDRED YARDS OF THE HOTEL FAT AGAIN.
NOT UNLESS I BREAK IN ONE NIGHT WITH A BATCH OF DYNAMITE STRAPPED TO A BUNCH OF DEAD WEASELS TO CREATE AN EXPLOSIVE MEAT GEYSER ALL OVER YOUR LOBBY.
YOU'RE SECRET SERVICE?
YES SIR, MR. JERUSALEM. STAND STILL WHILE WE GIVE YOU THE ONCE-OVER.
WHAT'S THIS?
mutter
I CAN'T HEAR YOU, SIR.

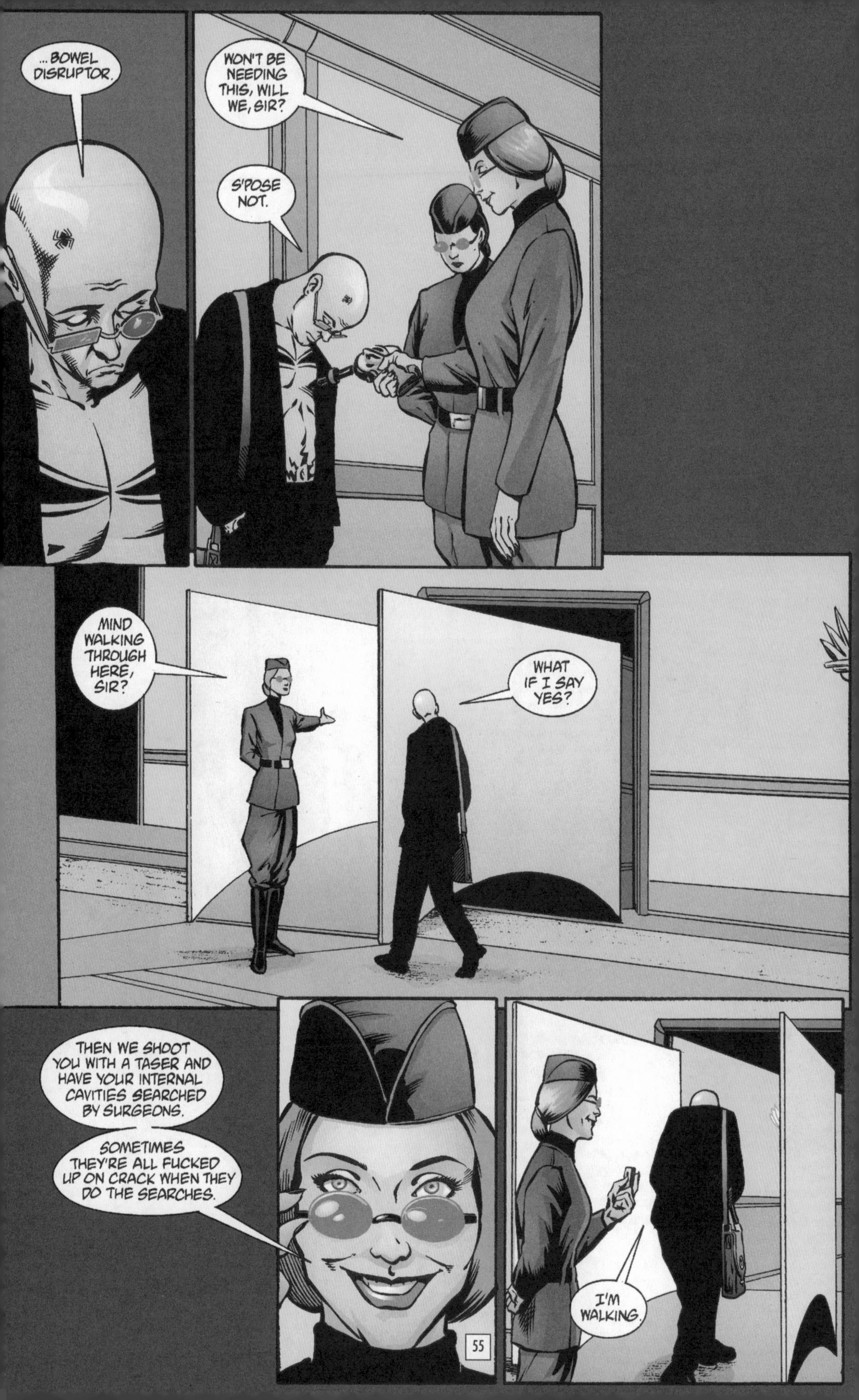
...BOWEL DISRUPTOR.
WON'T BE NEEDING THIS, WILL WE, SIR?
S'POSE NOT.
MIND WALKING THROUGH HERE, SIR?
WHAT IF I SAY YES?
THEN WE SHOOT YOU WITH A TASER AND HAVE YOUR INTERNAL CAVITIES SEARCHED BY SURGEONS.
SOMETIMES THEY'RE ALL FUCKED UP ON CRACK WHEN THEY DO THE SEARCHES.
I'M WALKING.

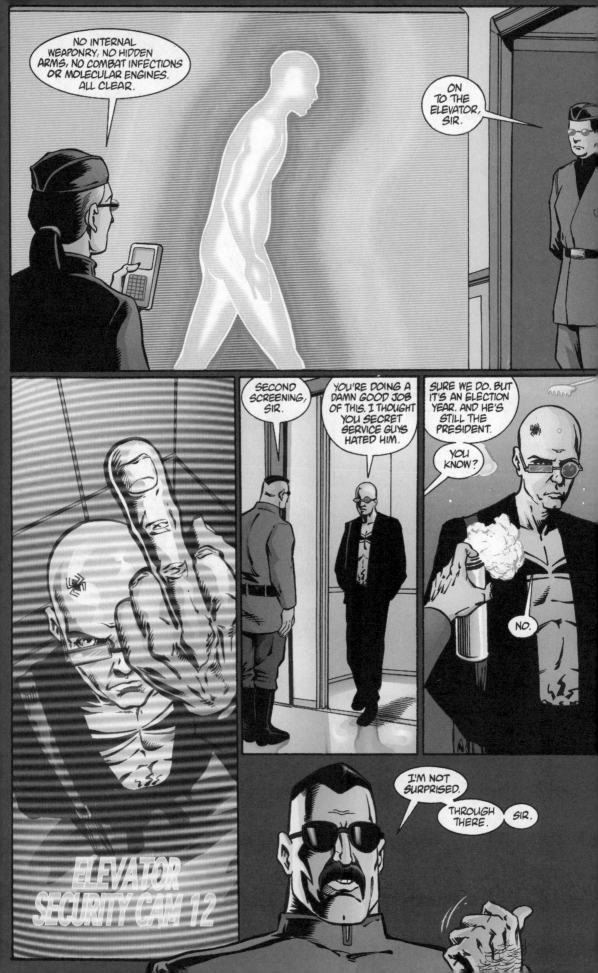

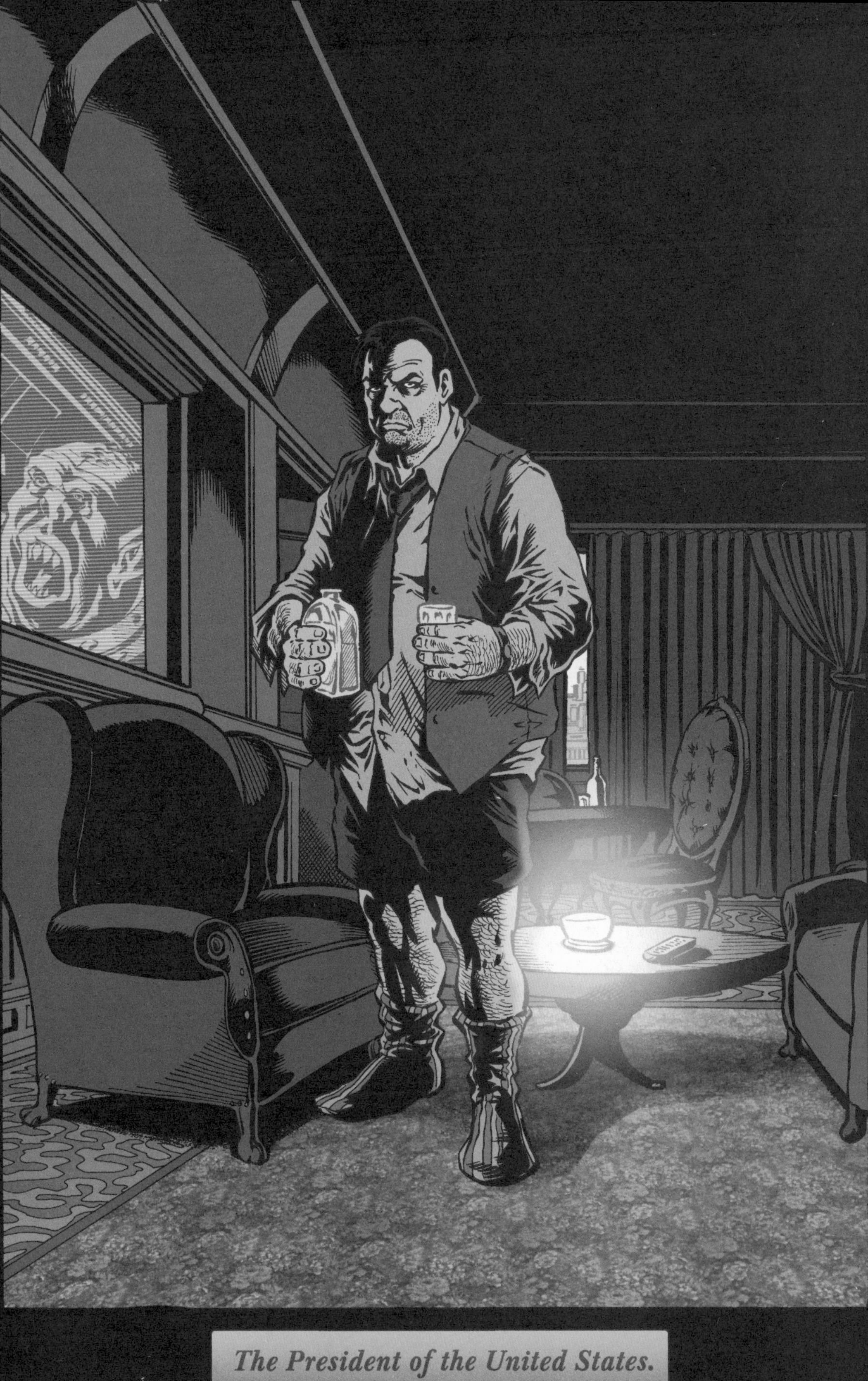
The President of the United States.

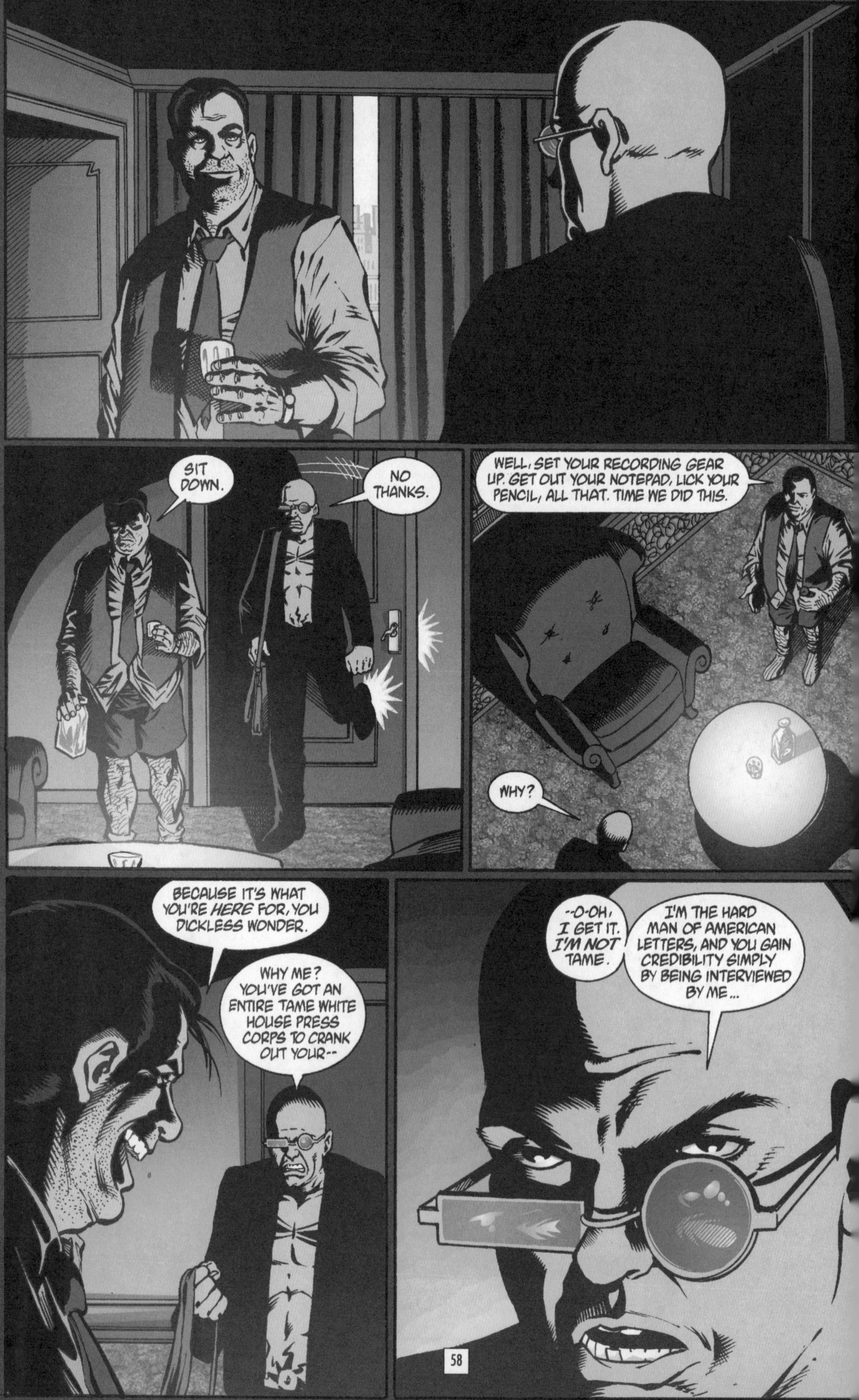
SIT DOWN.
NO THANKS.
WELL. SET YOUR RECORDING GEAR UP. GET OUT YOUR NOTEPAD, LICK YOUR PENCIL, ALL THAT. TIME WE DID THIS.
WHY?
BECAUSE IT'S WHAT YOU'RE *HERE* FOR, YOU DICKLESS WONDER.
WHY ME? YOU'VE GOT AN ENTIRE TAME WHITE HOUSE PRESS CORPS TO CRANK OUT YOUR--
--O-OH, I GET IT. *I'M NOT* TAME.
I'M THE HARD MAN OF AMERICAN LETTERS, AND YOU GAIN CREDIBILITY SIMPLY BY BEING INTERVIEWED BY ME...

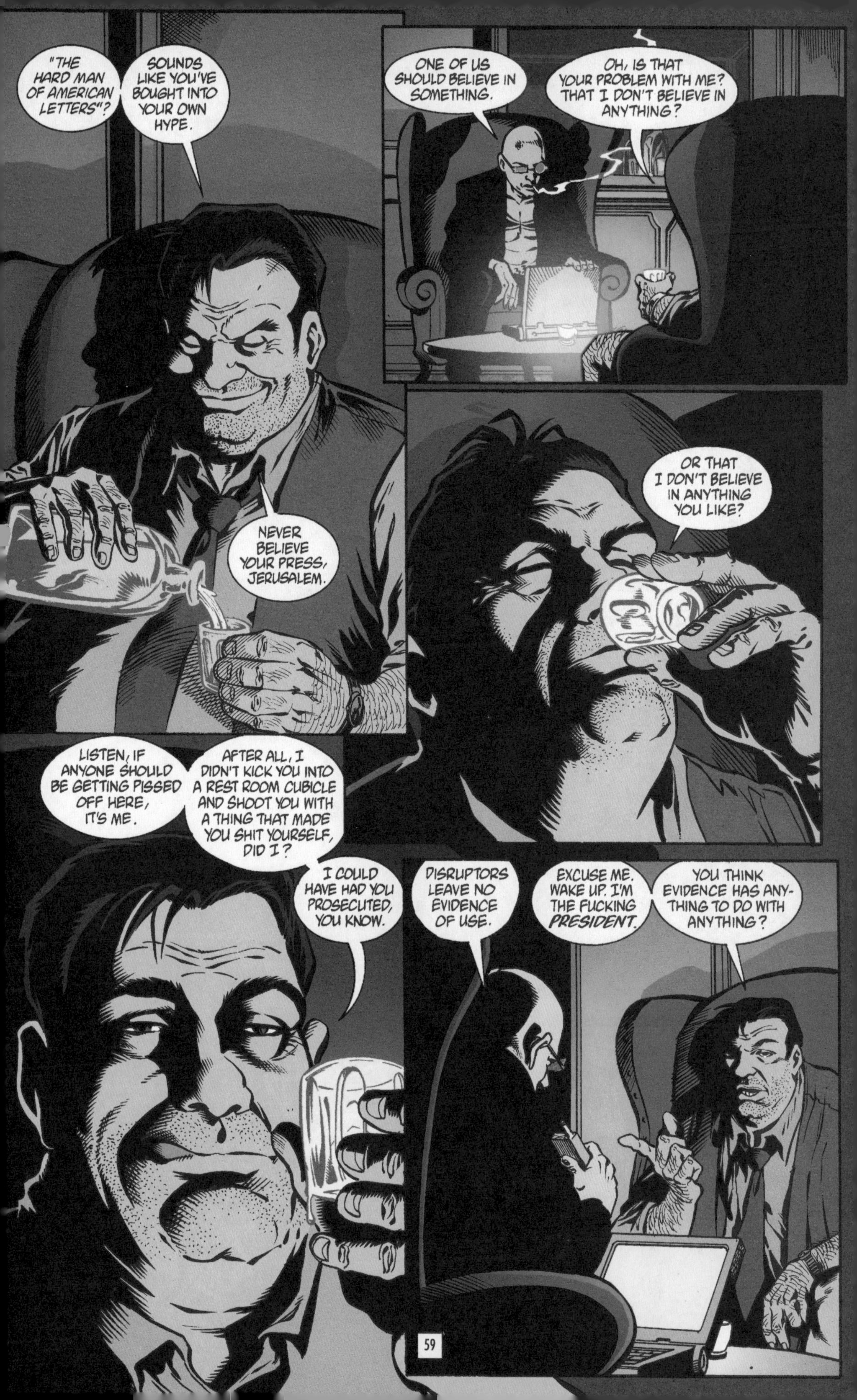
"THE HARD MAN OF AMERICAN LETTERS"?
SOUNDS LIKE YOU'VE BOUGHT INTO YOUR OWN HYPE.
ONE OF US SHOULD BELIEVE IN SOMETHING.
OH, IS THAT YOUR PROBLEM WITH ME? THAT I DON'T BELIEVE IN ANYTHING?
NEVER BELIEVE YOUR PRESS, JERUSALEM.
OR THAT I DON'T BELIEVE IN ANYTHING YOU LIKE?
LISTEN, IF ANYONE SHOULD BE GETTING PISSED OFF HERE, IT'S ME.
AFTER ALL, I DIDN'T KICK YOU INTO A REST ROOM CUBICLE AND SHOOT YOU WITH A THING THAT MADE YOU SHIT YOURSELF, DID I?
I COULD HAVE HAD YOU PROSECUTED, YOU KNOW.
DISRUPTORS LEAVE NO EVIDENCE OF USE.
EXCUSE ME. WAKE UP. I'M THE FUCKING *PRESIDENT*.
YOU THINK EVIDENCE HAS ANYTHING TO DO WITH ANYTHING?

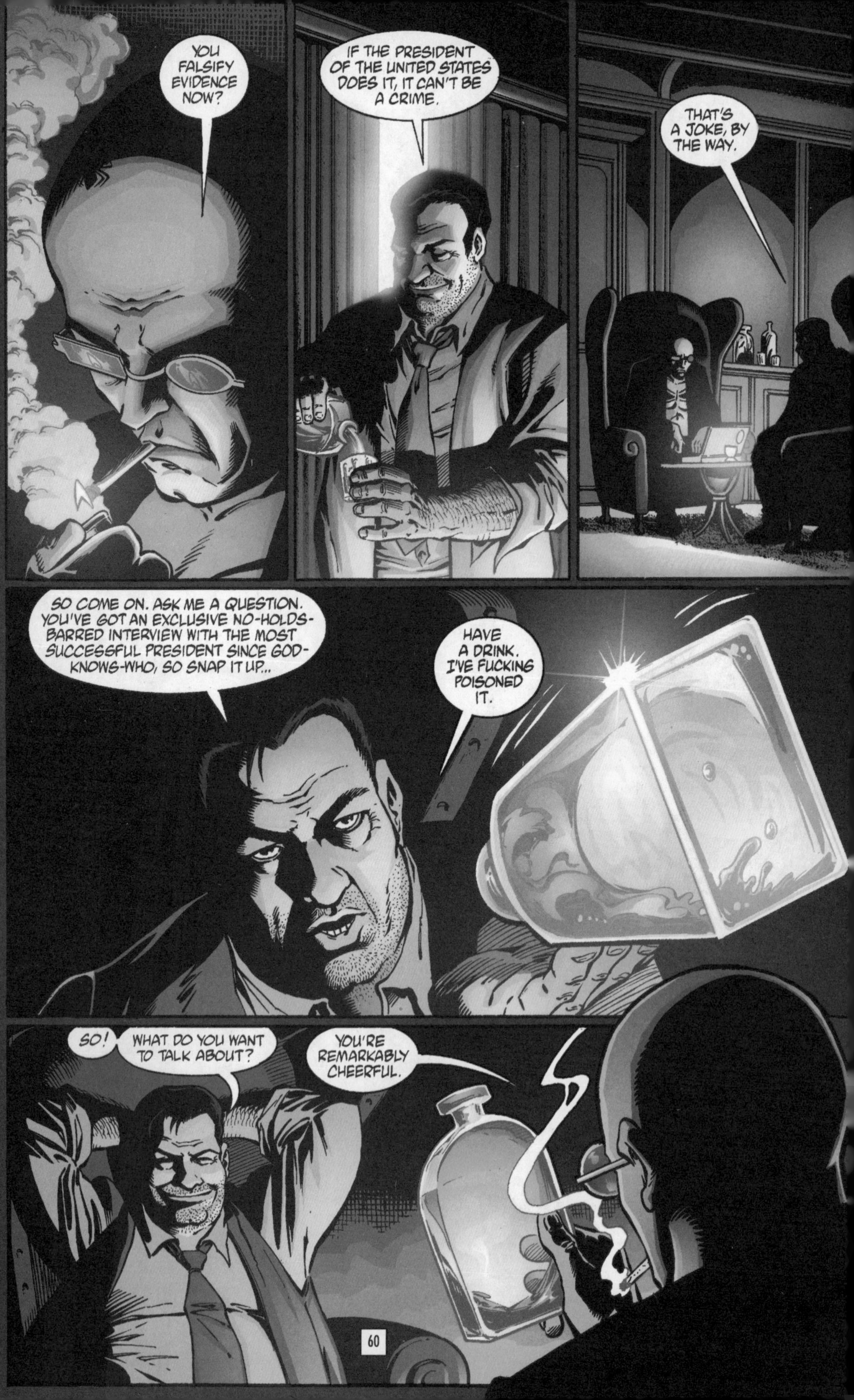

YOU FALSIFY EVIDENCE NOW?
IF THE PRESIDENT OF THE UNITED STATES DOES IT, IT CAN'T BE A CRIME.
THAT'S A JOKE, BY THE WAY.
SO COME ON. ASK ME A QUESTION. YOU'VE GOT AN EXCLUSIVE NO-HOLDS-BARRED INTERVIEW WITH THE MOST SUCCESSFUL PRESIDENT SINCE GOD-KNOWS-WHO, SO SNAP IT UP...
HAVE A DRINK. I'VE FUCKING POISONED IT.
SO!
WHAT DO YOU WANT TO TALK ABOUT?
YOU'RE REMARKABLY CHEERFUL.

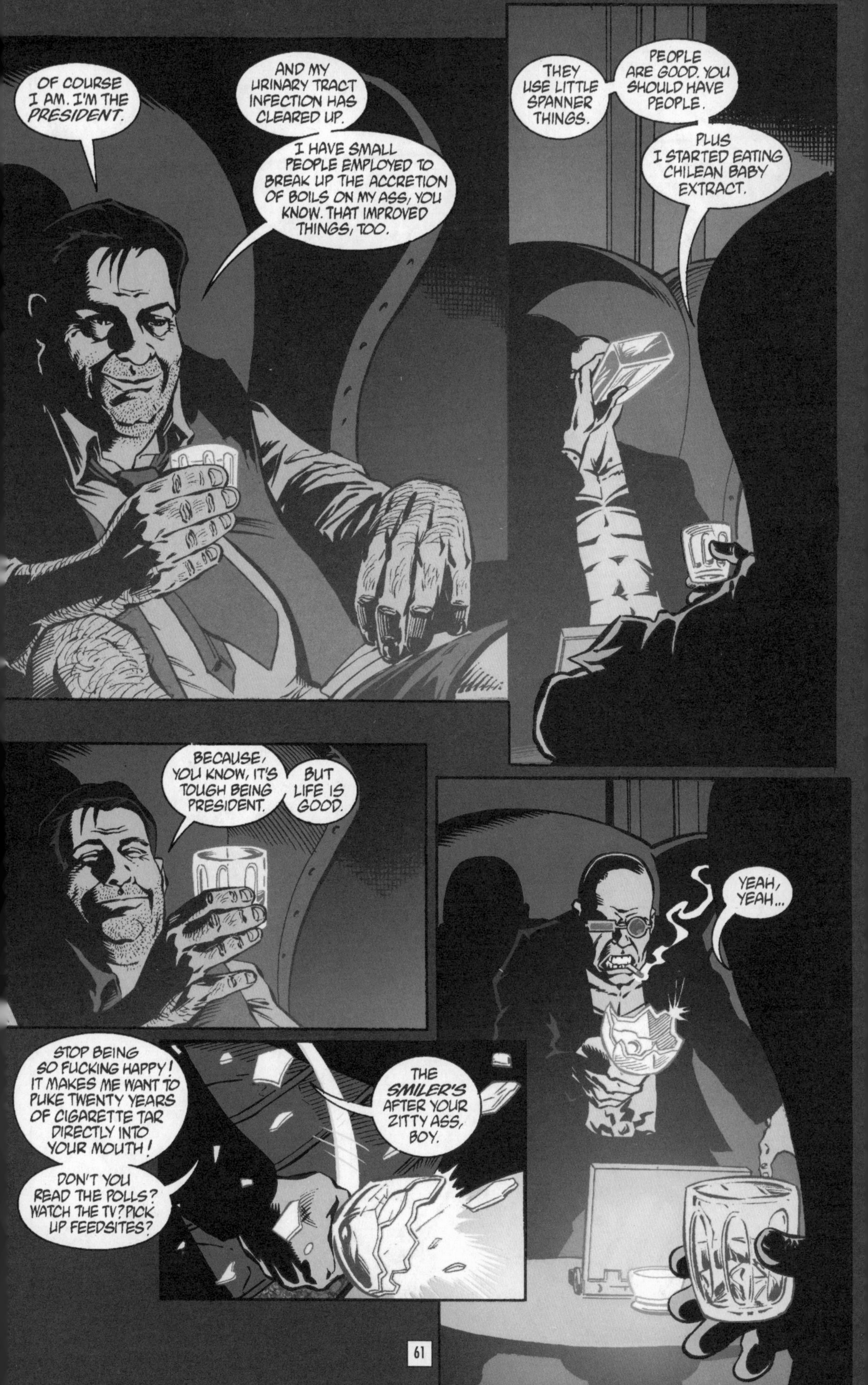

OF COURSE I AM. I'M THE PRESIDENT.
AND MY URINARY TRACT INFECTION HAS CLEARED UP.
I HAVE SMALL PEOPLE EMPLOYED TO BREAK UP THE ACCRETION OF BOILS ON MY ASS, YOU KNOW. THAT IMPROVED THINGS, TOO.
THEY USE LITTLE SPANNER THINGS.
PEOPLE ARE GOOD. YOU SHOULD HAVE PEOPLE.
PLUS I STARTED EATING CHILEAN BABY EXTRACT.
BECAUSE, YOU KNOW, IT'S TOUGH BEING PRESIDENT.
BUT LIFE IS GOOD.
YEAH, YEAH...
STOP BEING SO FUCKING HAPPY! IT MAKES ME WANT TO PUKE TWENTY YEARS OF CIGARETTE TAR DIRECTLY INTO YOUR MOUTH!
DON'T YOU READ THE POLLS? WATCH THE TV? PICK UP FEEDSITES?
THE SMILER'S AFTER YOUR ZITTY ASS, BOY.

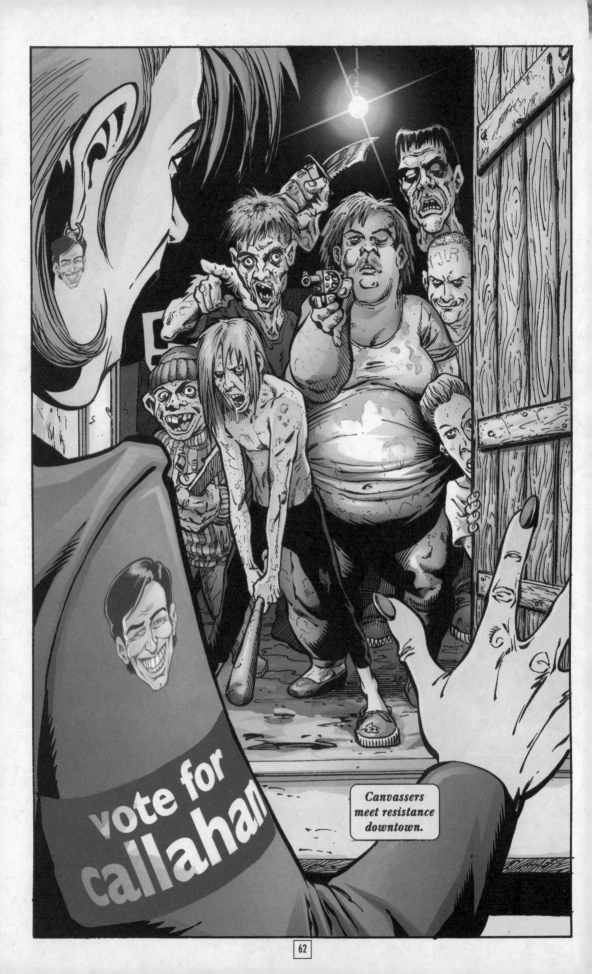

Canvassers meet resistance downtown.

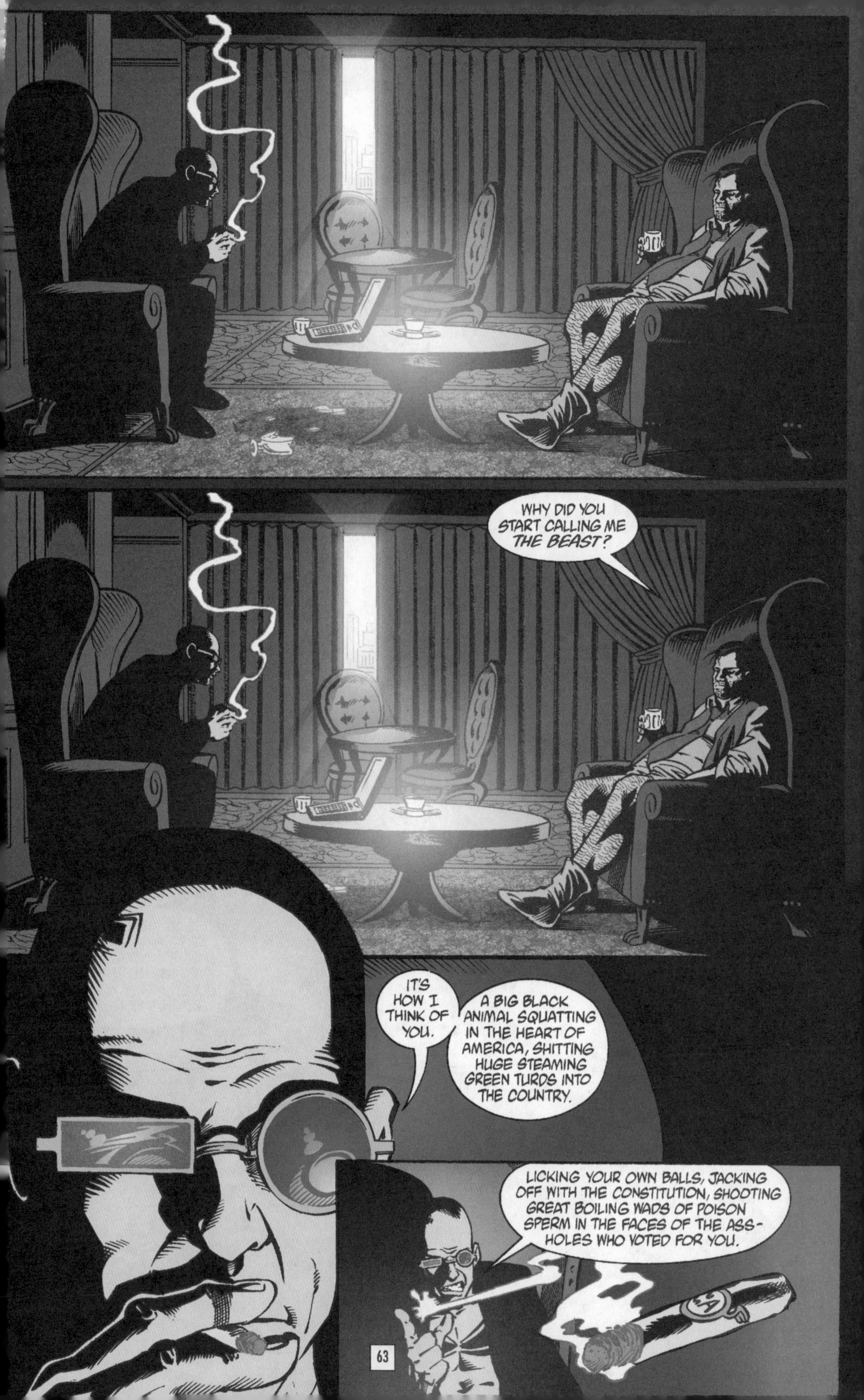

WHY DID YOU START CALLING ME THE BEAST?
IT'S HOW I THINK OF YOU.
A BIG BLACK ANIMAL SQUATTING IN THE HEART OF AMERICA, SHITTING HUGE STEAMING GREEN TURDS INTO THE COUNTRY.
LICKING YOUR OWN BALLS, JACKING OFF WITH THE CONSTITUTION, SHOOTING GREAT BOILING WADS OF POISON SPERM IN THE FACES OF THE ASS-HOLES WHO VOTED FOR YOU.

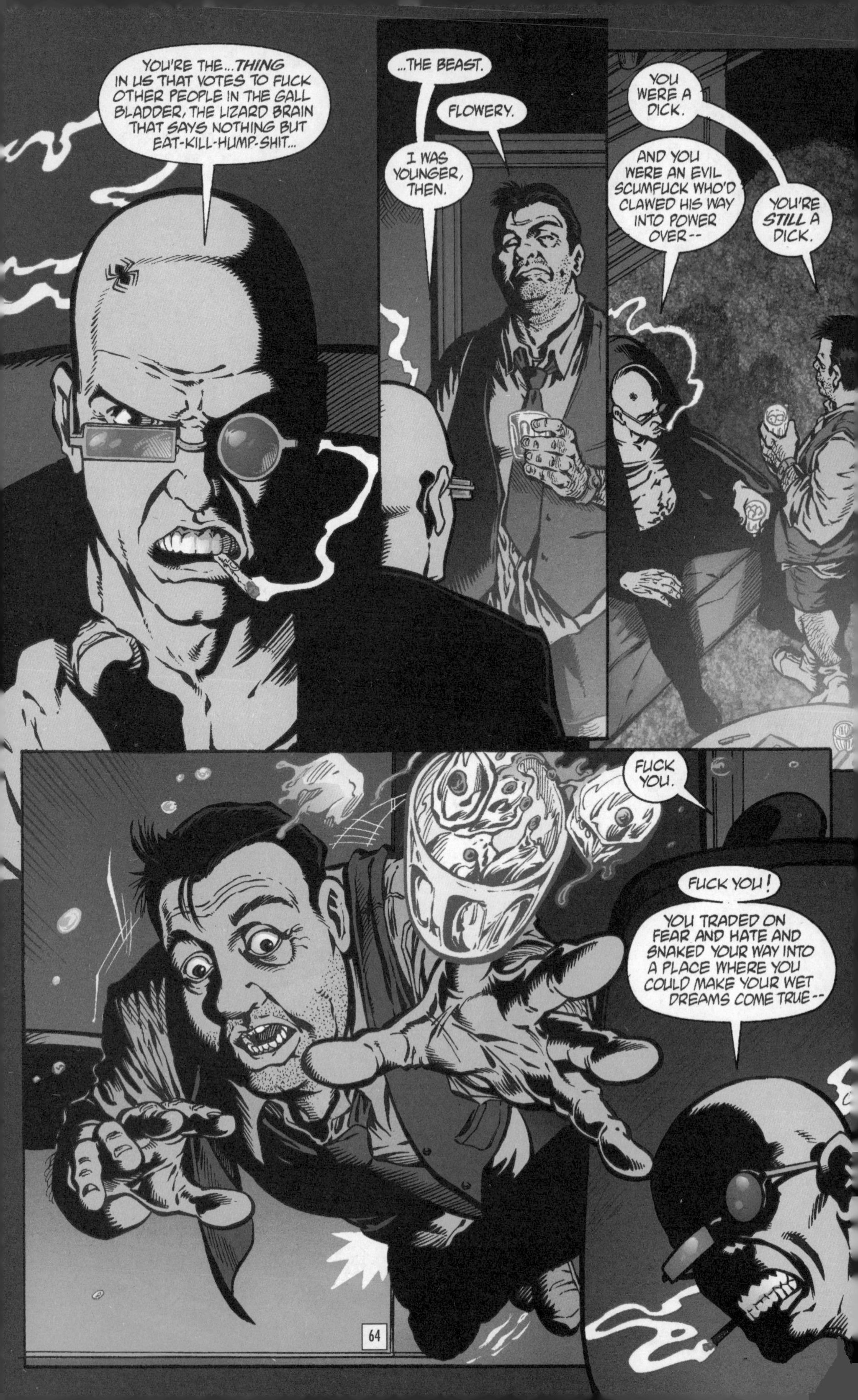
YOU'RE THE... THING IN US THAT VOTES TO FUCK OTHER PEOPLE IN THE GALL BLADDER, THE LIZARD BRAIN THAT SAYS NOTHING BUT EAT-KILL-HUMP-SHIT...
...THE BEAST.
FLOWERY.
I WAS YOUNGER, THEN.
YOU WERE A DICK.
AND YOU WERE AN EVIL SCUMFUCK WHO'D CLAWED HIS WAY INTO POWER OVER--
YOU'RE STILL A DICK.
FUCK YOU.
FUCK YOU!
YOU TRADED ON FEAR AND HATE AND SNAKED YOUR WAY INTO A PLACE WHERE YOU COULD MAKE YOUR WET DREAMS COME TRUE--

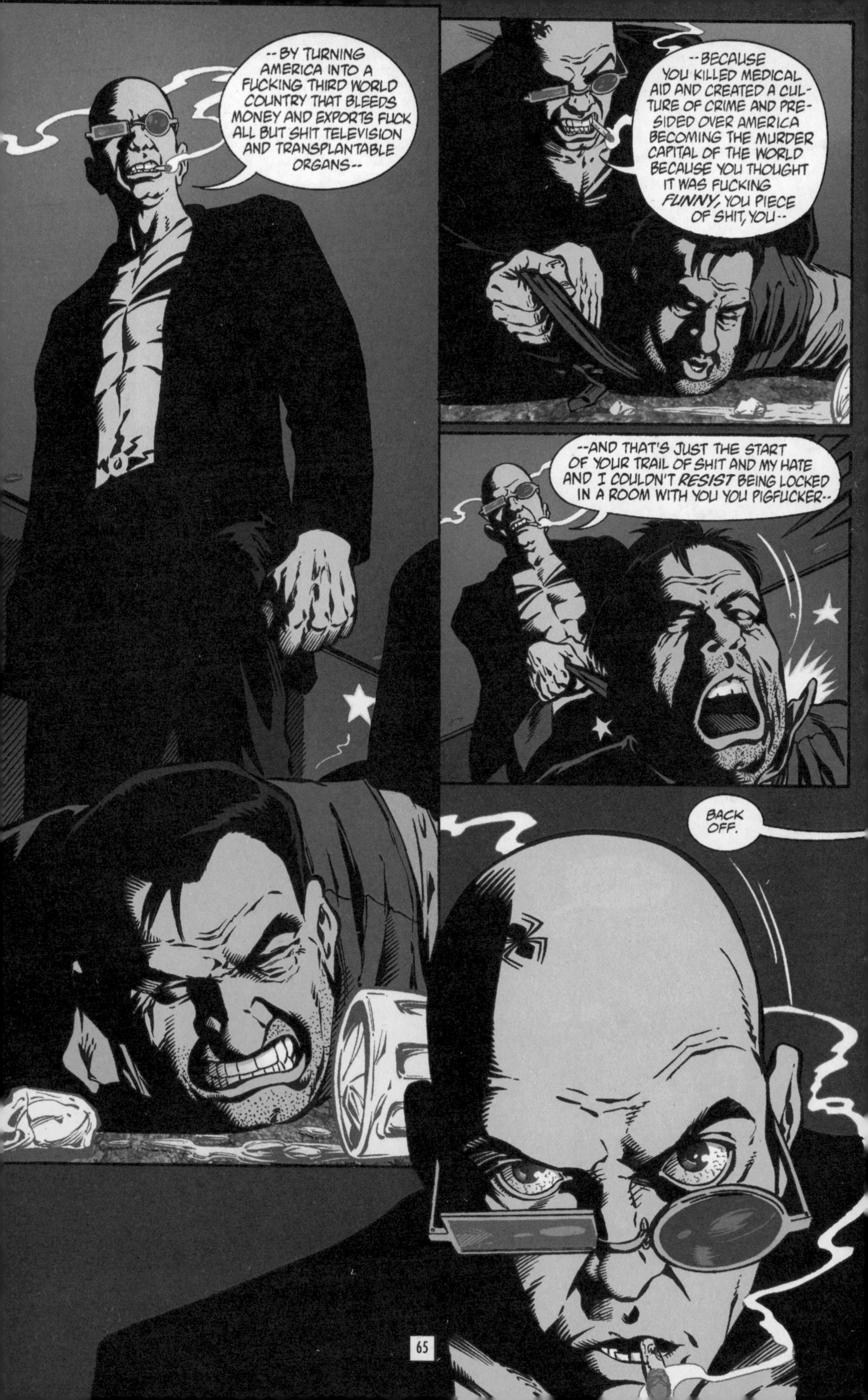
--BY TURNING AMERICA INTO A FUCKING THIRD WORLD COUNTRY THAT BLEEDS MONEY AND EXPORTS FUCK ALL BUT SHIT TELEVISION AND TRANSPLANTABLE ORGANS--
--BECAUSE YOU KILLED MEDICAL AID AND CREATED A CULTURE OF CRIME AND PRESIDED OVER AMERICA BECOMING THE MURDER CAPITAL OF THE WORLD BECAUSE YOU THOUGHT IT WAS FUCKING *FUNNY,* YOU PIECE OF SHIT, YOU--
--AND THAT'S JUST THE START OF YOUR TRAIL OF SHIT AND MY HATE AND I COULDN'T *RESIST* BEING LOCKED IN A ROOM WITH YOU YOU PIGFUCKER--
BACK OFF.

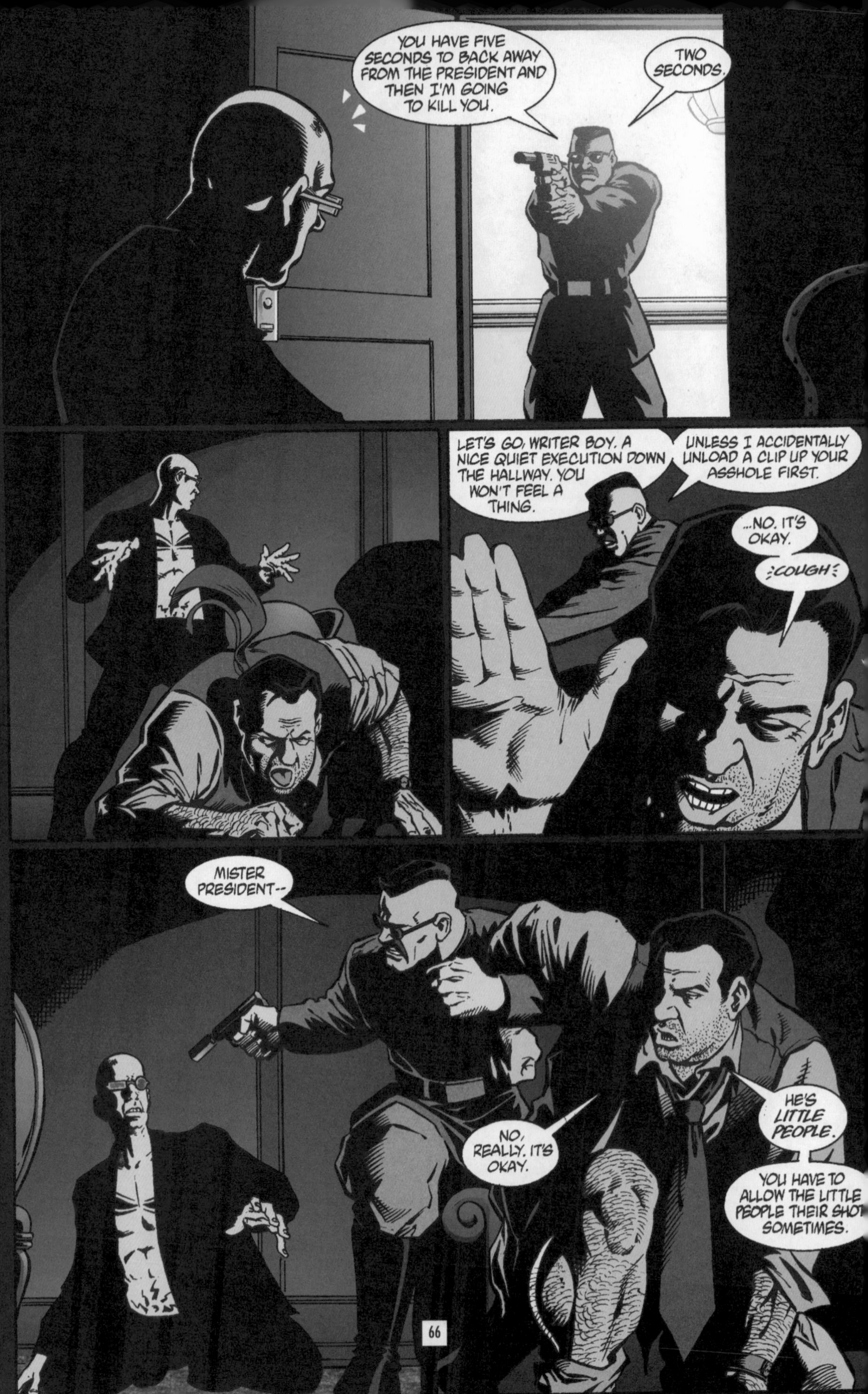
YOU HAVE FIVE SECONDS TO BACK AWAY FROM THE PRESIDENT AND THEN I'M GOING TO KILL YOU.
TWO SECONDS.
LET'S GO, WRITER BOY. A NICE QUIET EXECUTION DOWN THE HALLWAY. YOU WON'T FEEL A THING.
UNLESS I ACCIDENTALLY UNLOAD A CLIP UP YOUR ASSHOLE FIRST.
...NO. IT'S OKAY.
COUGH
MISTER PRESIDENT--
NO, REALLY. IT'S OKAY.
HE'S LITTLE PEOPLE.
YOU HAVE TO ALLOW THE LITTLE PEOPLE THEIR SHOT SOMETIMES.

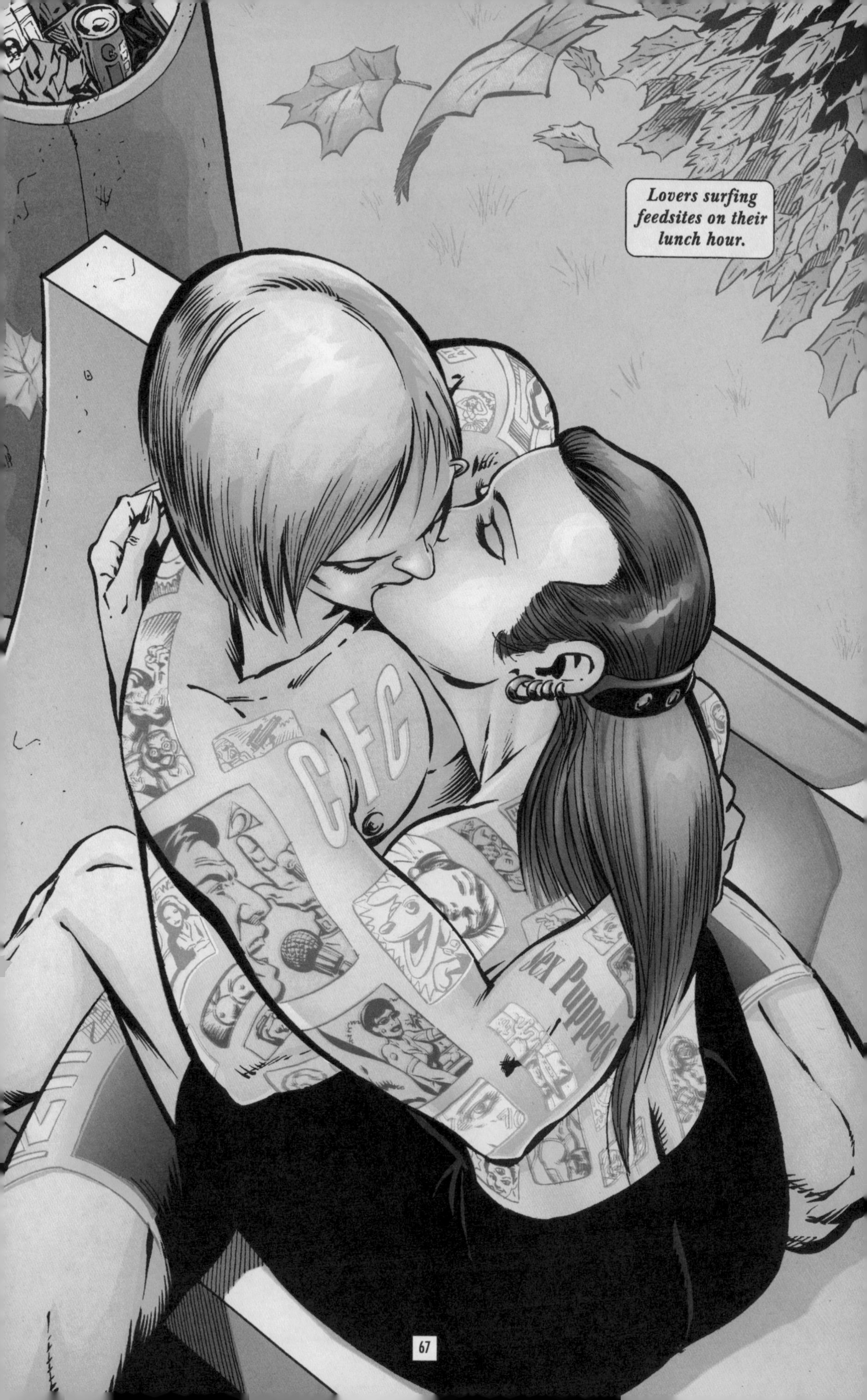
Lovers surfing feedsites on their lunch hour.
CFC
Sex Puppets

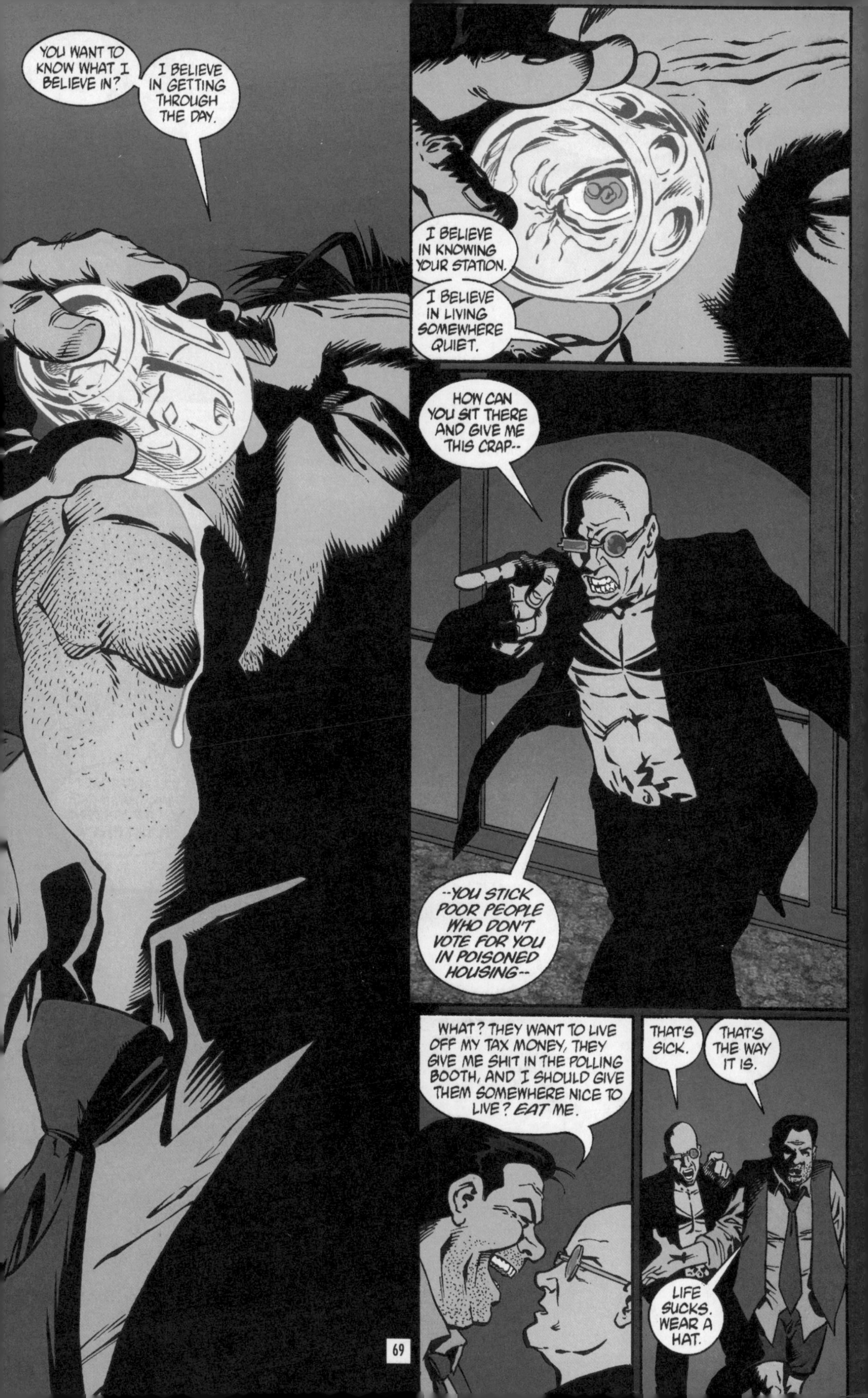
YOU WANT TO KNOW WHAT I BELIEVE IN?
I BELIEVE IN GETTING THROUGH THE DAY.
I BELIEVE IN KNOWING YOUR STATION.
I BELIEVE IN LIVING SOMEWHERE QUIET.
HOW CAN YOU SIT THERE AND GIVE ME THIS CRAP--
--YOU STICK POOR PEOPLE WHO DON'T VOTE FOR YOU IN POISONED HOUSING--
WHAT? THEY WANT TO LIVE OFF MY TAX MONEY, THEY GIVE ME SHIT IN THE POLLING BOOTH, AND I SHOULD GIVE THEM SOMEWHERE NICE TO LIVE? EAT ME.
THAT'S SICK.
THAT'S THE WAY IT IS.
LIFE SUCKS. WEAR A HAT.

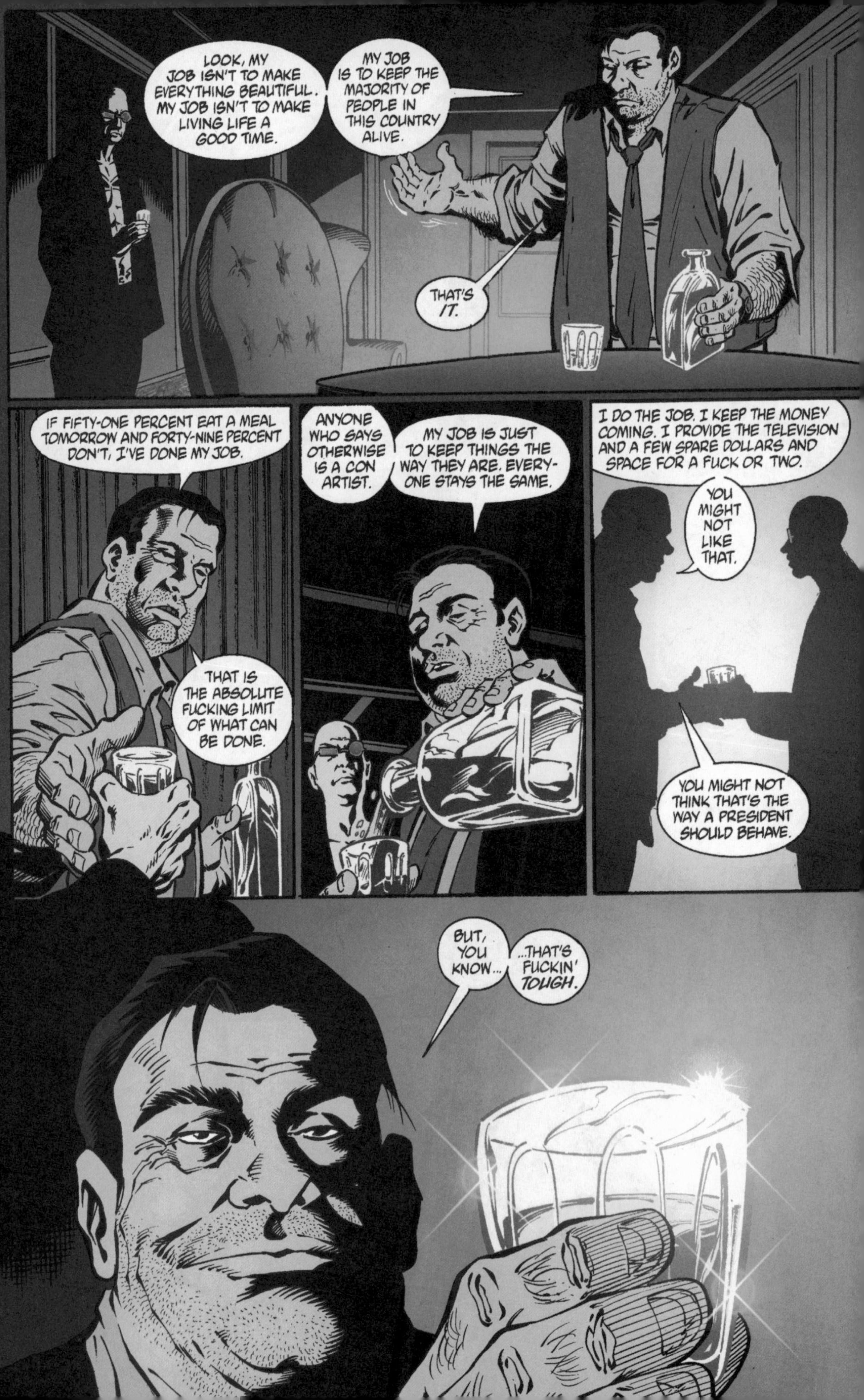
LOOK, MY JOB ISN'T TO MAKE EVERYTHING BEAUTIFUL. MY JOB ISN'T TO MAKE LIVING LIFE A GOOD TIME.
MY JOB IS TO KEEP THE MAJORITY OF PEOPLE IN THIS COUNTRY ALIVE.
THAT'S *IT*.
IF FIFTY-ONE PERCENT EAT A MEAL TOMORROW AND FORTY-NINE PERCENT DON'T, I'VE DONE MY JOB.
THAT IS THE ABSOLUTE FUCKING LIMIT OF WHAT CAN BE DONE.
ANYONE WHO SAYS OTHERWISE IS A CON ARTIST.
MY JOB IS JUST TO KEEP THINGS THE WAY THEY ARE. EVERY-ONE STAYS THE SAME.
I DO THE JOB. I KEEP THE MONEY COMING. I PROVIDE THE TELEVISION AND A FEW SPARE DOLLARS AND SPACE FOR A FUCK OR TWO.
YOU MIGHT NOT LIKE THAT.
YOU MIGHT NOT THINK THAT'S THE WAY A PRESIDENT SHOULD BEHAVE.
BUT, YOU KNOW...
...THAT'S FUCKIN' *TOUGH*.

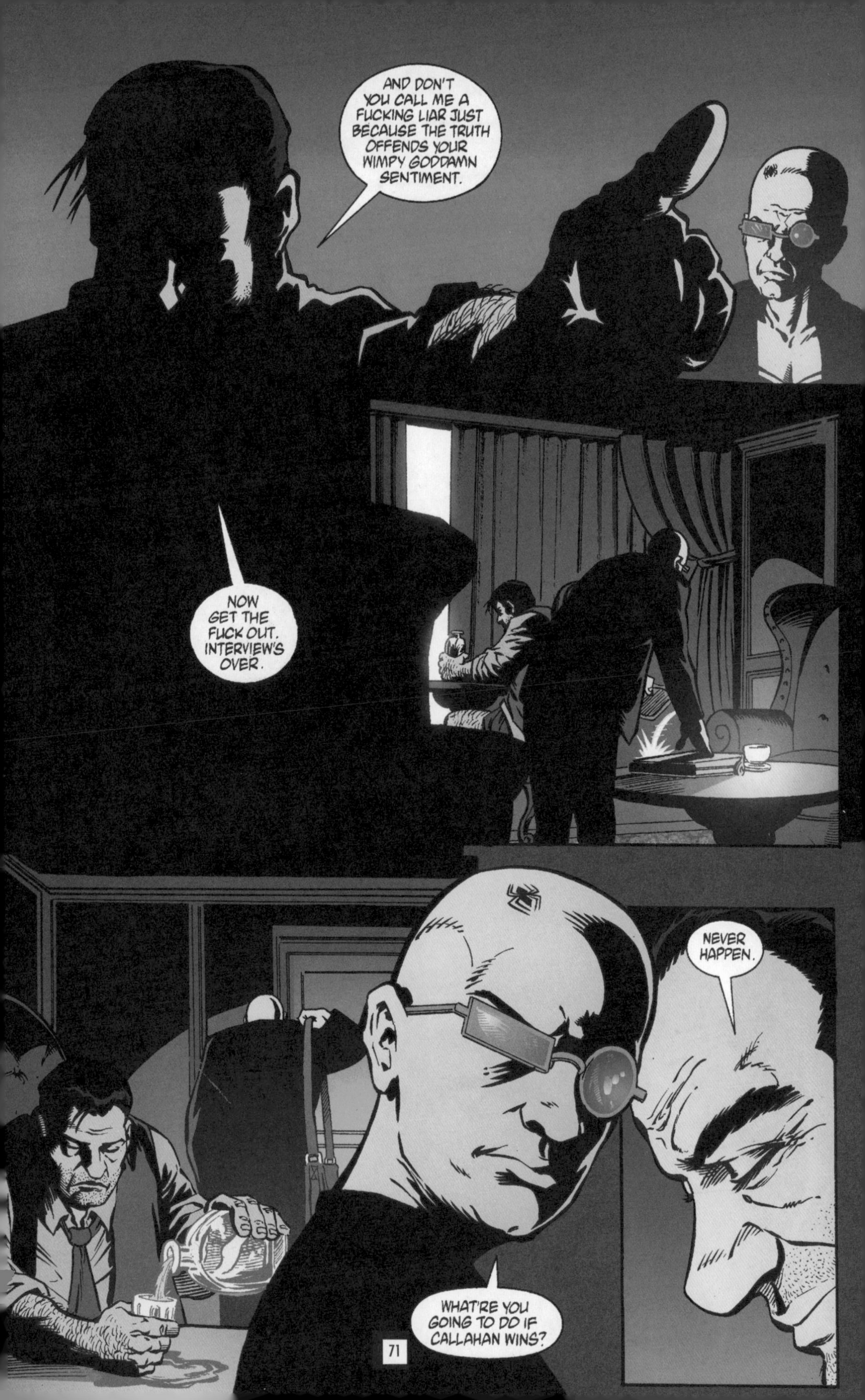
AND DON'T YOU CALL ME A FUCKING LIAR JUST BECAUSE THE TRUTH OFFENDS YOUR WIMPY GODDAMN SENTIMENT.
NOW GET THE FUCK OUT. INTERVIEW'S OVER.
WHAT'RE YOU GOING TO DO IF CALLAHAN WINS?
NEVER HAPPEN.

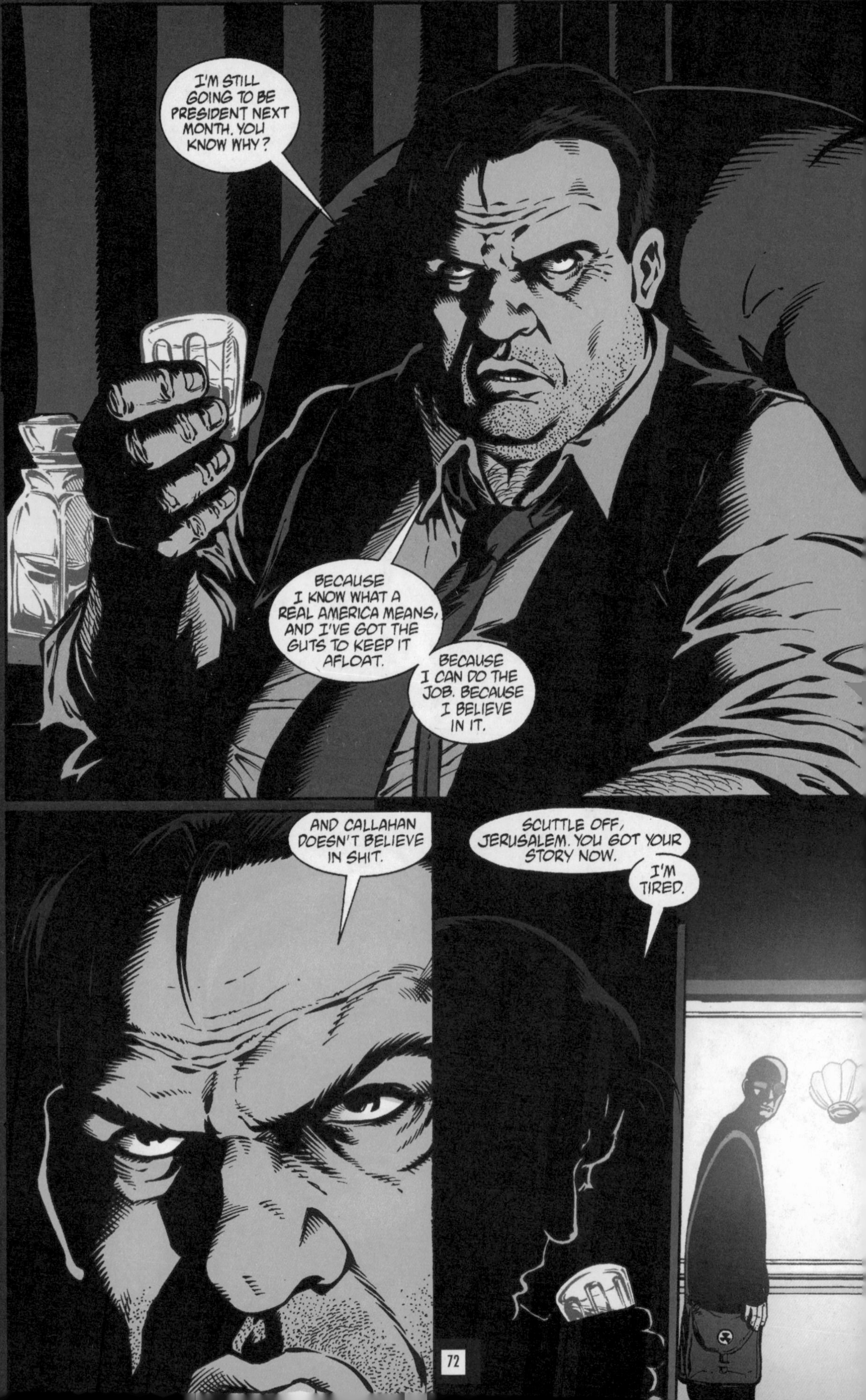
I'M STILL GOING TO BE PRESIDENT NEXT MONTH. YOU KNOW WHY?
BECAUSE I KNOW WHAT A REAL AMERICA MEANS, AND I'VE GOT THE GUTS TO KEEP IT AFLOAT.
BECAUSE I CAN DO THE JOB. BECAUSE I BELIEVE IN IT.
AND CALLAHAN DOESN'T BELIEVE IN SHIT.
SCUTTLE OFF, JERUSALEM. YOU GOT YOUR STORY NOW.
I'M TIRED.

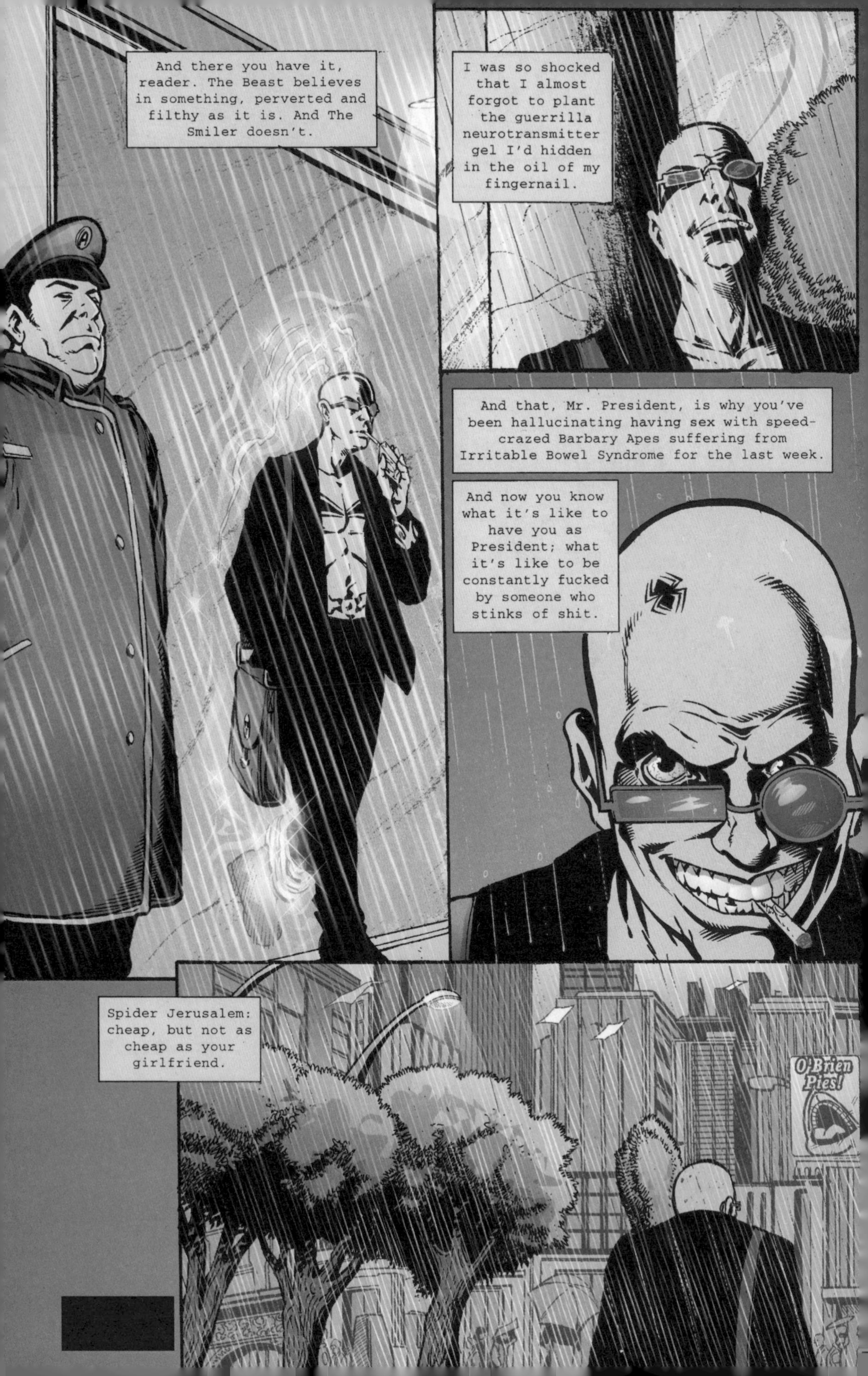
And there you have it, reader. The Beast believes in something, perverted and filthy as it is. And The Smiler doesn't.
I was so shocked that I almost forgot to plant the guerrilla neurotransmitter gel I'd hidden in the oil of my fingernail.
And that, Mr. President, is why you've been hallucinating having sex with speed-crazed Barbary Apes suffering from Irritable Bowel Syndrome for the last week.
And now you know what it's like to have you as President; what it's like to be constantly fucked by someone who stinks of shit.
Spider Jerusalem: cheap, but not as cheap as your girlfriend.
O'Brien Pies!

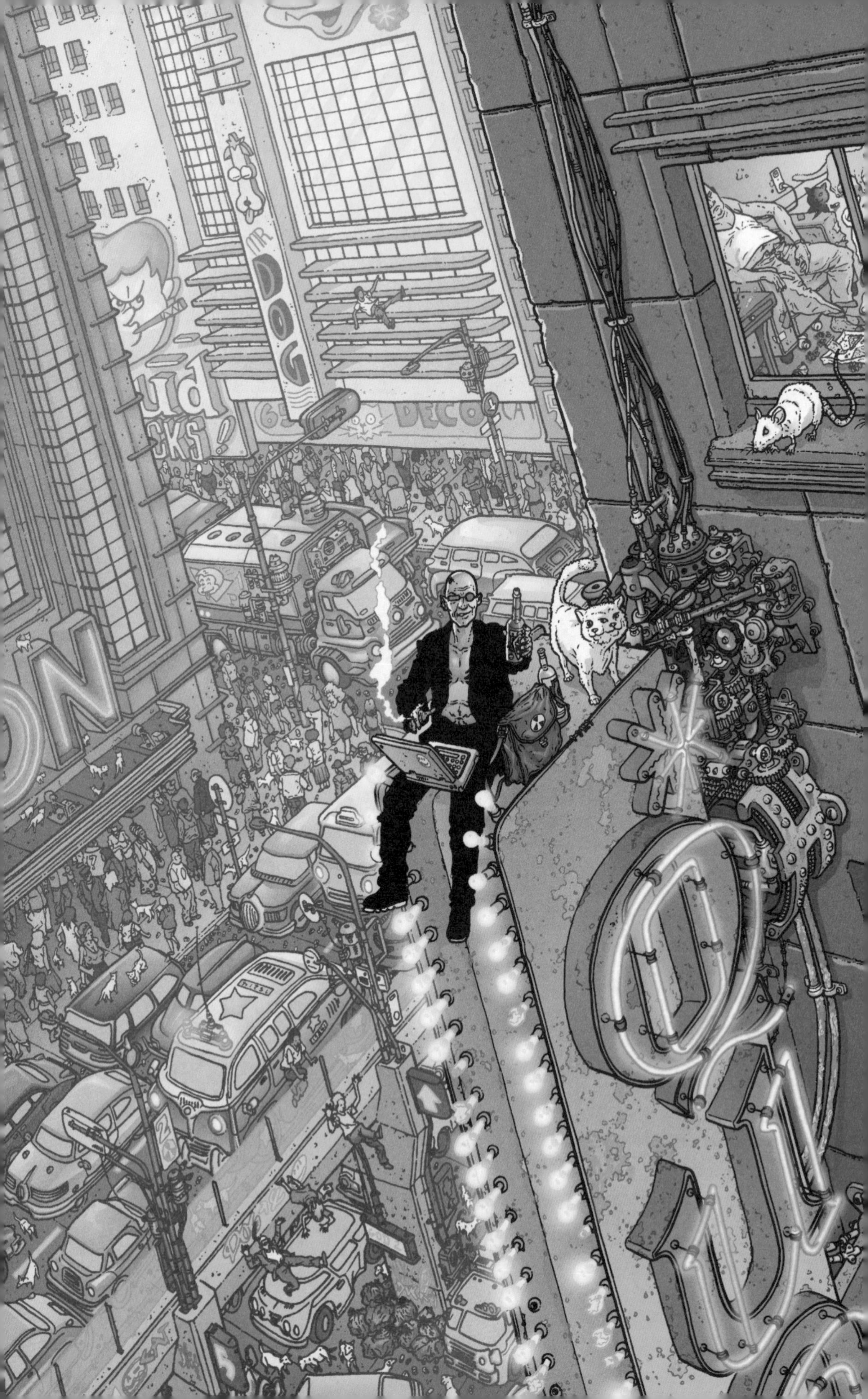
MR DOG
DECO

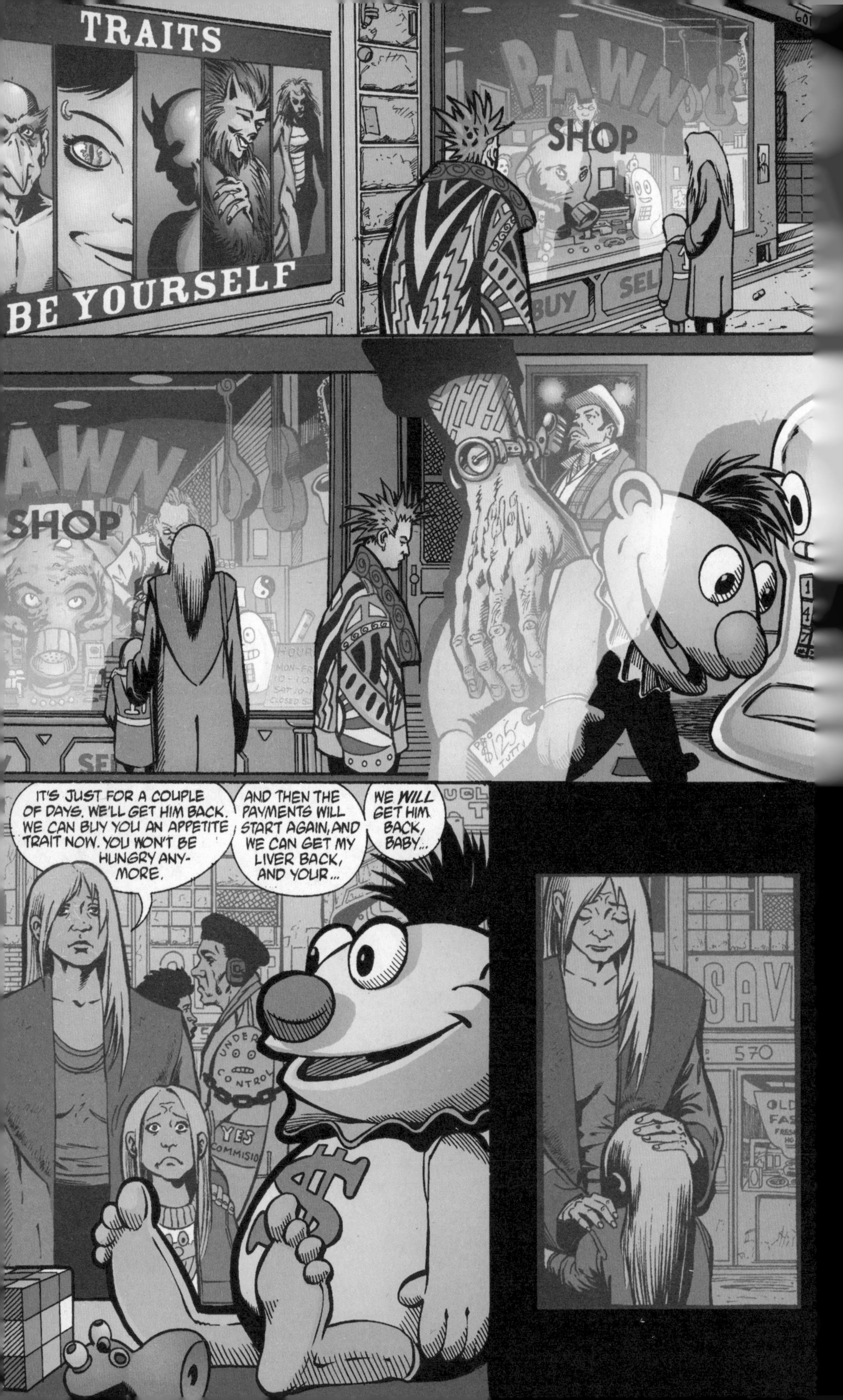
TRAITS
BE YOURSELF
PAWN
SHOP
BUY
SELL
SHOP
$125
IT'S JUST FOR A COUPLE OF DAYS. WE'LL GET HIM BACK. WE CAN BUY YOU AN APPETITE TRAIT NOW. YOU WON'T BE HUNGRY ANY-MORE.
AND THEN THE PAYMENTS WILL START AGAIN, AND WE CAN GET MY LIVER BACK, AND YOUR...
WE WILL GET HIM BACK, BABY...
UNDER CONTROL
YES
570

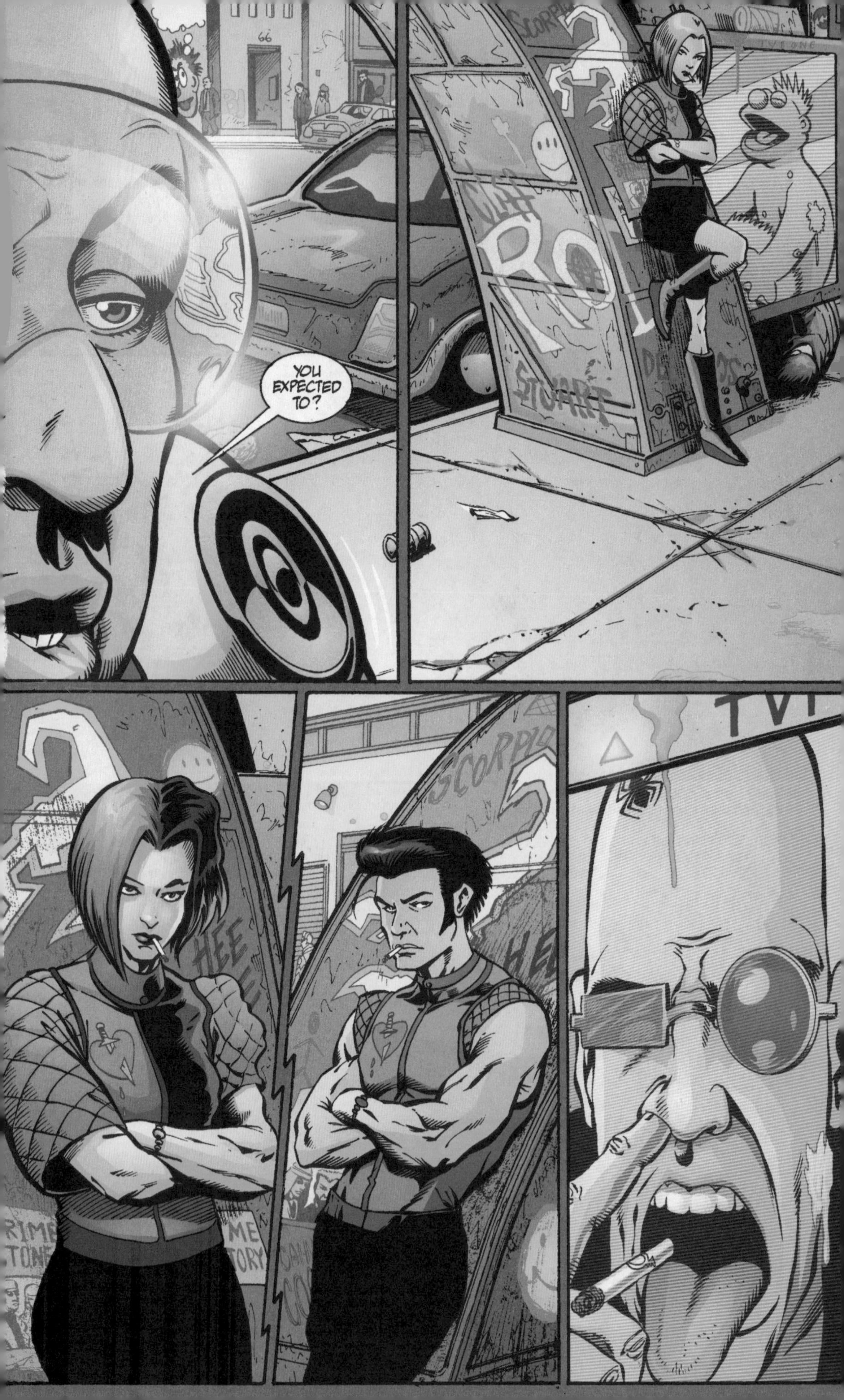
YOU EXPECTED TO?

WARREN ELLIS WRITES AND DARICK ROBERTSON PENCILS

THE NEW SCUM

4: NEW STREETS

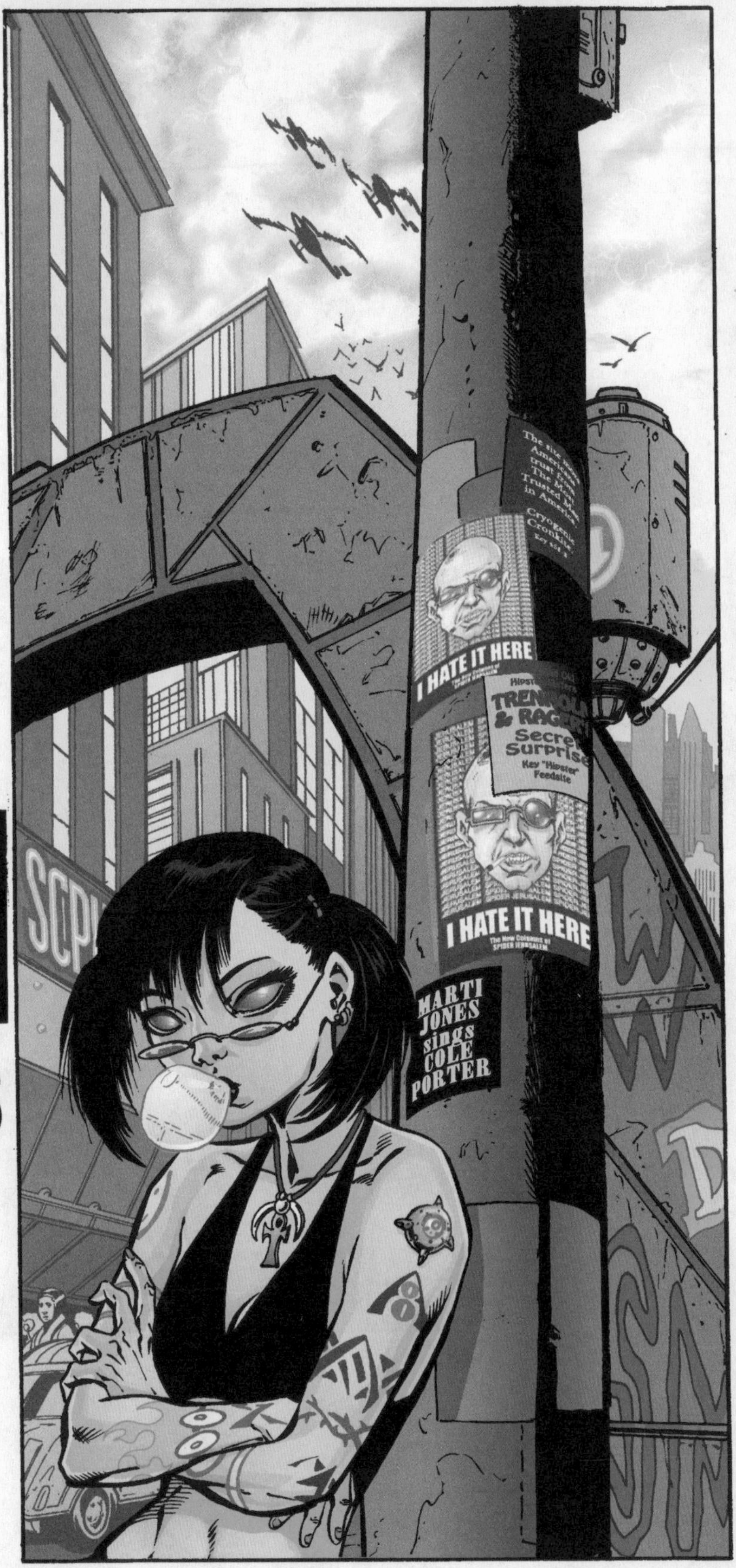

Cryogenic Cronkite
I HATE IT HERE
Secret Surprise
Key "Hipster" Feedsite
I HATE IT HERE
The New Columns of SPIDER JERUSALEM
MARTI JONES sings COLE PORTER

RODNEY RAMOS
INKER

CLEM ROBINS
LETTERER

NATHAN EYRING
COLOR & SEPARATIONS

GEOF DARROW
COVER

CLIFF CHIANG
ASSISTANT EDITOR

STUART MOORE
EDITOR

TRANSMETROPOLITAN
created by WARREN ELLIS
& DARICK ROBERTSON

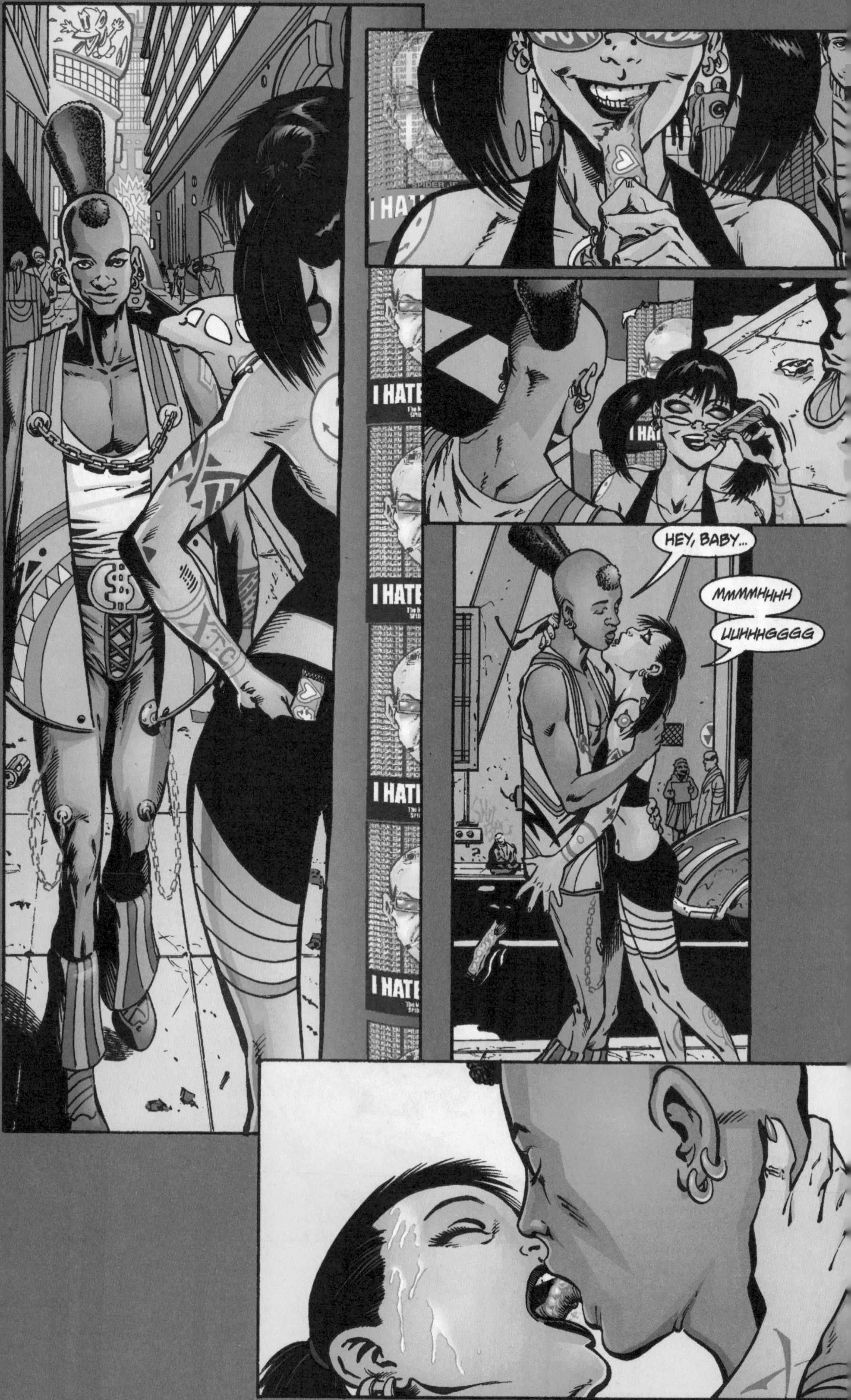
HEY, BABY...
MMMMHHHH
UUHHHGGGG

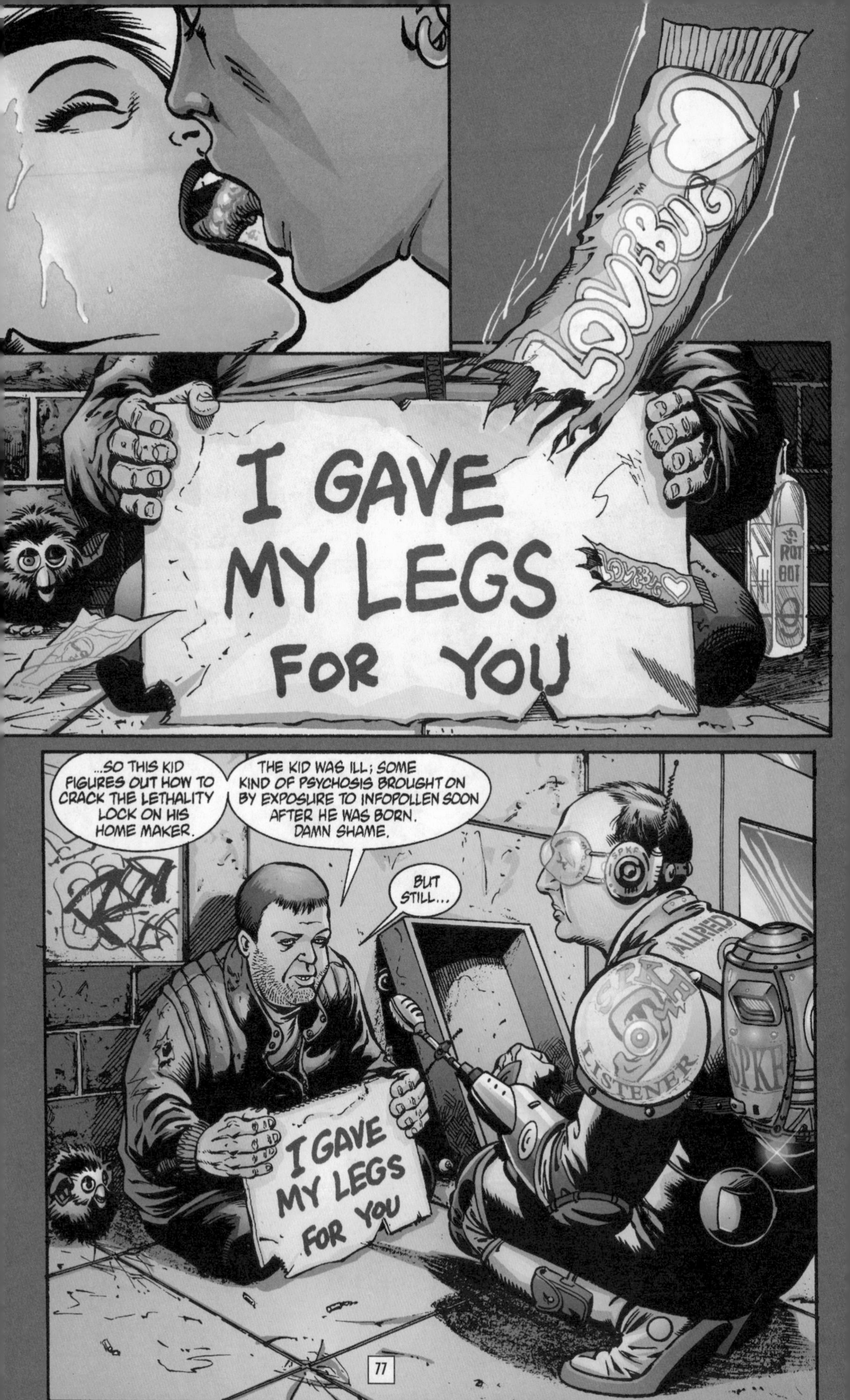
LOVEBUG
I GAVE MY LEGS FOR YOU
ROT GUT
...SO THIS KID FIGURES OUT HOW TO CRACK THE LETHALITY LOCK ON HIS HOME MAKER.
THE KID WAS ILL; SOME KIND OF PSYCHOSIS BROUGHT ON BY EXPOSURE TO INFOPOLLEN SOON AFTER HE WAS BORN. DAMN SHAME.
BUT STILL...
I GAVE MY LEGS FOR YOU
ALLPIED
SPKF
LISTENER
SPKF

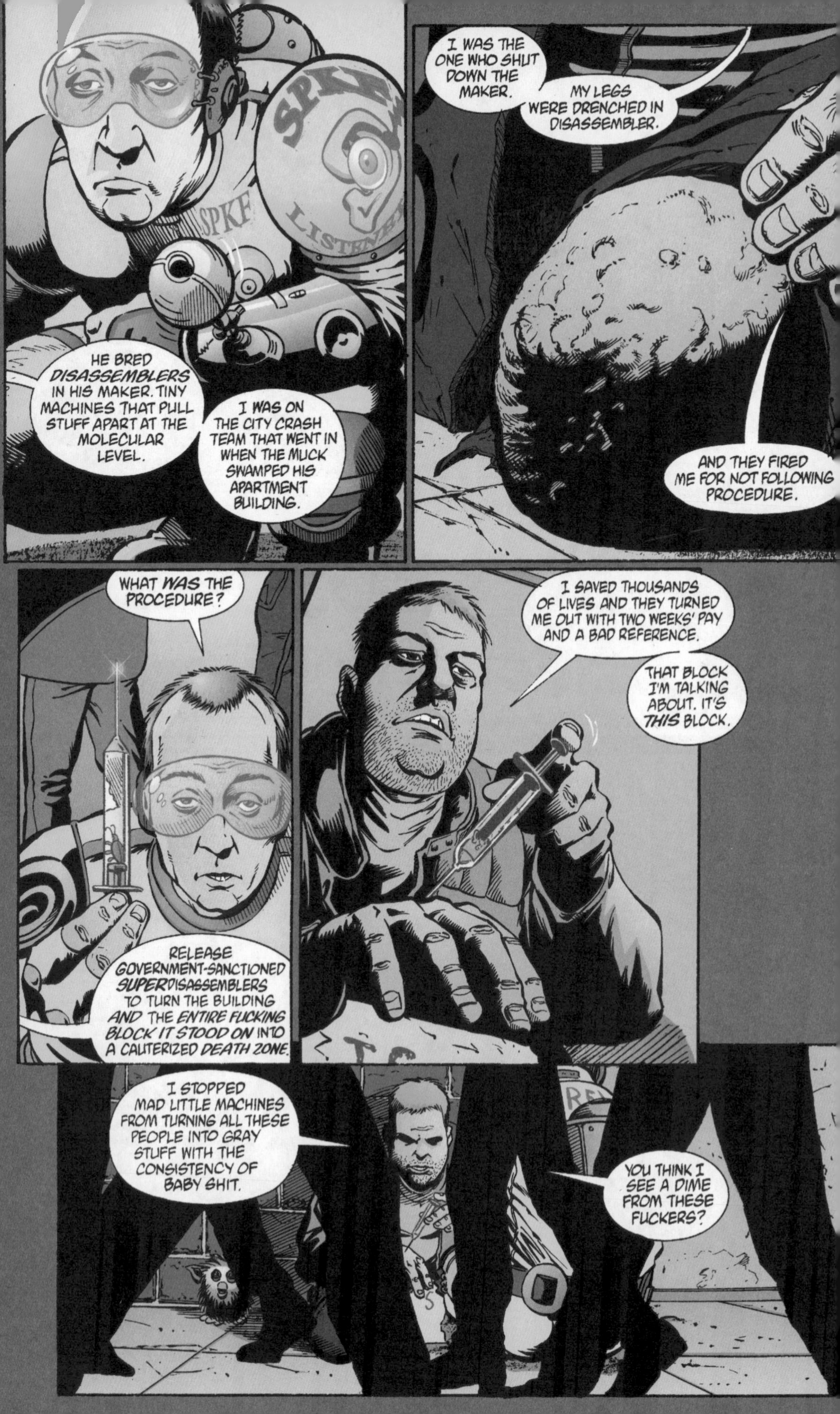
SPKF
LISTENER
SPKF
HE BRED DISASSEMBLERS IN HIS MAKER. TINY MACHINES THAT PULL STUFF APART AT THE MOLECULAR LEVEL.
I WAS ON THE CITY CRASH TEAM THAT WENT IN WHEN THE MUCK SWAMPED HIS APARTMENT BUILDING.
I WAS THE ONE WHO SHUT DOWN THE MAKER.
MY LEGS WERE DRENCHED IN DISASSEMBLER.
AND THEY FIRED ME FOR NOT FOLLOWING PROCEDURE.
WHAT WAS THE PROCEDURE?
RELEASE GOVERNMENT-SANCTIONED SUPERDISASSEMBLERS TO TURN THE BUILDING AND THE ENTIRE FUCKING BLOCK IT STOOD ON INTO A CAUTERIZED DEATH ZONE.
I SAVED THOUSANDS OF LIVES AND THEY TURNED ME OUT WITH TWO WEEKS' PAY AND A BAD REFERENCE.
THAT BLOCK I'M TALKING ABOUT. IT'S THIS BLOCK.
I STOPPED MAD LITTLE MACHINES FROM TURNING ALL THESE PEOPLE INTO GRAY STUFF WITH THE CONSISTENCY OF BABY SHIT.
YOU THINK I SEE A DIME FROM THESE FUCKERS?

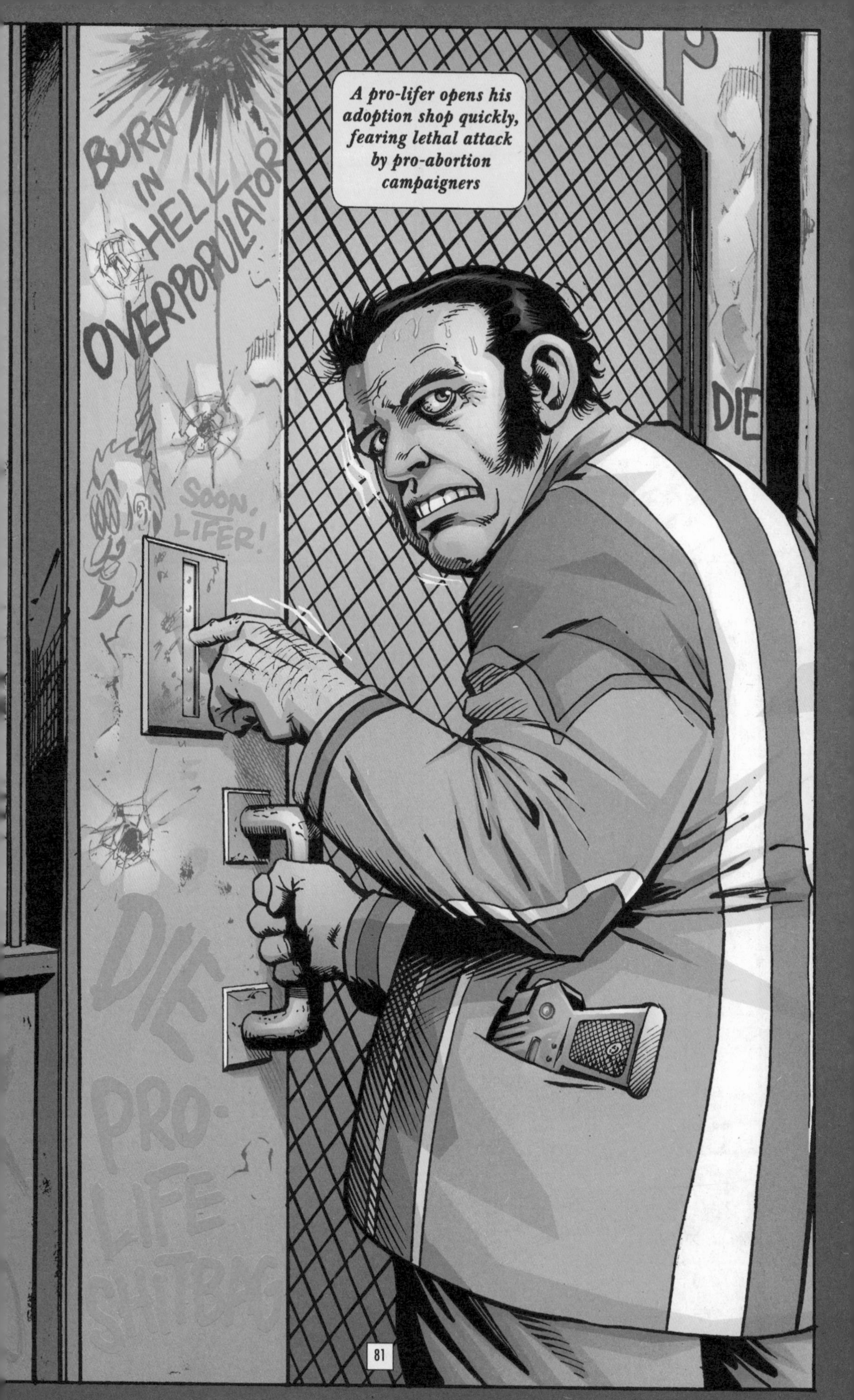
A pro-lifer opens his adoption shop quickly, fearing lethal attack by pro-abortion campaigners
BURN IN HELL OVERPOPULATOR
SOON, LIFER!
DIE
DIE PRO-LIFE

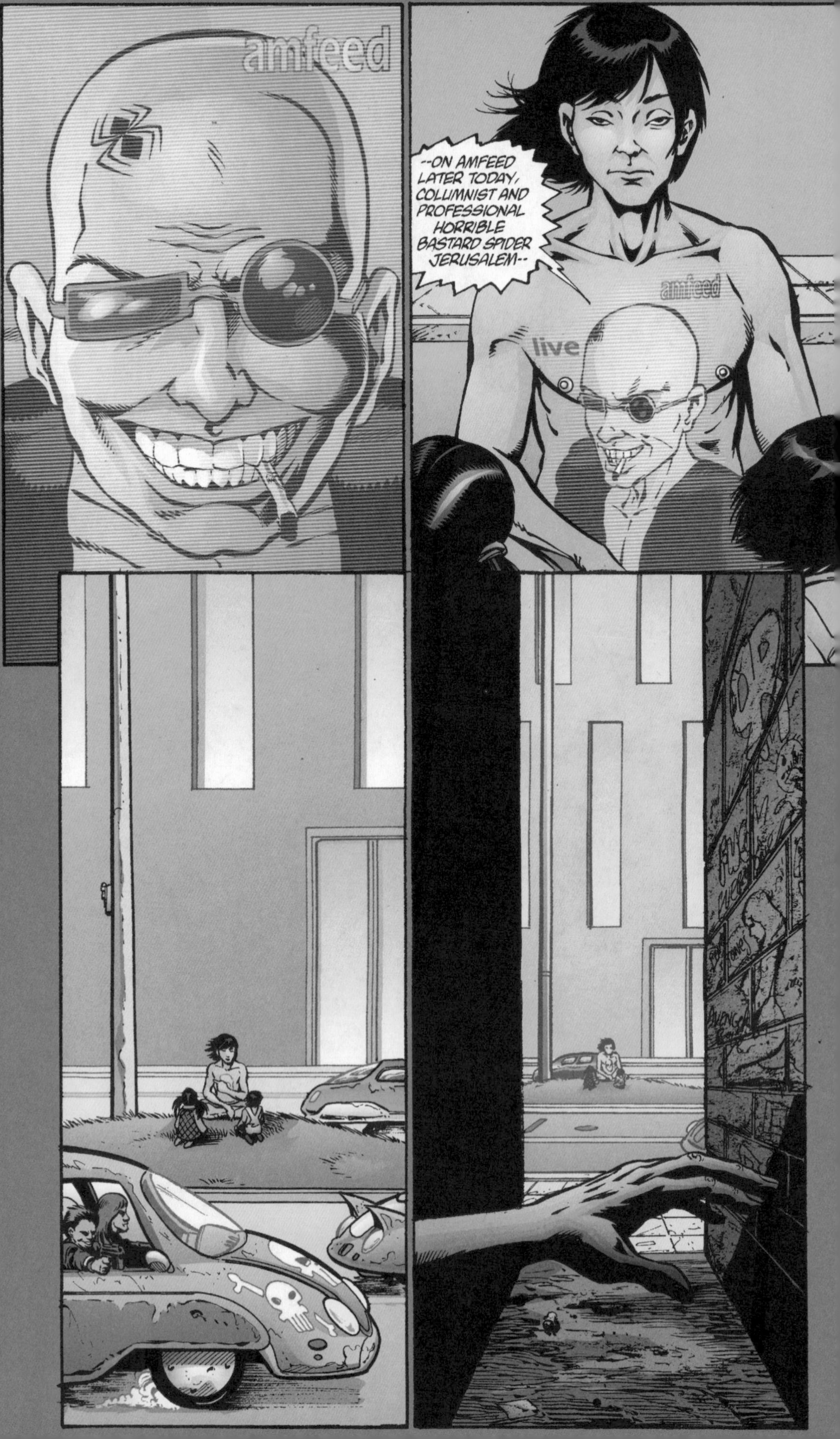
amfeed
--ON AMFEED LATER TODAY, COLUMNIST AND PROFESSIONAL HORRIBLE BASTARD SPIDER JERUSALEM--
amfeed
live

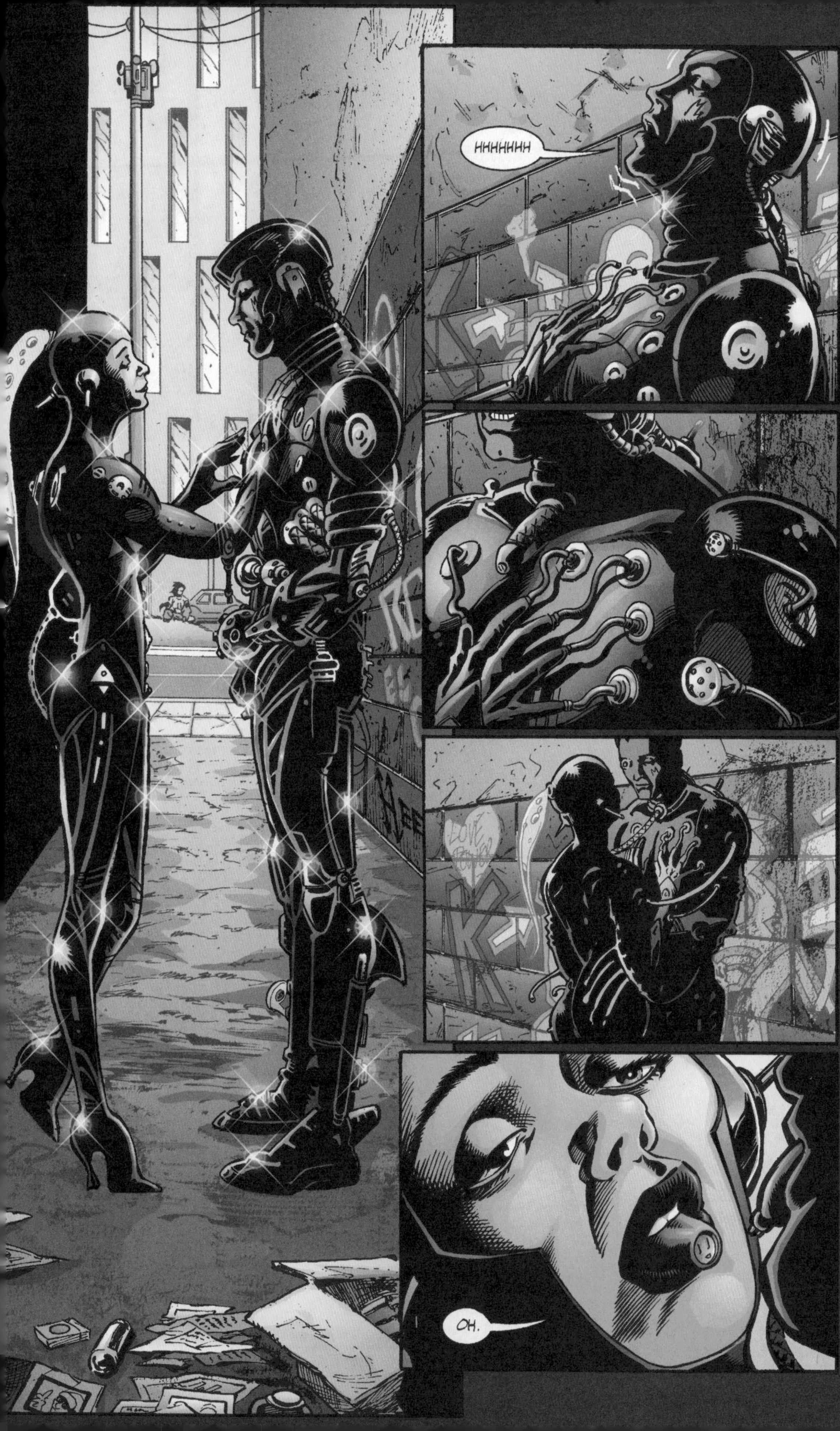
HHHHHHH
LOVE
OH.

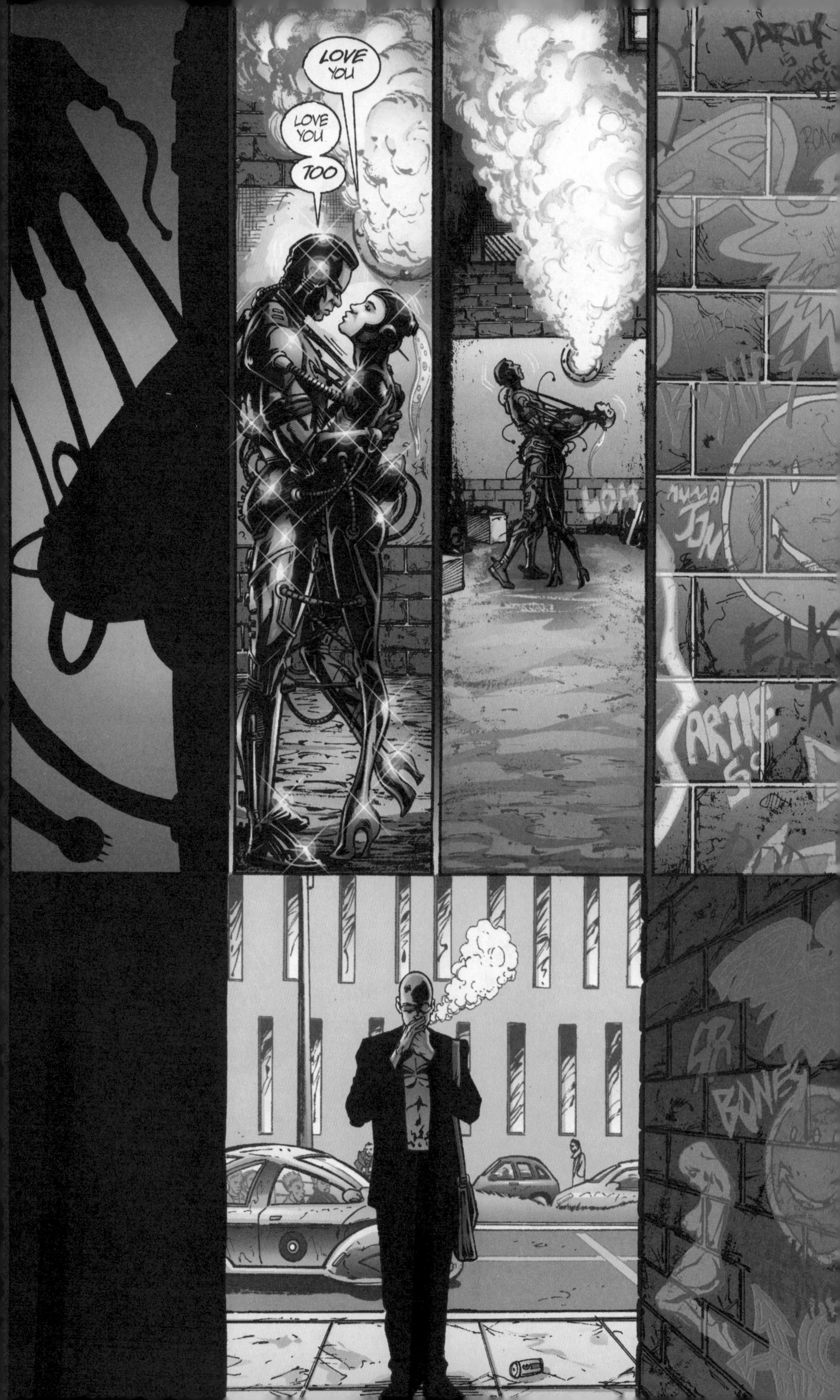
LOVE YOU
LOVE YOU TOO

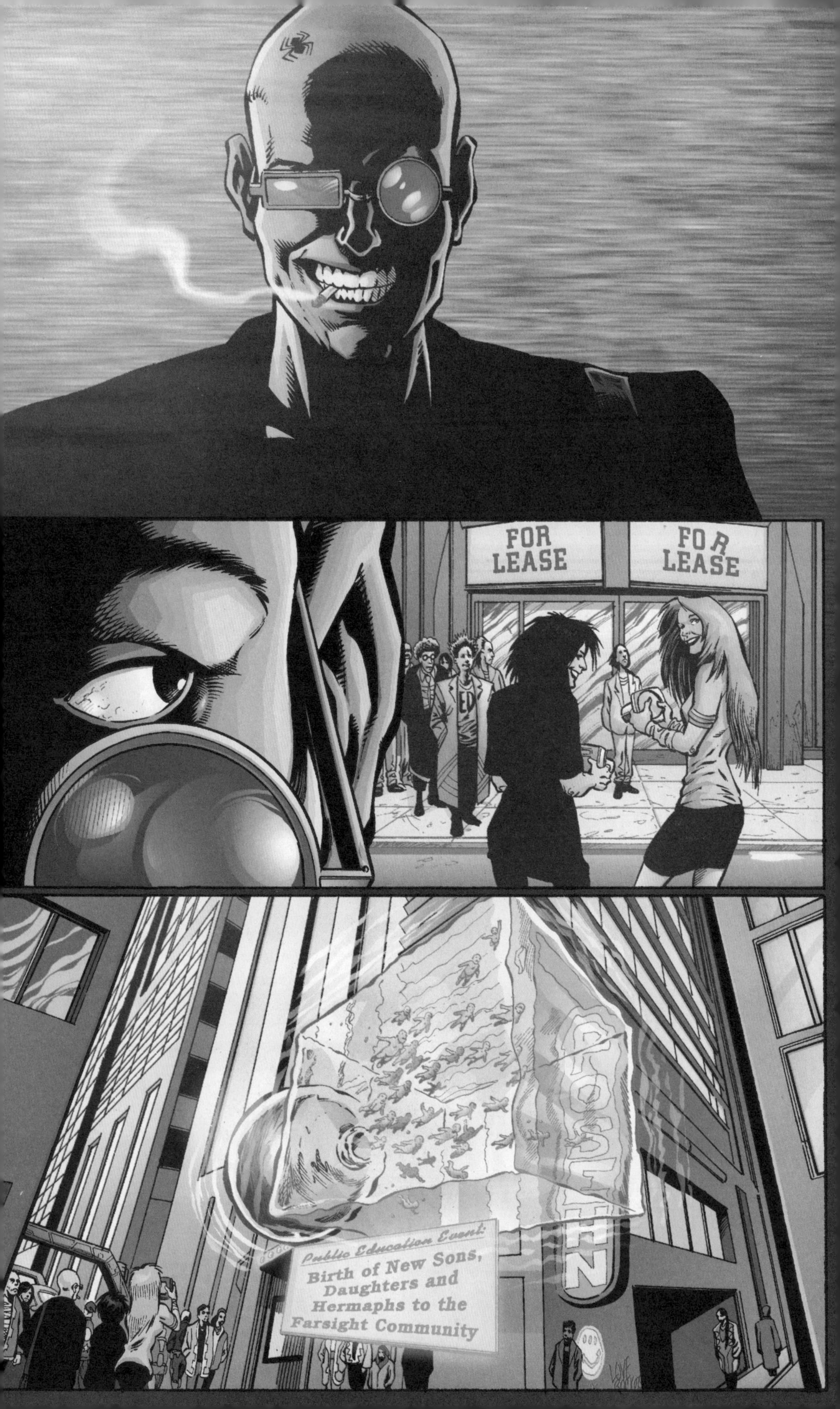

FOR LEASE
FOR LEASE
Public Education Event:
Birth of New Sons, Daughters and Hermaphs to the Farsight Community

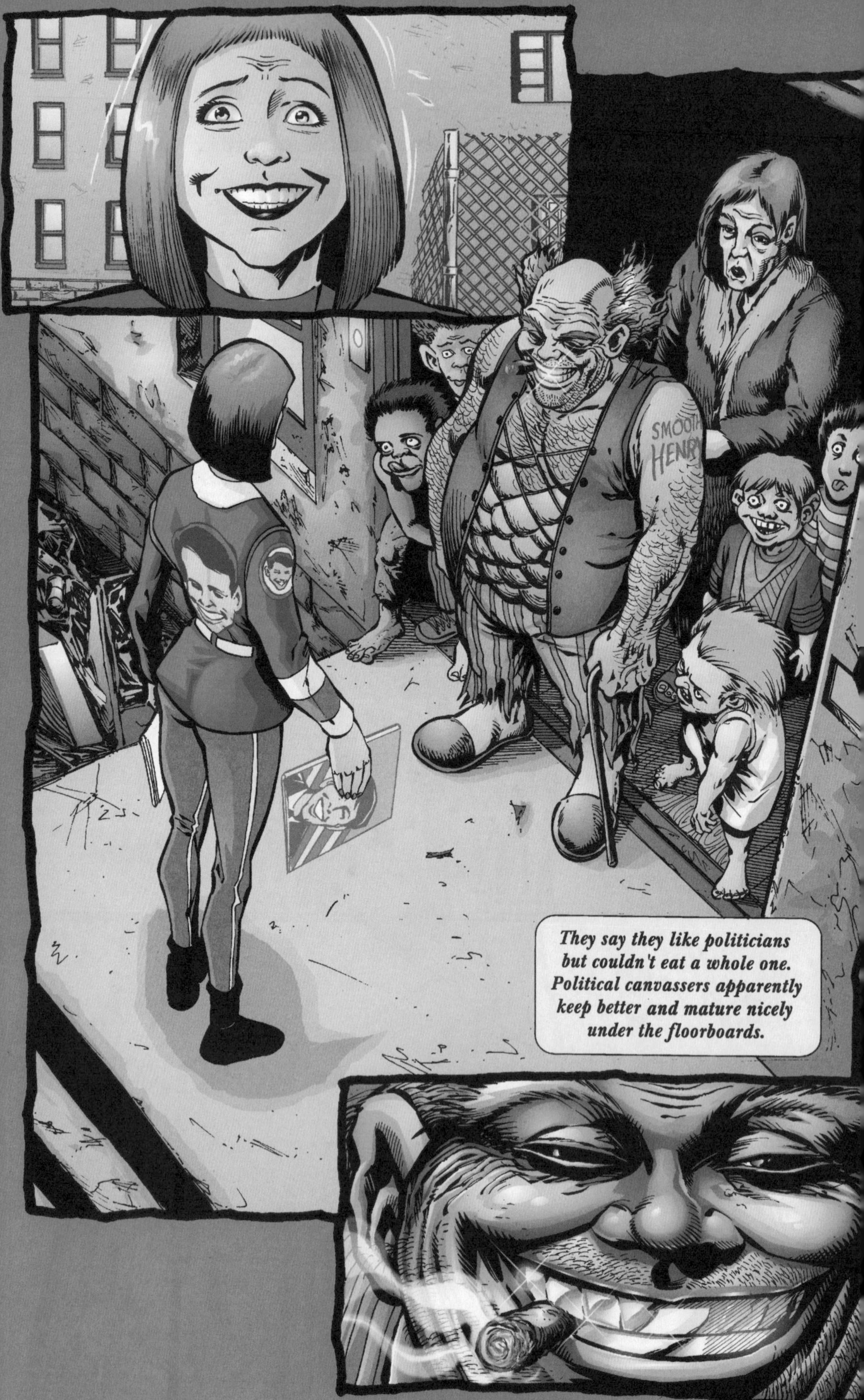
SMOOTH HENRY
They say they like politicians but couldn't eat a whole one. Political canvassers apparently keep better and mature nicely under the floorboards.

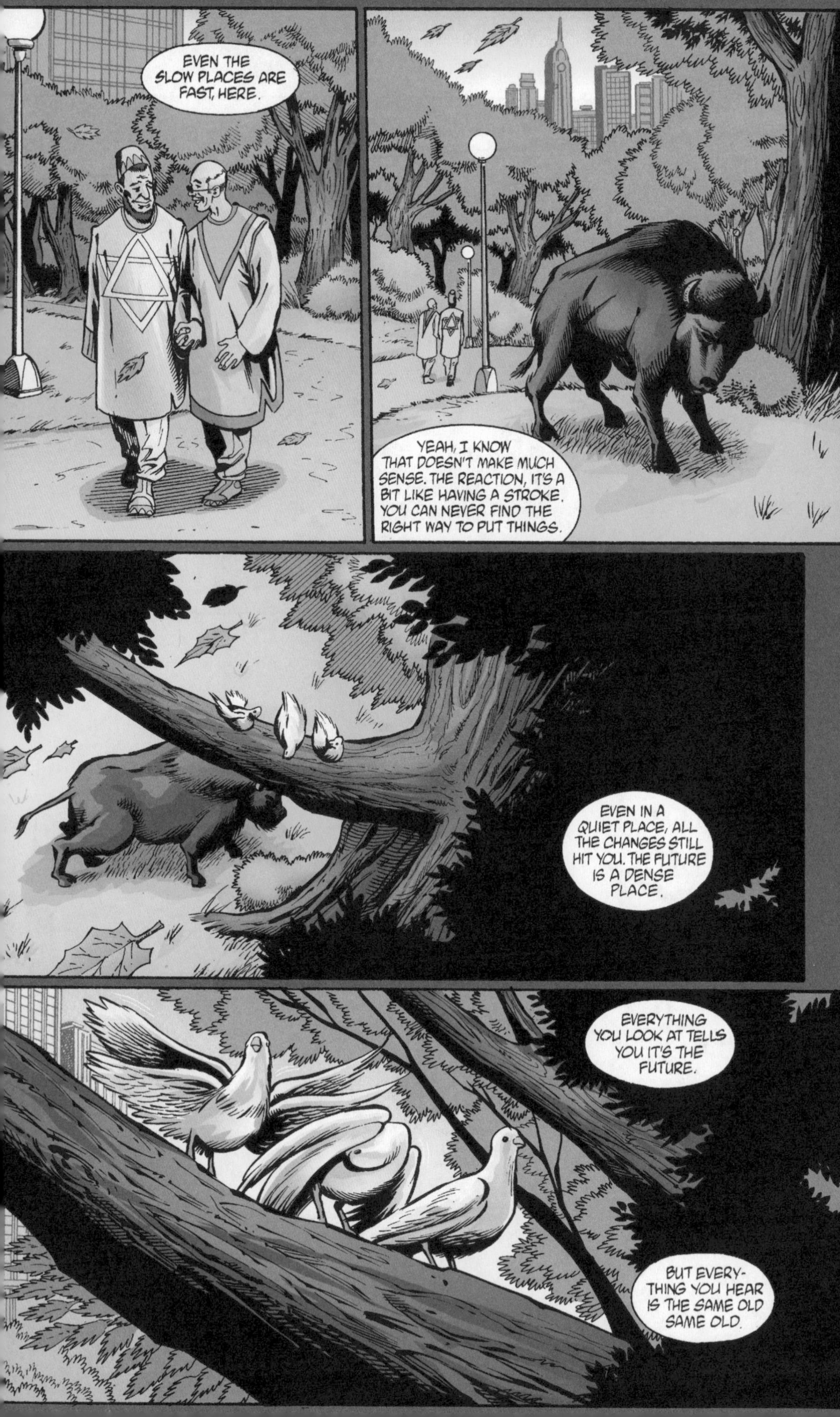
EVEN THE SLOW PLACES ARE FAST, HERE.
YEAH, I KNOW THAT DOESN'T MAKE MUCH SENSE. THE REACTION, IT'S A BIT LIKE HAVING A STROKE. YOU CAN NEVER FIND THE RIGHT WAY TO PUT THINGS.
EVEN IN A QUIET PLACE, ALL THE CHANGES STILL HIT YOU. THE FUTURE IS A DENSE PLACE.
EVERYTHING YOU LOOK AT TELLS YOU IT'S THE FUTURE.
BUT EVERY-THING YOU HEAR IS THE SAME OLD SAME OLD.

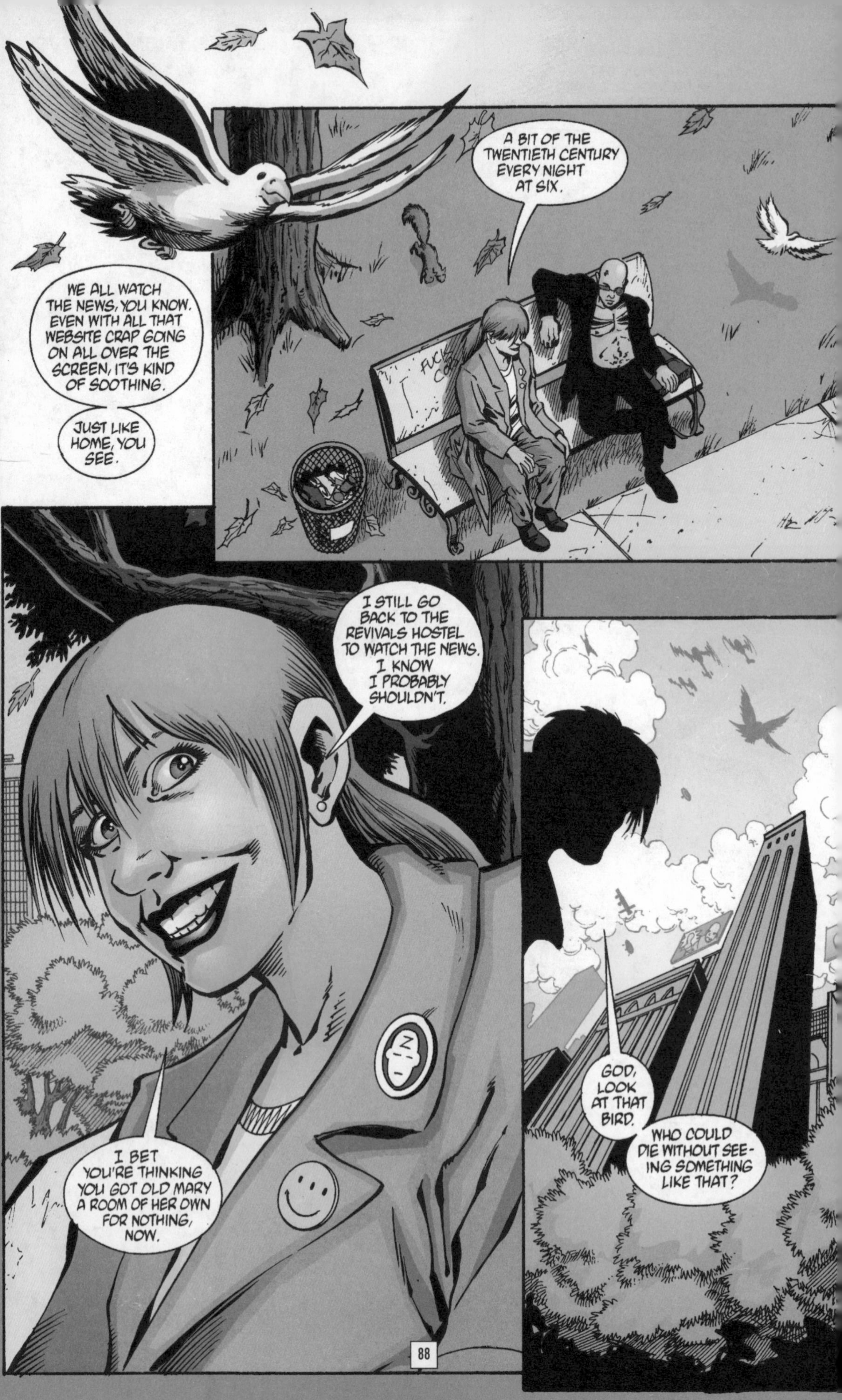
WE ALL WATCH THE NEWS, YOU KNOW. EVEN WITH ALL THAT WEBSITE CRAP GOING ON ALL OVER THE SCREEN, IT'S KIND OF SOOTHING.
JUST LIKE HOME, YOU SEE.
A BIT OF THE TWENTIETH CENTURY EVERY NIGHT AT SIX.
I STILL GO BACK TO THE REVIVALS HOSTEL TO WATCH THE NEWS. I KNOW I PROBABLY SHOULDN'T.
I BET YOU'RE THINKING YOU GOT OLD MARY A ROOM OF HER OWN FOR NOTHING, NOW.
GOD, LOOK AT THAT BIRD.
WHO COULD DIE WITHOUT SEEING SOMETHING LIKE THAT?

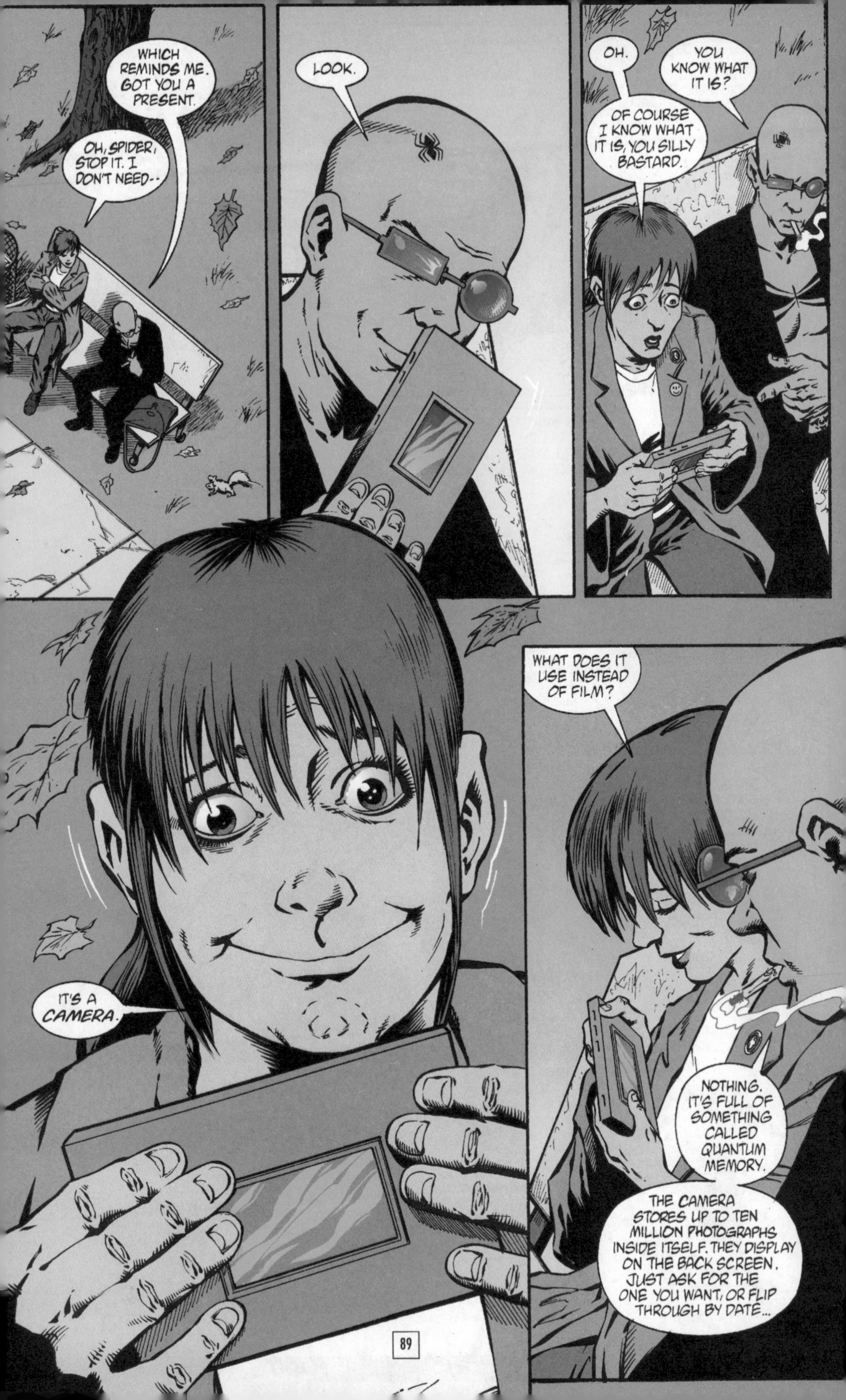

WHICH REMINDS ME. GOT YOU A PRESENT.
OH, SPIDER, STOP IT. I DON'T NEED--
LOOK.
OH.
YOU KNOW WHAT IT IS?
OF COURSE I KNOW WHAT IT IS, YOU SILLY BASTARD.
IT'S A CAMERA.
WHAT DOES IT USE INSTEAD OF FILM?
NOTHING. IT'S FULL OF SOMETHING CALLED QUANTUM MEMORY.
THE CAMERA STORES UP TO TEN MILLION PHOTOGRAPHS INSIDE ITSELF. THEY DISPLAY ON THE BACK SCREEN. JUST ASK FOR THE ONE YOU WANT, OR FLIP THROUGH BY DATE...

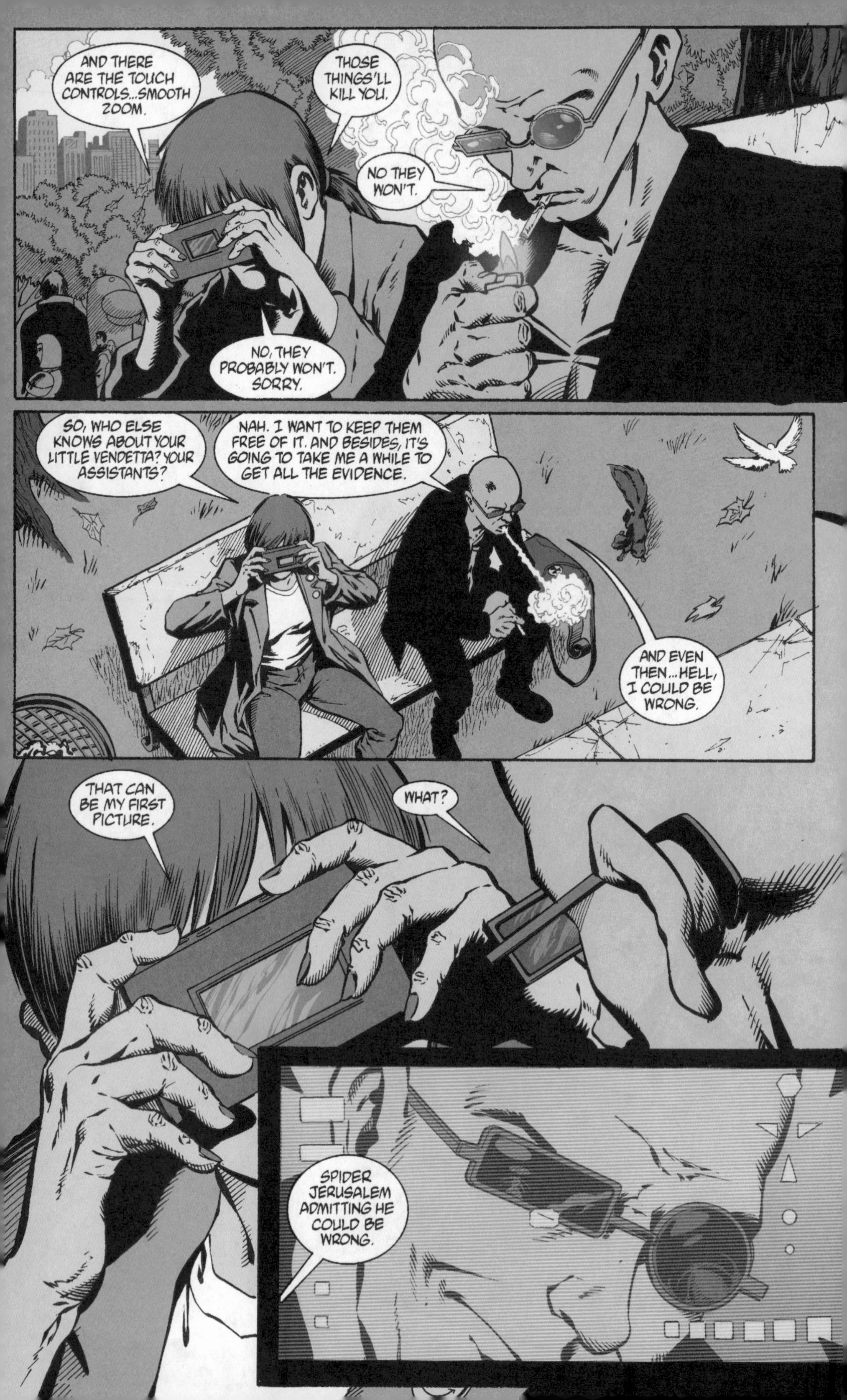

AND THERE ARE THE TOUCH CONTROLS...SMOOTH ZOOM.
THOSE THINGS'LL KILL YOU.
NO THEY WON'T.
NO, THEY PROBABLY WON'T. SORRY.
SO, WHO ELSE KNOWS ABOUT YOUR LITTLE VENDETTA? YOUR ASSISTANTS?
NAH. I WANT TO KEEP THEM FREE OF IT. AND BESIDES, IT'S GOING TO TAKE ME A WHILE TO GET ALL THE EVIDENCE.
AND EVEN THEN...HELL, I COULD BE WRONG.
THAT CAN BE MY FIRST PICTURE.
WHAT?
SPIDER JERUSALEM ADMITTING HE COULD BE WRONG.

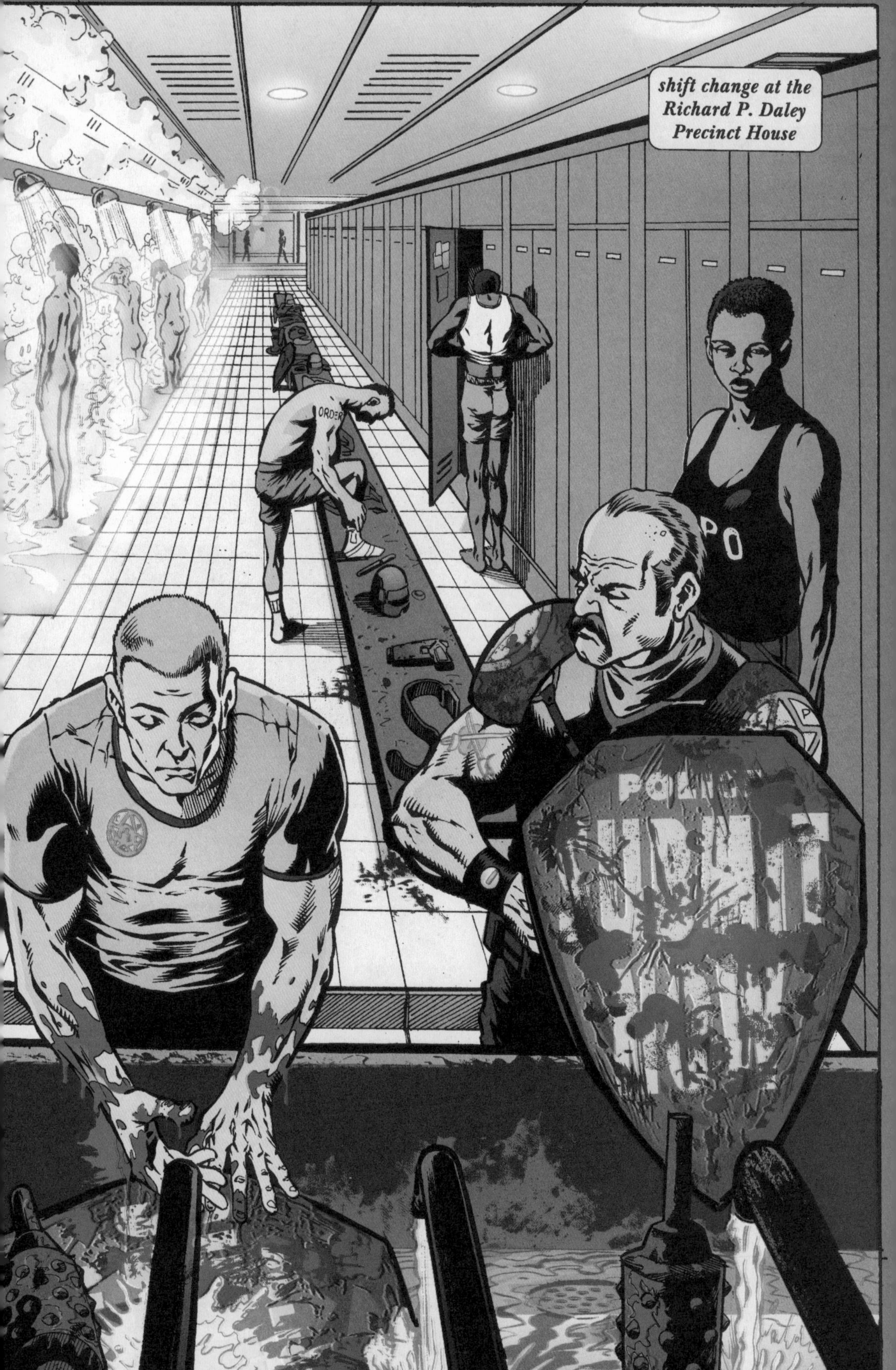
shift change at the Richard P. Daley Precinct House
ORDER
PO

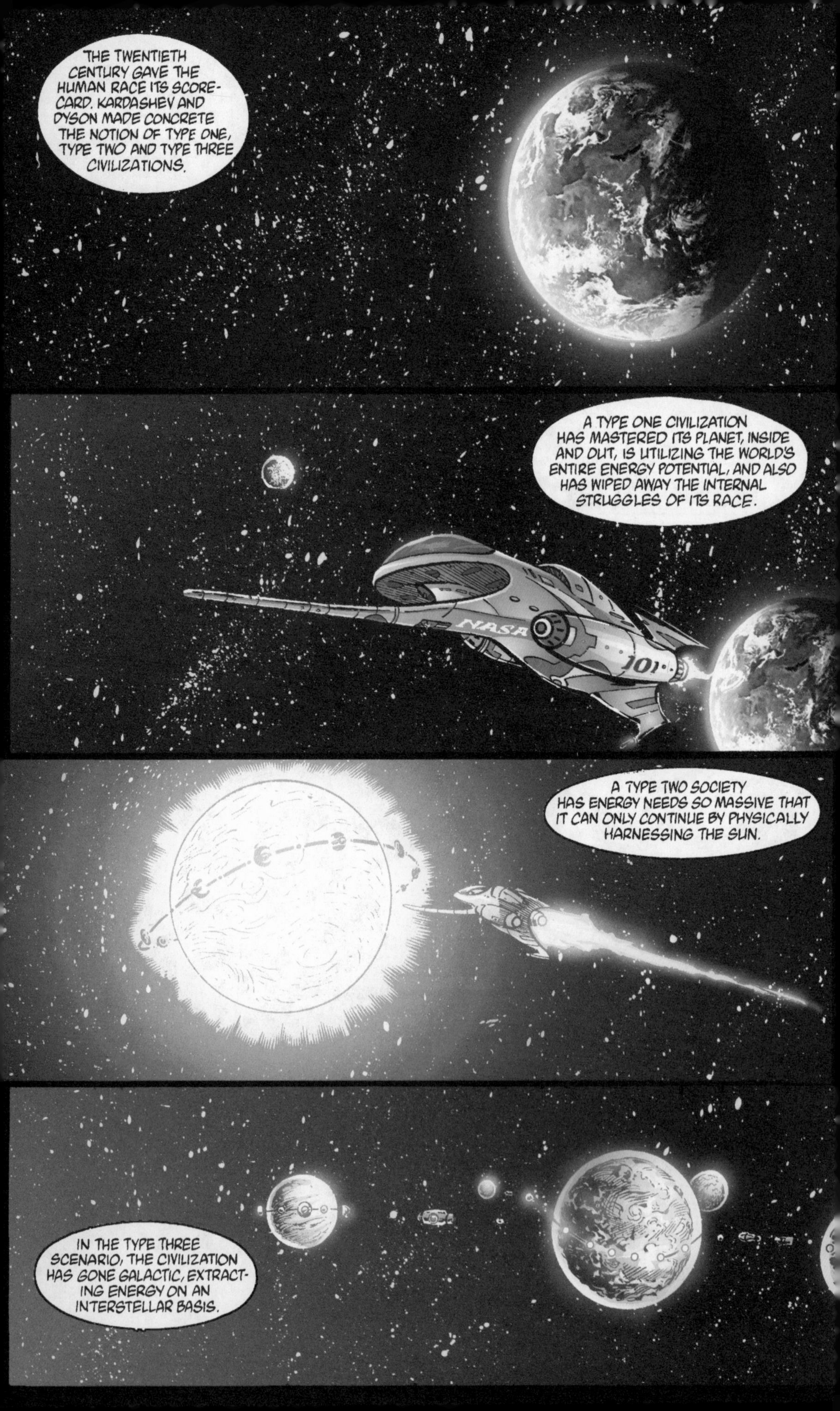
THE TWENTIETH CENTURY GAVE THE HUMAN RACE ITS SCORE-CARD. KARDASHEV AND DYSON MADE CONCRETE THE NOTION OF TYPE ONE, TYPE TWO AND TYPE THREE CIVILIZATIONS.
A TYPE ONE CIVILIZATION HAS MASTERED ITS PLANET, INSIDE AND OUT, IS UTILIZING THE WORLD'S ENTIRE ENERGY POTENTIAL, AND ALSO HAS WIPED AWAY THE INTERNAL STRUGGLES OF ITS RACE.
NASA
101
A TYPE TWO SOCIETY HAS ENERGY NEEDS SO MASSIVE THAT IT CAN ONLY CONTINUE BY PHYSICALLY HARNESSING THE SUN.
IN THE TYPE THREE SCENARIO, THE CIVILIZATION HAS GONE GALACTIC, EXTRACT-ING ENERGY ON AN INTERSTELLAR BASIS.

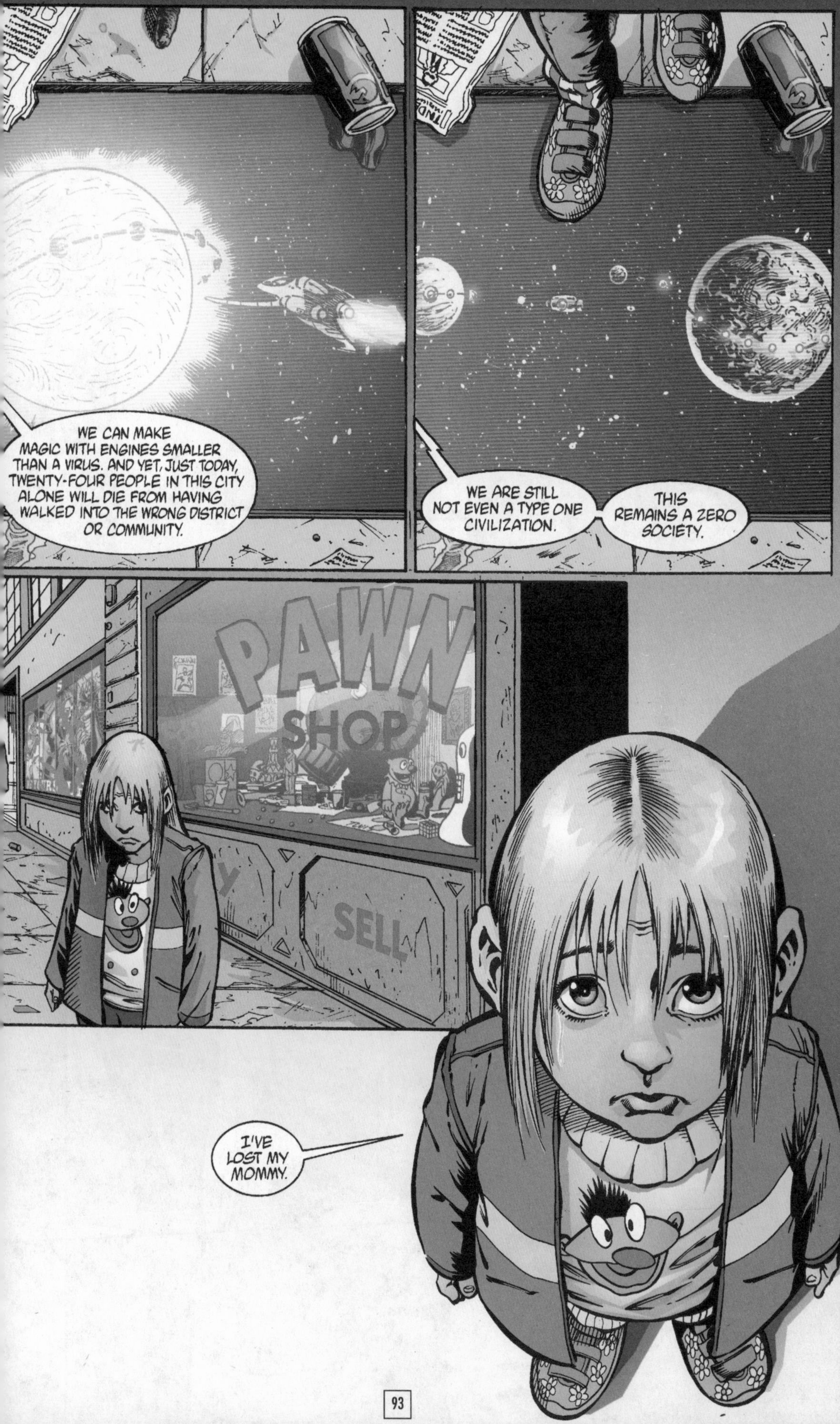
WE CAN MAKE MAGIC WITH ENGINES SMALLER THAN A VIRUS. AND YET, JUST TODAY, TWENTY-FOUR PEOPLE IN THIS CITY ALONE WILL DIE FROM HAVING WALKED INTO THE WRONG DISTRICT OR COMMUNITY.
WE ARE STILL NOT EVEN A TYPE ONE CIVILIZATION.
THIS REMAINS A ZERO SOCIETY.
PAWN
SHOP
SELL
I'VE LOST MY MOMMY.

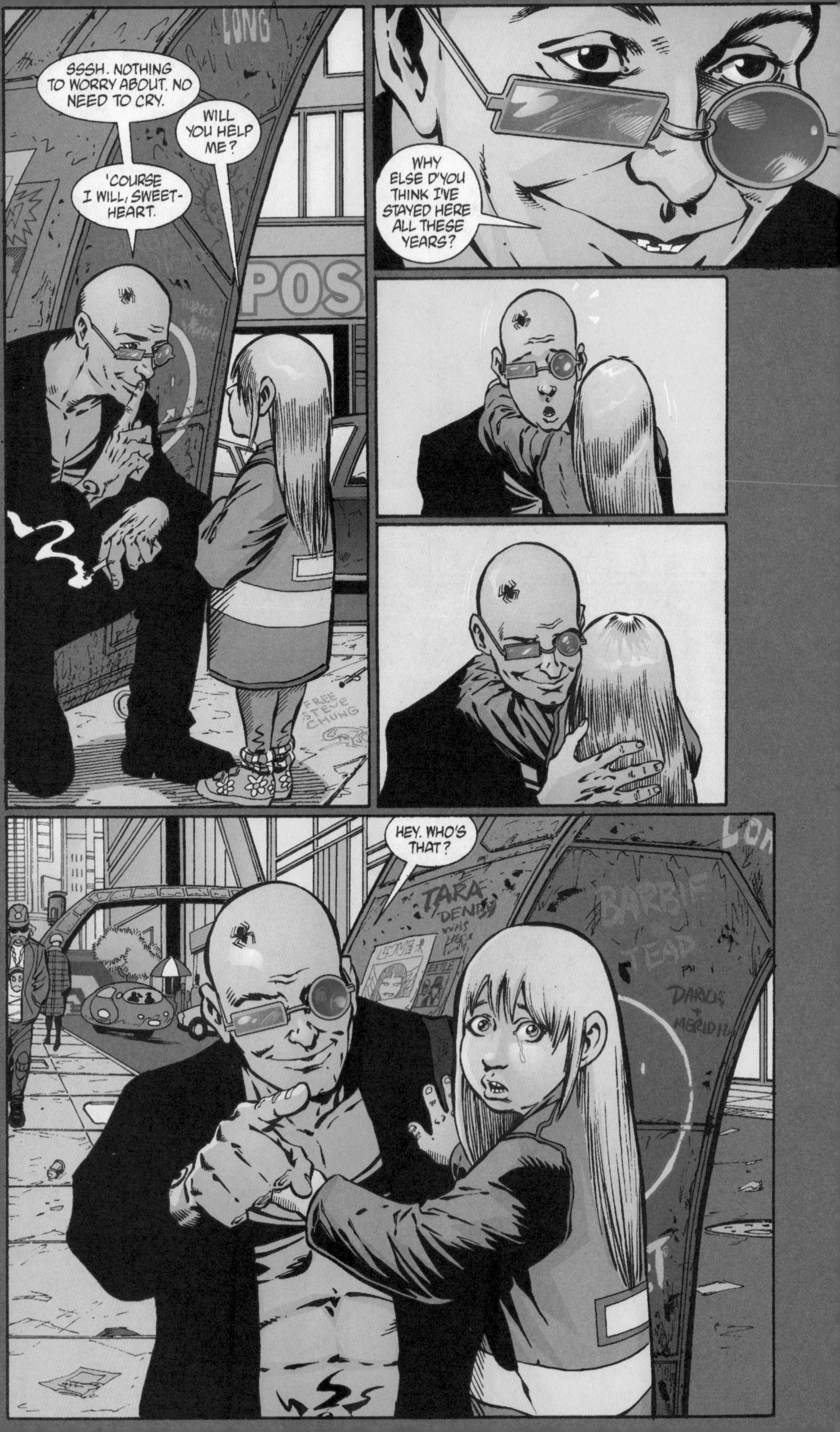
SSSH. NOTHING TO WORRY ABOUT. NO NEED TO CRY.
WILL YOU HELP ME?
'COURSE I WILL, SWEET-HEART.
WHY ELSE D'YOU THINK I'VE STAYED HERE ALL THESE YEARS?
HEY. WHO'S THAT?

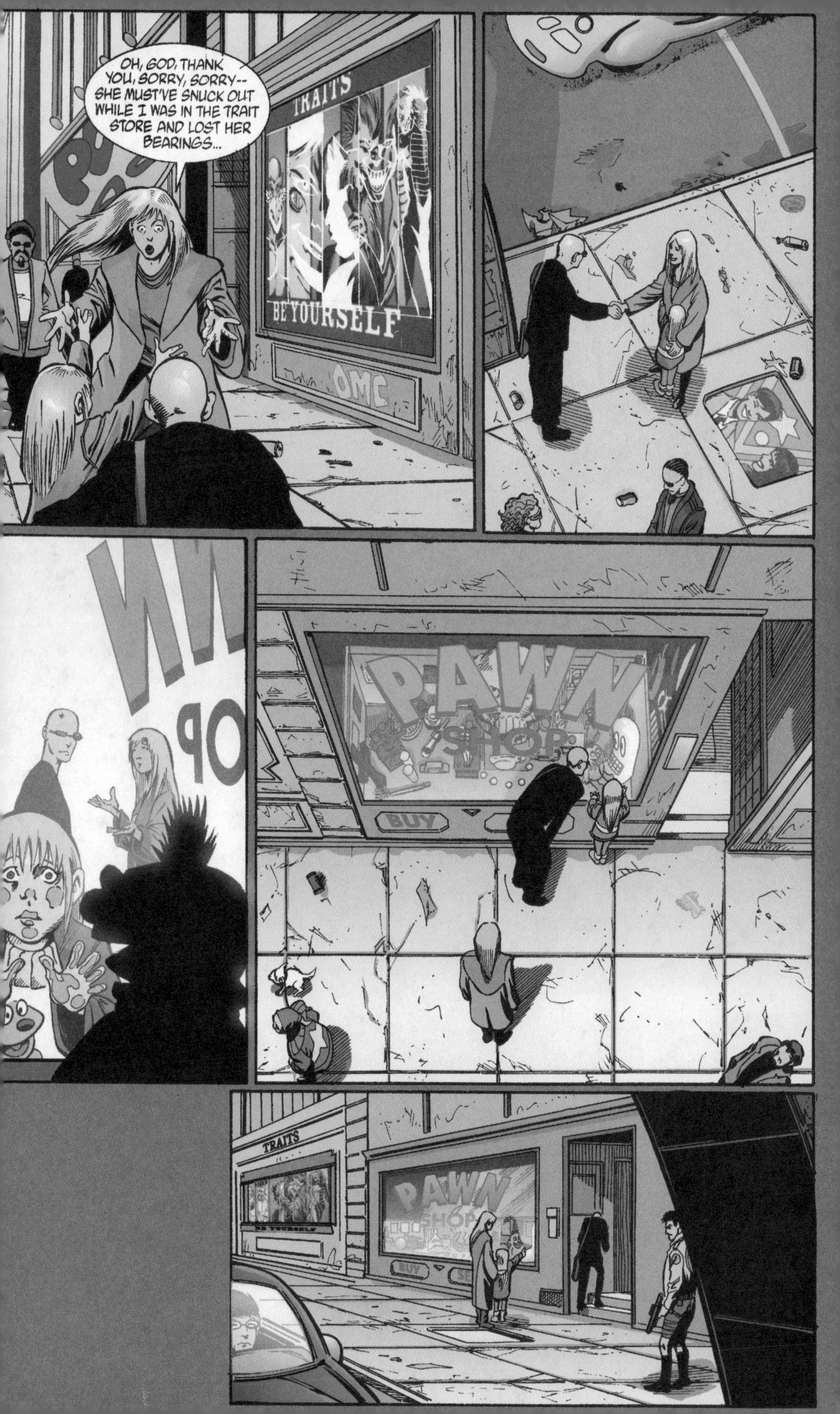
OH, GOD, THANK YOU, SORRY, SORRY-- SHE MUST'VE SNUCK OUT WHILE I WAS IN THE TRAIT STORE AND LOST HER BEARINGS...
TRAITS
BE YOURSELF
OMC
PAWN SHOP
BUY
TRAITS
PAWN SHOP
BUY

THESE ARE THE NEW STREETS OF THIS CITY,
WHERE THE NEW SCUM TRY TO LIVE. YOU AND ME.
AND HERE IN THESE STREETS ARE THE THINGS
THAT WE WANT: SEX AND BIRTH, VOTES AND TRAIT-
MONEY AND GUILT, TELEVISION AND TEDDY BEARS

BUT ALL WE'VE ACTUALLY GOT IS EACH OTHER.

YOU DECIDE WHAT THAT MEANS.

_ SPIDER JERUSALEM
"I HATE IT HERE"
THE WORD

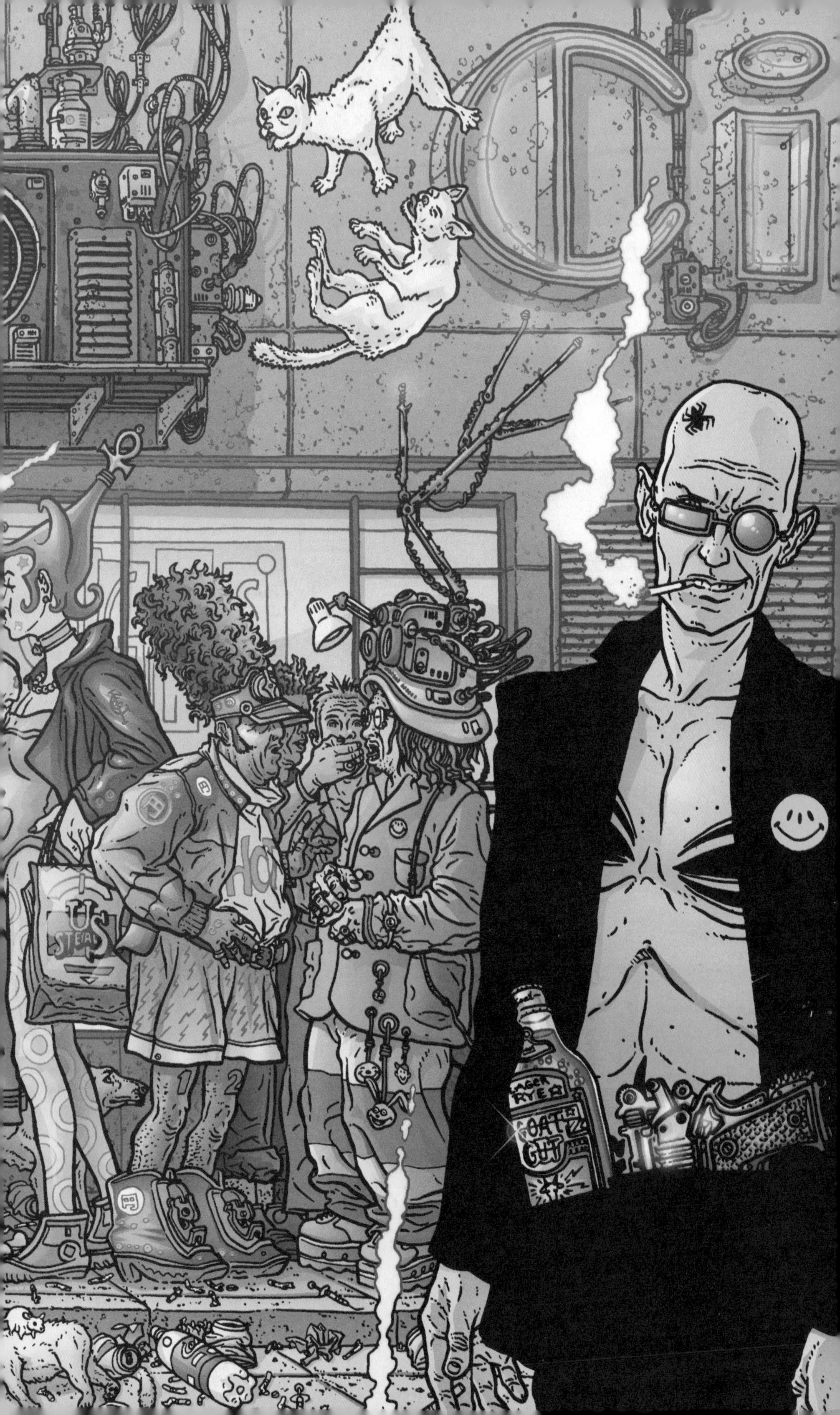
LAGER RYE
GOAT GUT

WARREN ELLIS writes and **DARICK ROBERTSON** pencils

THE NEW SCUM 5: NEW BOSS

RODNEY RAMOS inker   **NATHAN EYRING** color & separations   **CLEM ROBINS** letterer   **GEOF DARROW** cover artist   **CLIFF CHIANG** ass't editor   **STUART MOORE** editor

TRANSMETROPOLITAN created by WARREN ELLIS & DARICK ROBERTSON

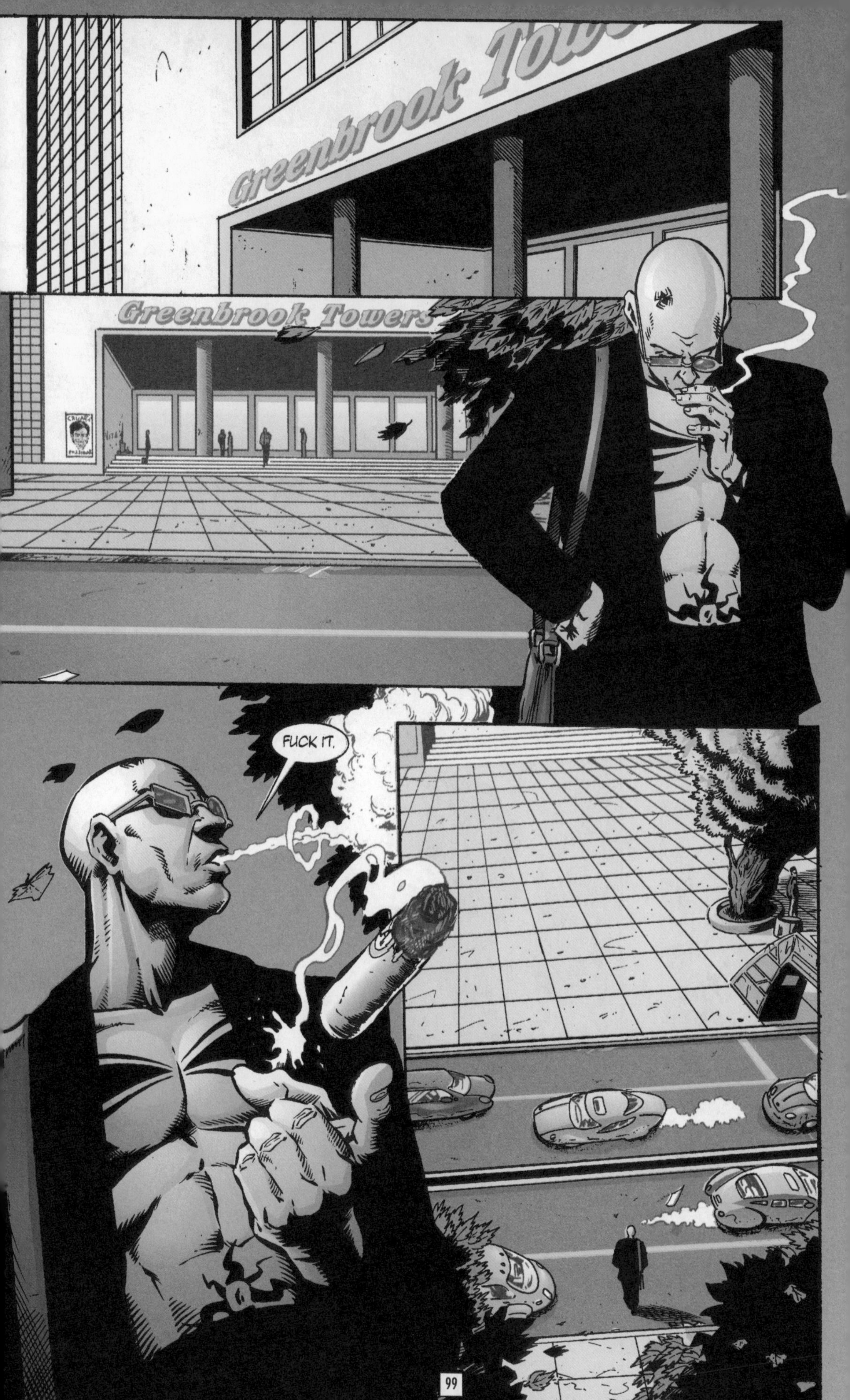
Greenbrook Towers
Greenbrook Towers
FUCK IT.

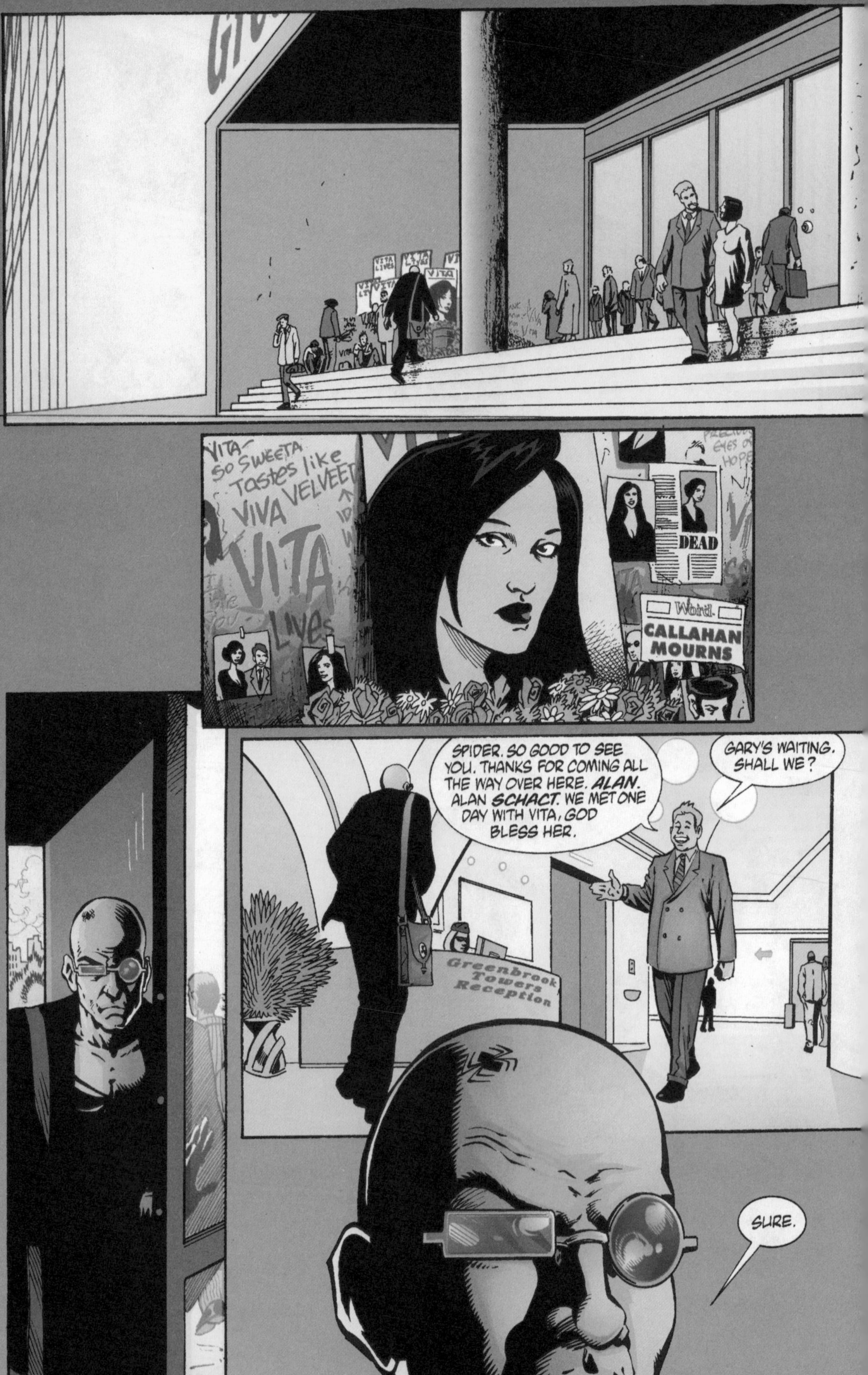

VITA LIVES
VITA- So SWEETA Tastes like VELVEET
VIVA
VITA
LIVES
DEAD
World
CALLAHAN MOURNS
Greenbrook Towers Reception
SPIDER. SO GOOD TO SEE YOU. THANKS FOR COMING ALL THE WAY OVER HERE. ALAN. ALAN SCHACT. WE MET ONE DAY WITH VITA, GOD BLESS HER.
GARY'S WAITING. SHALL WE?
SURE.

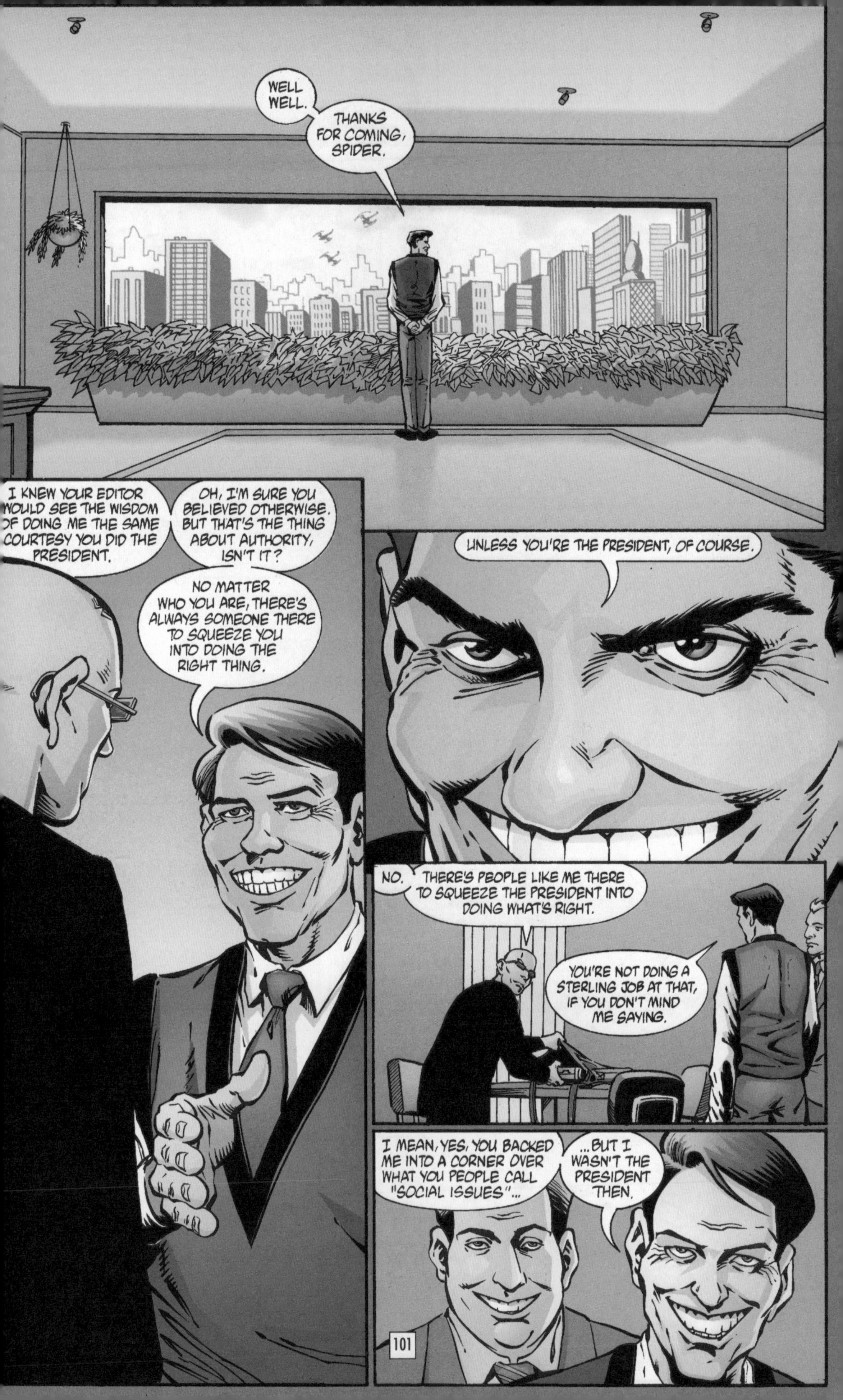
WELL WELL.
THANKS FOR COMING, SPIDER.
I KNEW YOUR EDITOR WOULD SEE THE WISDOM OF DOING ME THE SAME COURTESY YOU DID THE PRESIDENT.
OH, I'M SURE YOU BELIEVED OTHERWISE. BUT THAT'S THE THING ABOUT AUTHORITY, ISN'T IT?
NO MATTER WHO YOU ARE, THERE'S ALWAYS SOMEONE THERE TO SQUEEZE YOU INTO DOING THE RIGHT THING.
UNLESS YOU'RE THE PRESIDENT, OF COURSE.
NO.
THERE'S PEOPLE LIKE ME THERE TO SQUEEZE THE PRESIDENT INTO DOING WHAT'S RIGHT.
YOU'RE NOT DOING A STERLING JOB AT THAT, IF YOU DON'T MIND ME SAYING.
I MEAN, YES, YOU BACKED ME INTO A CORNER OVER WHAT YOU PEOPLE CALL "SOCIAL ISSUES"...
...BUT I WASN'T THE PRESIDENT THEN.

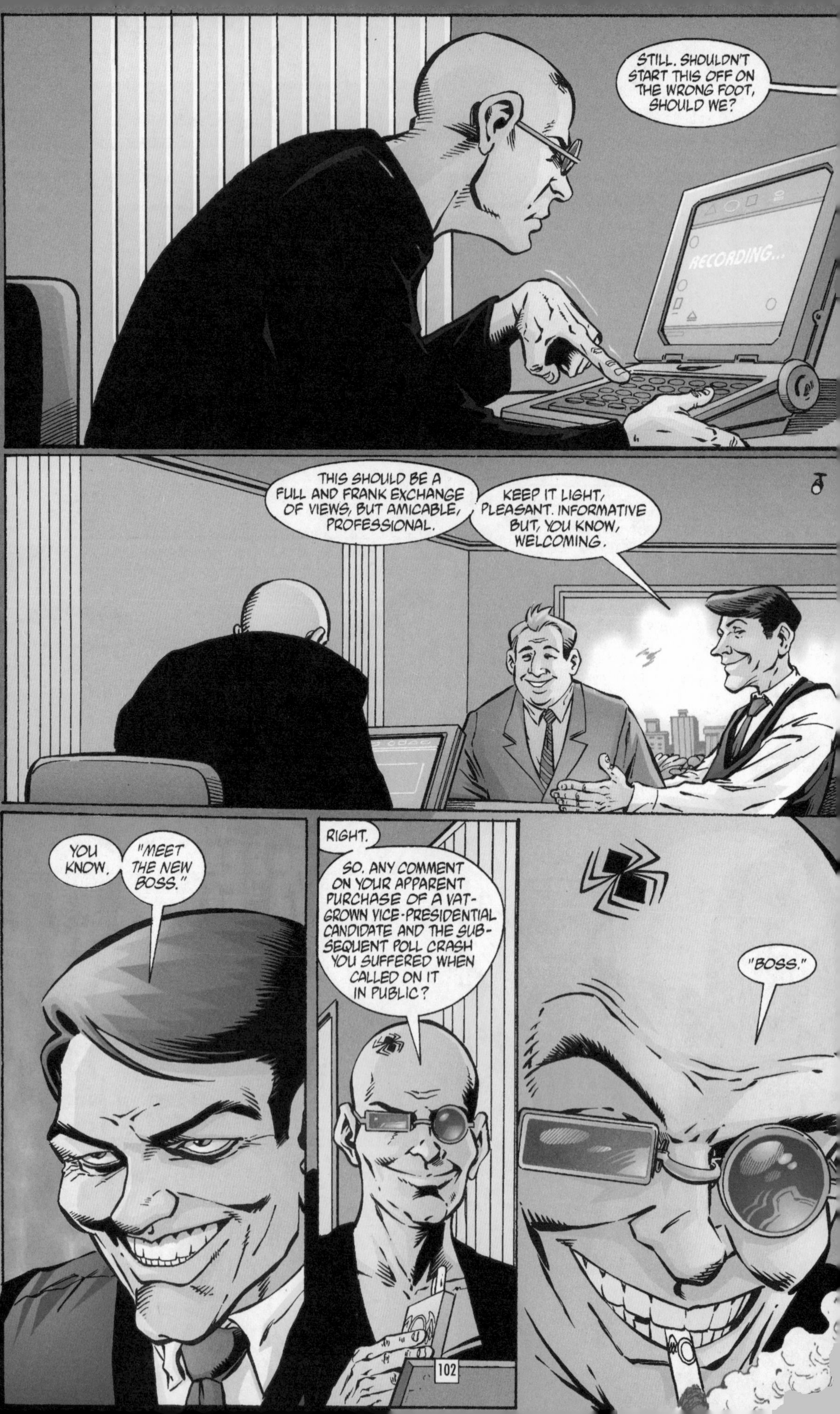
STILL. SHOULDN'T START THIS OFF ON THE WRONG FOOT, SHOULD WE?
RECORDING...
THIS SHOULD BE A FULL AND FRANK EXCHANGE OF VIEWS, BUT AMICABLE, PROFESSIONAL.
KEEP IT LIGHT, PLEASANT. INFORMATIVE BUT, YOU KNOW, WELCOMING.
YOU KNOW.
"MEET THE NEW BOSS."
RIGHT.
SO. ANY COMMENT ON YOUR APPARENT PURCHASE OF A VAT-GROWN VICE-PRESIDENTIAL CANDIDATE AND THE SUBSEQUENT POLL CRASH YOU SUFFERED WHEN CALLED ON IT IN PUBLIC?
"BOSS."

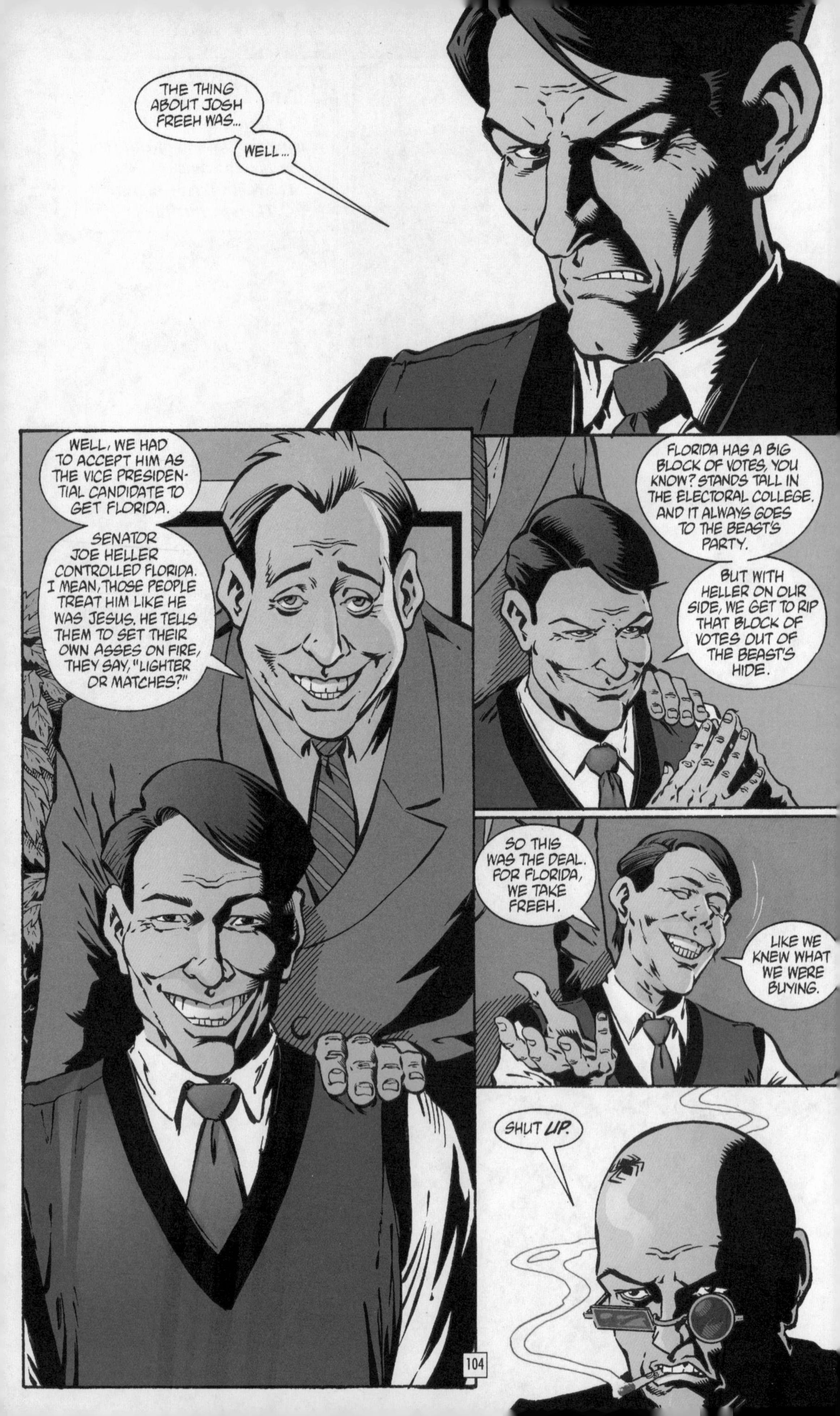
THE THING ABOUT JOSH FREEH WAS...
WELL...
WELL, WE HAD TO ACCEPT HIM AS THE VICE PRESIDENTIAL CANDIDATE TO GET FLORIDA.
SENATOR JOE HELLER CONTROLLED FLORIDA. I MEAN, THOSE PEOPLE TREAT HIM LIKE HE WAS JESUS. HE TELLS THEM TO SET THEIR OWN ASSES ON FIRE, THEY SAY, "LIGHTER OR MATCHES?"
FLORIDA HAS A BIG BLOCK OF VOTES, YOU KNOW? STANDS TALL IN THE ELECTORAL COLLEGE. AND IT ALWAYS GOES TO THE BEAST'S PARTY.
BUT WITH HELLER ON OUR SIDE, WE GET TO RIP THAT BLOCK OF VOTES OUT OF THE BEAST'S HIDE.
SO THIS WAS THE DEAL. FOR FLORIDA, WE TAKE FREEH.
LIKE WE KNEW WHAT WE WERE BUYING.
SHUT *UP*.

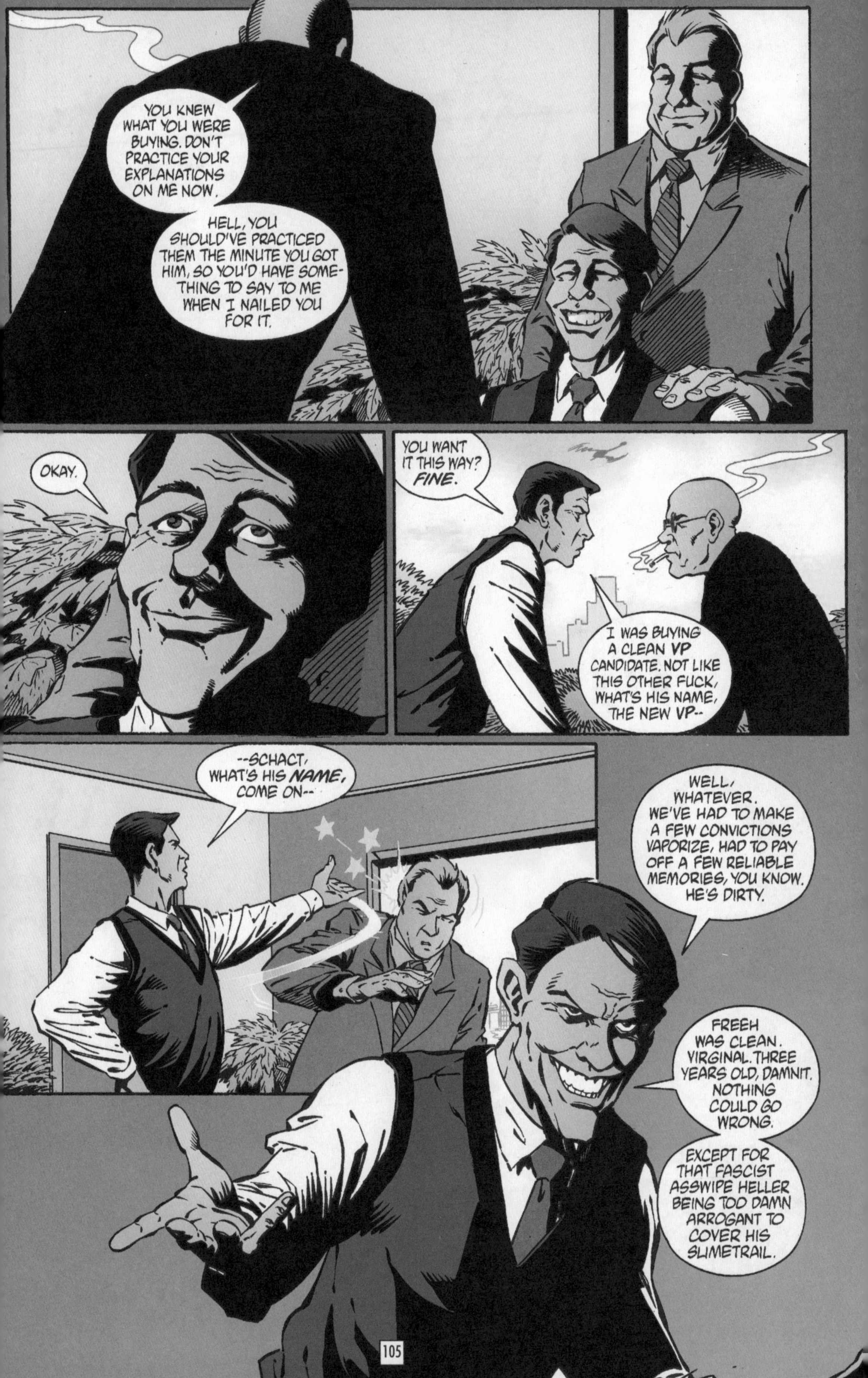
YOU KNEW WHAT YOU WERE BUYING. DON'T PRACTICE YOUR EXPLANATIONS ON ME NOW.
HELL, YOU SHOULD'VE PRACTICED THEM THE MINUTE YOU GOT HIM, SO YOU'D HAVE SOMETHING TO SAY TO ME WHEN I NAILED YOU FOR IT.
OKAY.
YOU WANT IT THIS WAY? FINE.
I WAS BUYING A CLEAN VP CANDIDATE. NOT LIKE THIS OTHER FUCK, WHAT'S HIS NAME, THE NEW VP--
--SCHACT, WHAT'S HIS NAME, COME ON--
WELL, WHATEVER. WE'VE HAD TO MAKE A FEW CONVICTIONS VAPORIZE, HAD TO PAY OFF A FEW RELIABLE MEMORIES, YOU KNOW. HE'S DIRTY.
FREEH WAS CLEAN. VIRGINAL. THREE YEARS OLD, DAMNIT. NOTHING COULD GO WRONG.
EXCEPT FOR THAT FASCIST ASSWIPE HELLER BEING TOO DAMN ARROGANT TO COVER HIS SLIMETRAIL.

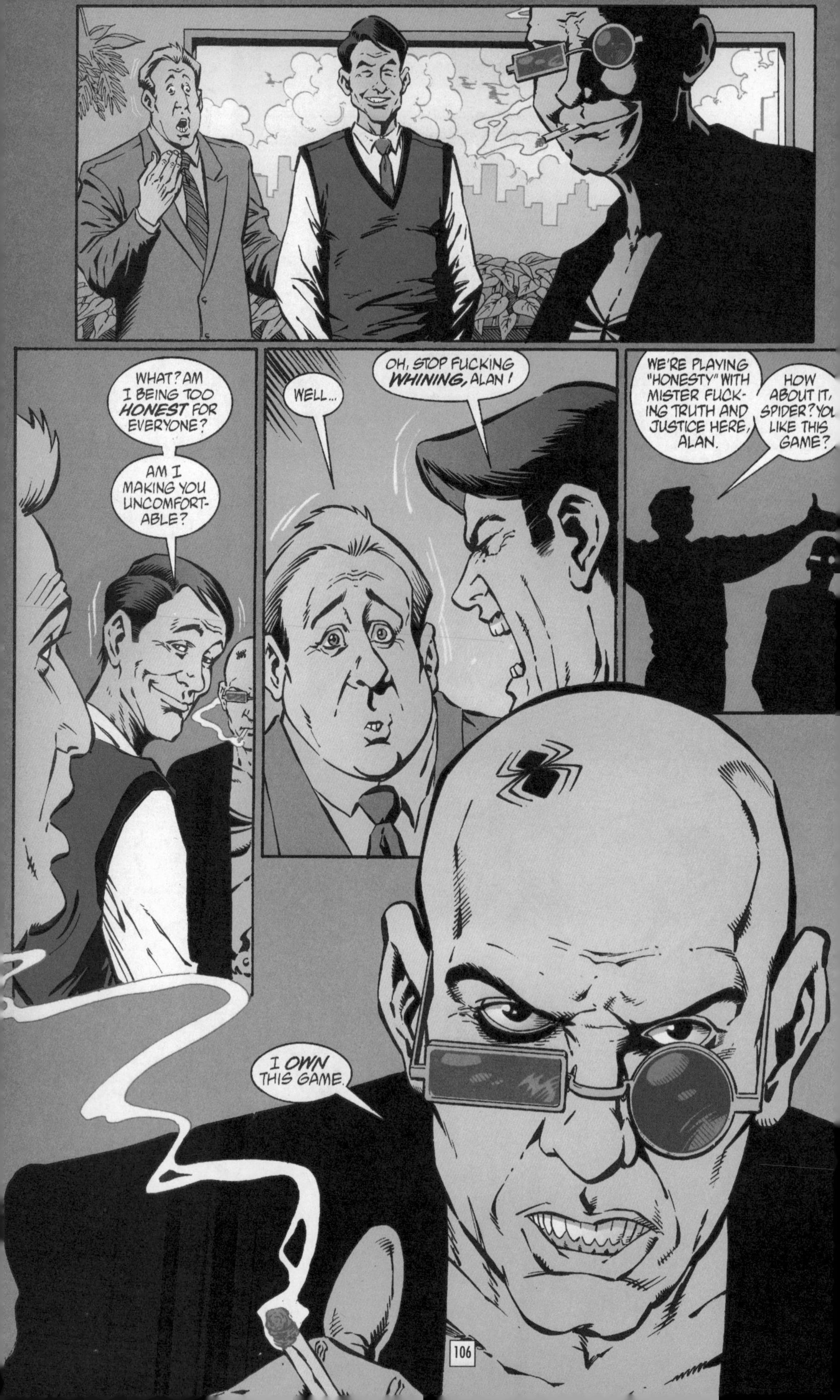
WHAT? AM I BEING TOO *HONEST* FOR EVERYONE?
AM I MAKING YOU UNCOMFORT-ABLE?
WELL...
OH, STOP FUCKING *WHINING*, ALAN!
WE'RE PLAYING "HONESTY" WITH MISTER FUCK-ING TRUTH AND JUSTICE HERE, ALAN.
HOW ABOUT IT, SPIDER? YOU LIKE THIS GAME?
I *OWN* THIS GAME.

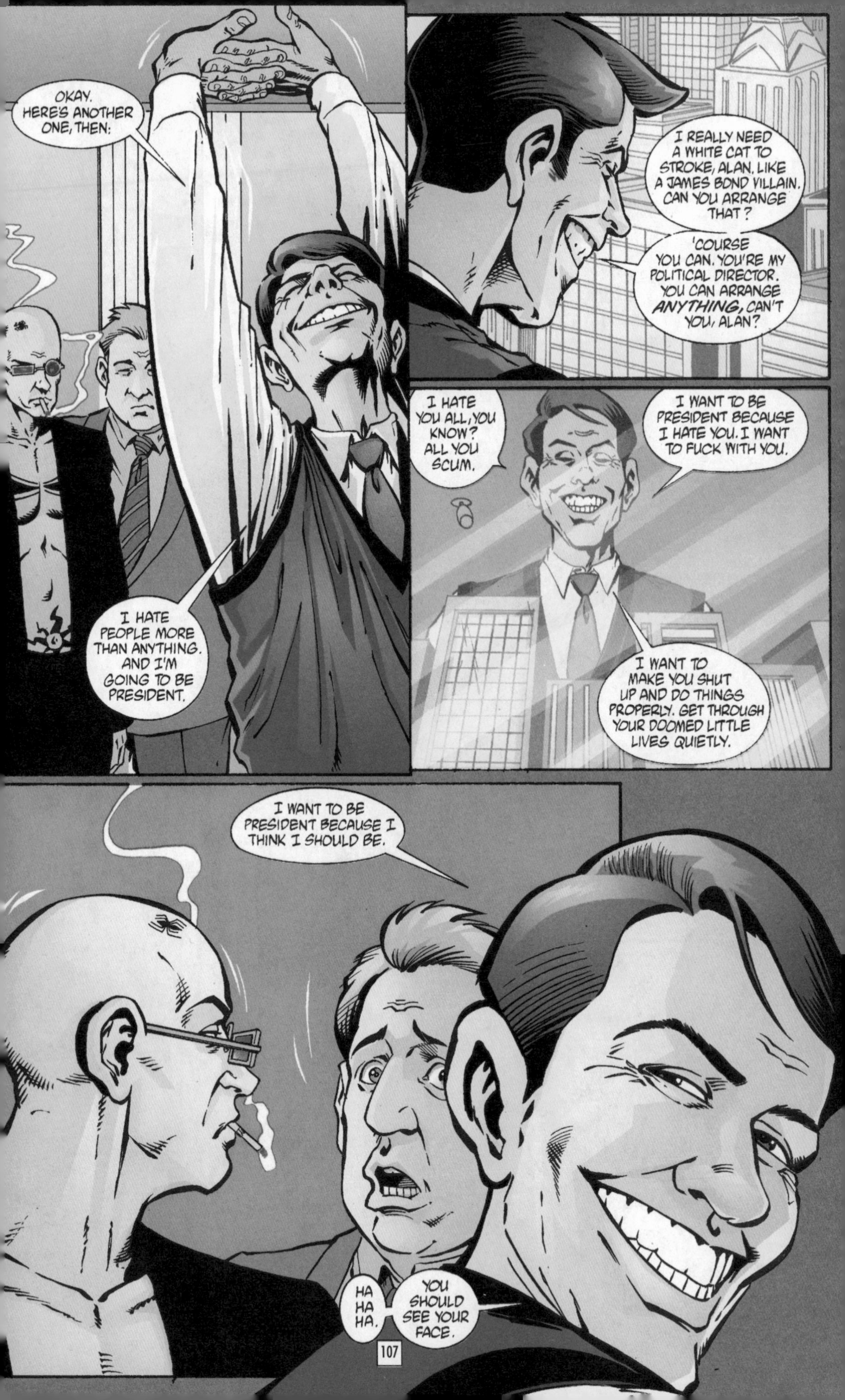

OKAY. HERE'S ANOTHER ONE, THEN:
I HATE PEOPLE MORE THAN ANYTHING. AND I'M GOING TO BE PRESIDENT.
I REALLY NEED A WHITE CAT TO STROKE, ALAN. LIKE A JAMES BOND VILLAIN. CAN YOU ARRANGE THAT?
'COURSE YOU CAN. YOU'RE MY POLITICAL DIRECTOR. YOU CAN ARRANGE *ANYTHING*, CAN'T YOU, ALAN?
I HATE YOU ALL, YOU KNOW? ALL YOU SCUM.
I WANT TO BE PRESIDENT BECAUSE I HATE YOU. I WANT TO FUCK WITH YOU.
I WANT TO MAKE YOU SHUT UP AND DO THINGS PROPERLY. GET THROUGH YOUR DOOMED LITTLE LIVES QUIETLY.
I WANT TO BE PRESIDENT BECAUSE I THINK I SHOULD BE.
HA HA HA.
YOU SHOULD SEE YOUR FACE.

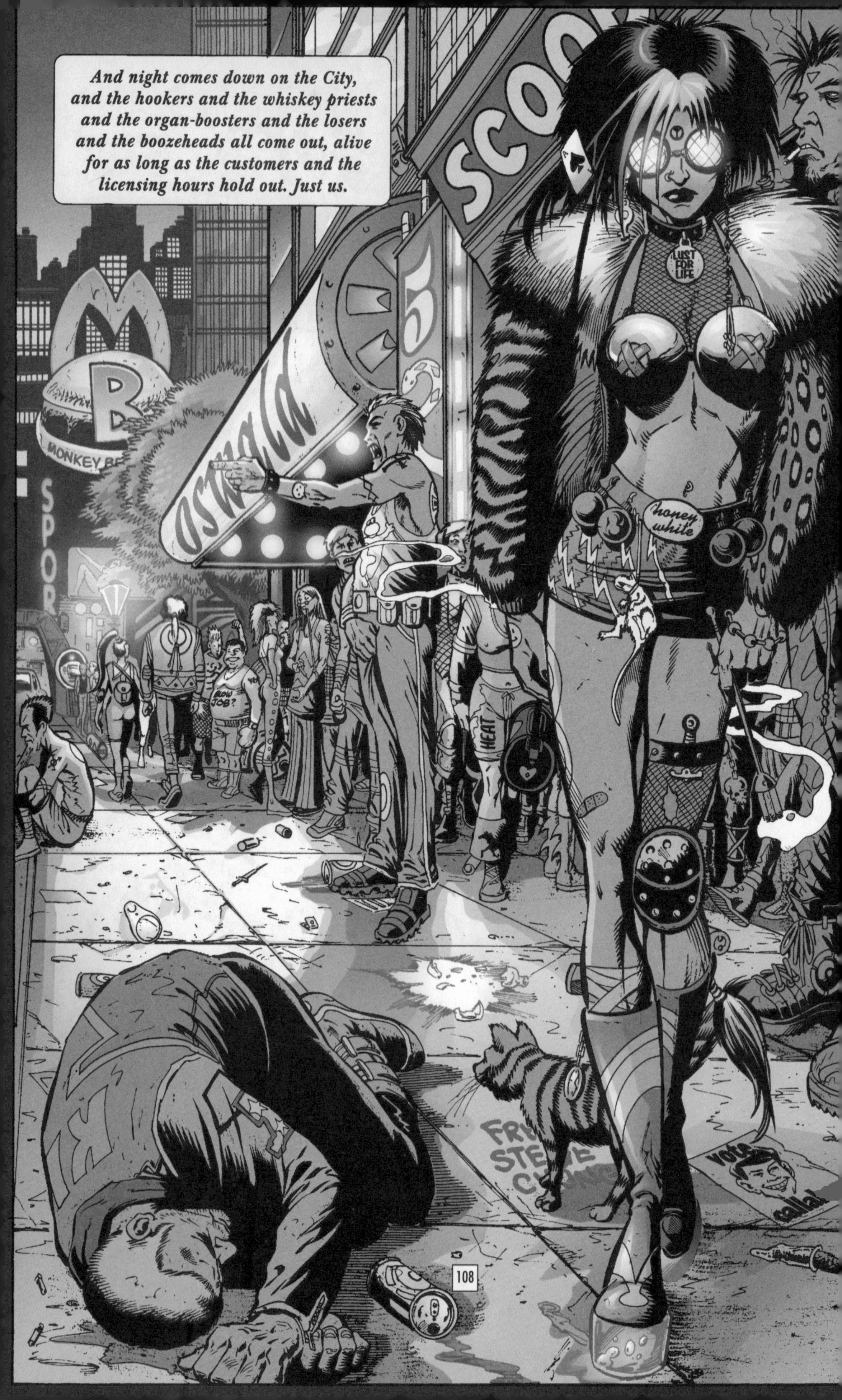

And night comes down on the City, and the hookers and the whiskey priests and the organ-boosters and the losers and the boozeheads all come out, alive for as long as the customers and the licensing hours hold out. Just us.
SCOO
Oswald
MONKEY B
SPOR
LUST FOR LIFE
honey white
BLOW JOB?
HEAT
Vote

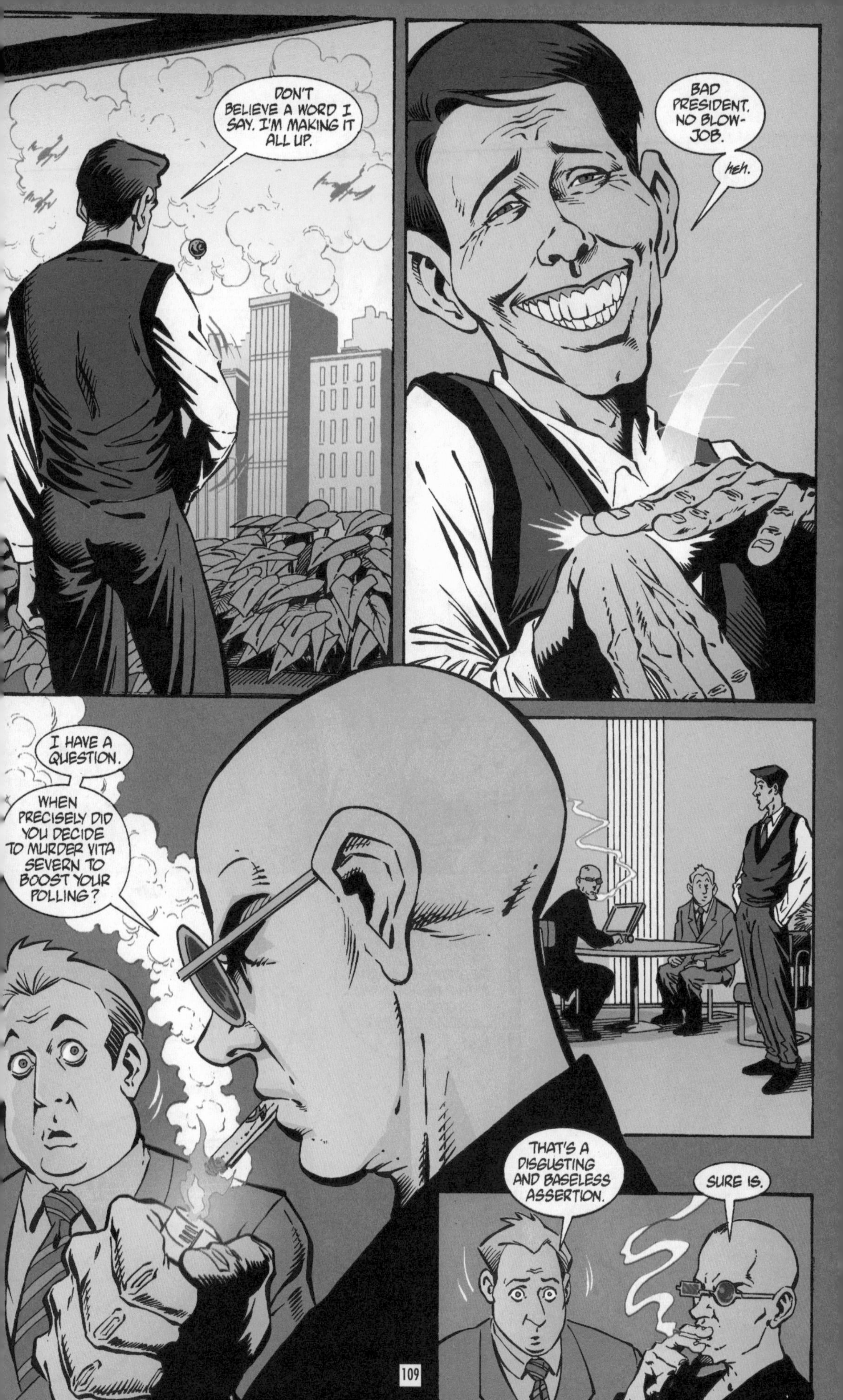

DON'T BELIEVE A WORD I SAY. I'M MAKING IT ALL UP.
BAD PRESIDENT. NO BLOW-JOB.
heh.
I HAVE A QUESTION.
WHEN PRECISELY DID YOU DECIDE TO MURDER VITA SEVERN TO BOOST YOUR POLLING?
THAT'S A DISGUSTING AND BASELESS ASSERTION.
SURE IS.

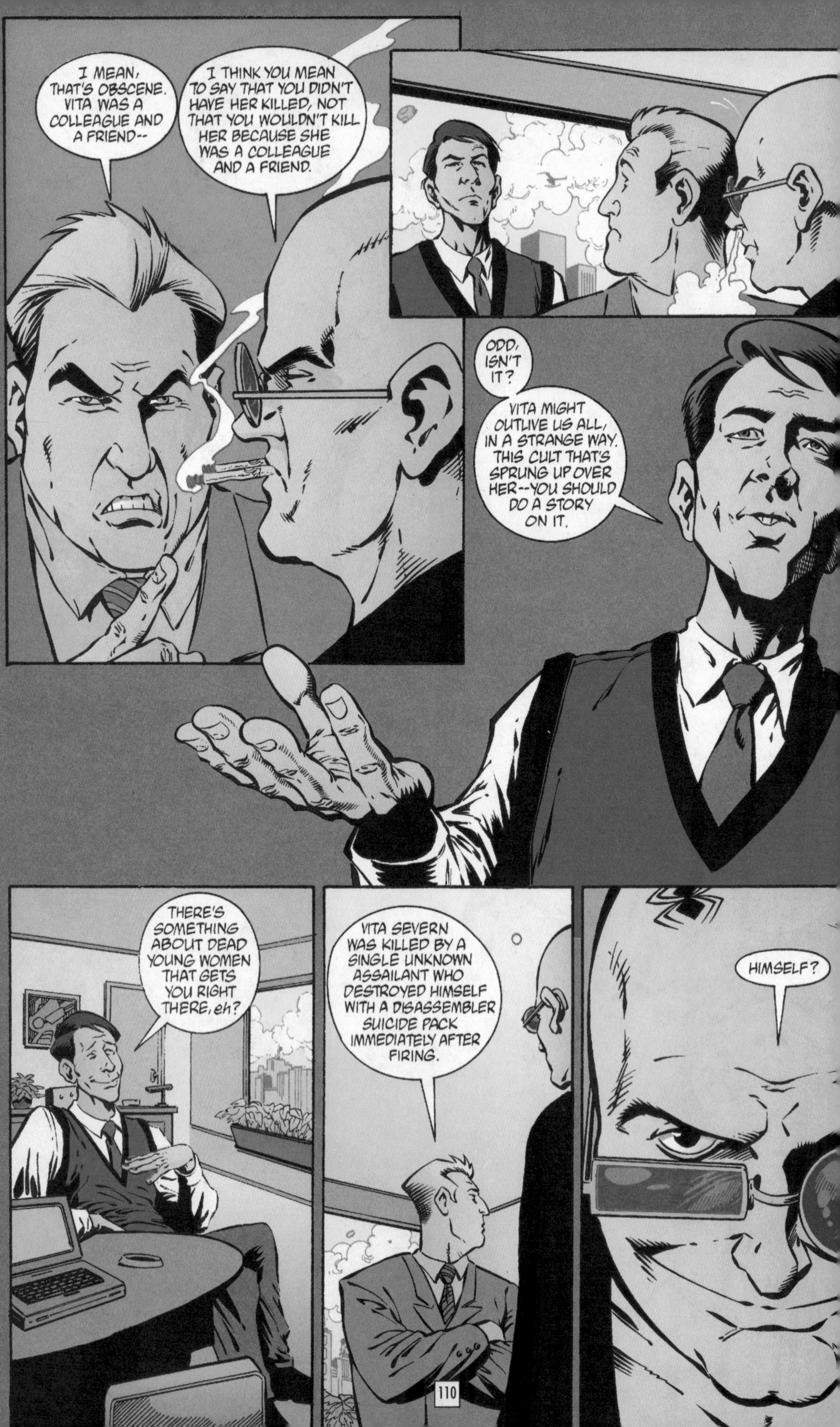
I MEAN, THAT'S OBSCENE. VITA WAS A COLLEAGUE AND A FRIEND--
I THINK YOU MEAN TO SAY THAT YOU DIDN'T HAVE HER KILLED, NOT THAT YOU WOULDN'T KILL HER BECAUSE SHE WAS A COLLEAGUE AND A FRIEND.
ODD, ISN'T IT?
VITA MIGHT OUTLIVE US ALL, IN A STRANGE WAY. THIS CULT THAT'S SPRUNG UP OVER HER--YOU SHOULD DO A STORY ON IT.
THERE'S SOMETHING ABOUT DEAD YOUNG WOMEN THAT GETS YOU RIGHT THERE, eh?
VITA SEVERN WAS KILLED BY A SINGLE UNKNOWN ASSAILANT WHO DESTROYED HIMSELF WITH A DISASSEMBLER SUICIDE PACK IMMEDIATELY AFTER FIRING.
HIMSELF?

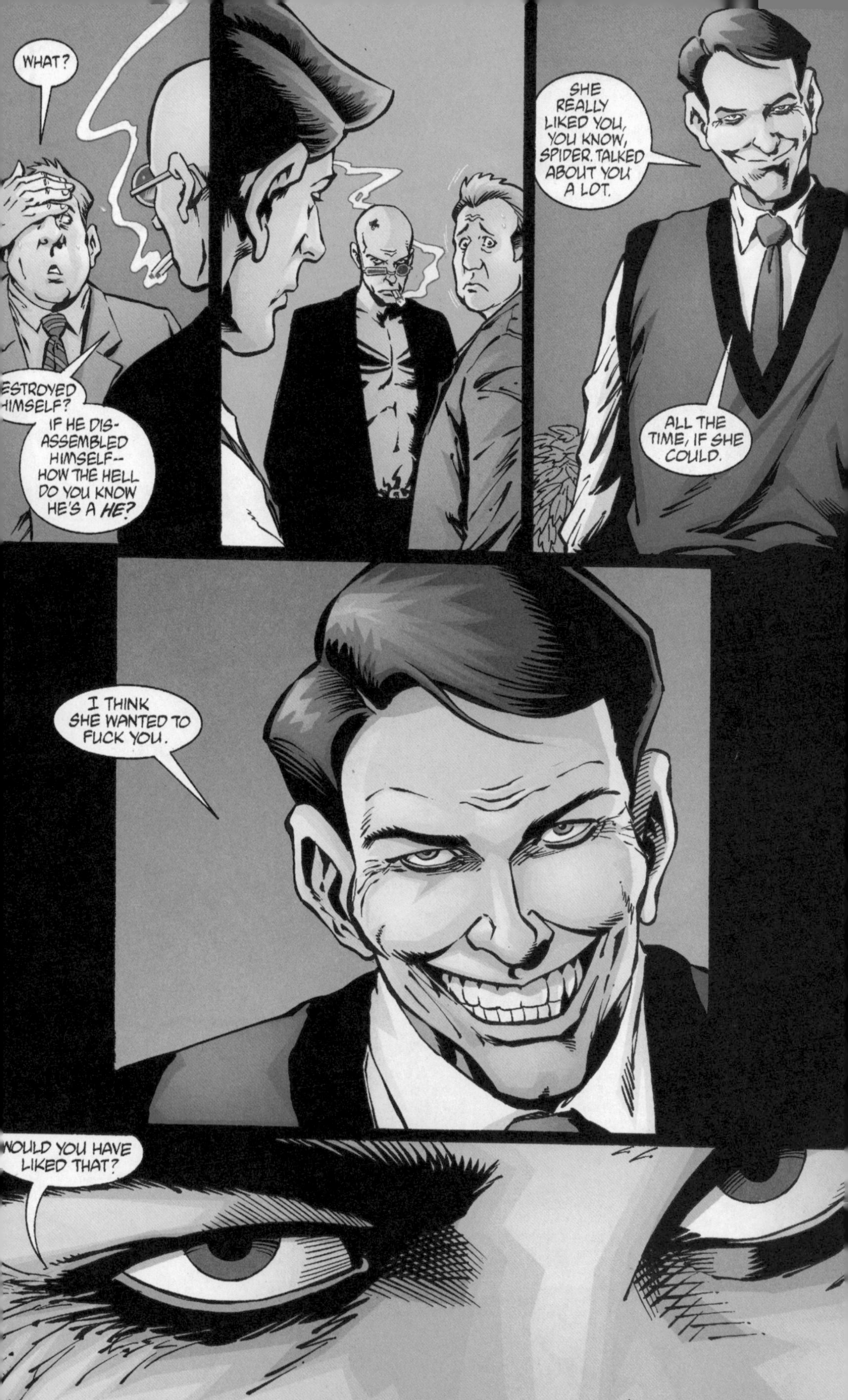
WHAT?
ESTROYED HIMSELF?
IF HE DIS-ASSEMBLED HIMSELF-- HOW THE HELL DO YOU KNOW HE'S A *HE?*
SHE REALLY LIKED YOU, YOU KNOW, SPIDER. TALKED ABOUT YOU A LOT.
ALL THE TIME, IF SHE COULD.
I THINK SHE WANTED TO FUCK YOU.
WOULD YOU HAVE LIKED THAT?

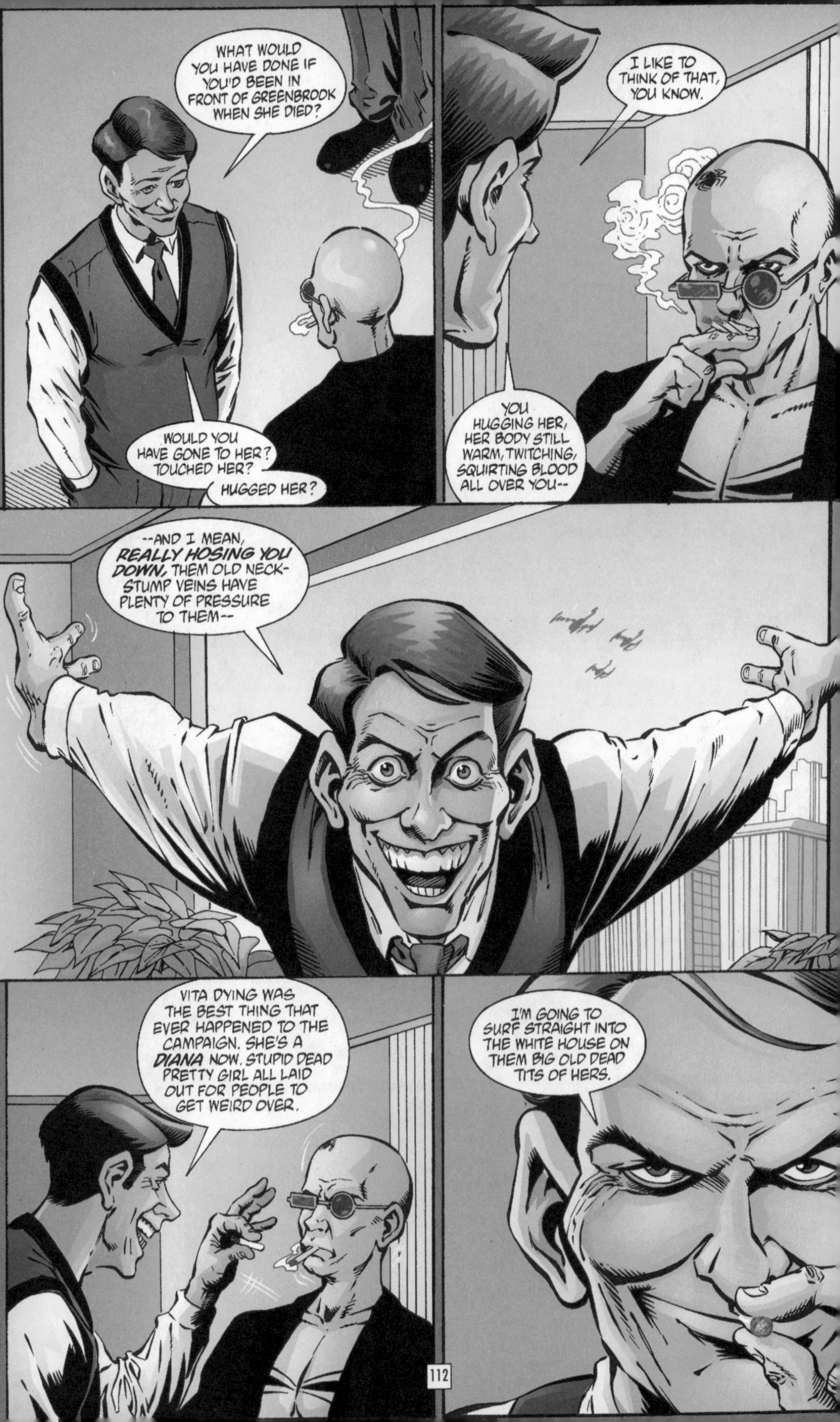
WHAT WOULD YOU HAVE DONE IF YOU'D BEEN IN FRONT OF GREENBROOK WHEN SHE DIED?
WOULD YOU HAVE GONE TO HER? TOUCHED HER?
HUGGED HER?
I LIKE TO THINK OF THAT, YOU KNOW.
YOU HUGGING HER, HER BODY STILL WARM, TWITCHING, SQUIRTING BLOOD ALL OVER YOU--
--AND I MEAN, ***REALLY HOSING YOU DOWN,*** THEM OLD NECK-STUMP VEINS HAVE PLENTY OF PRESSURE TO THEM--
VITA DYING WAS THE BEST THING THAT EVER HAPPENED TO THE CAMPAIGN. SHE'S A ***DIANA*** NOW. STUPID DEAD PRETTY GIRL ALL LAID OUT FOR PEOPLE TO GET WEIRD OVER.
I'M GOING TO SURF STRAIGHT INTO THE WHITE HOUSE ON THEM BIG OLD DEAD TITS OF HERS.

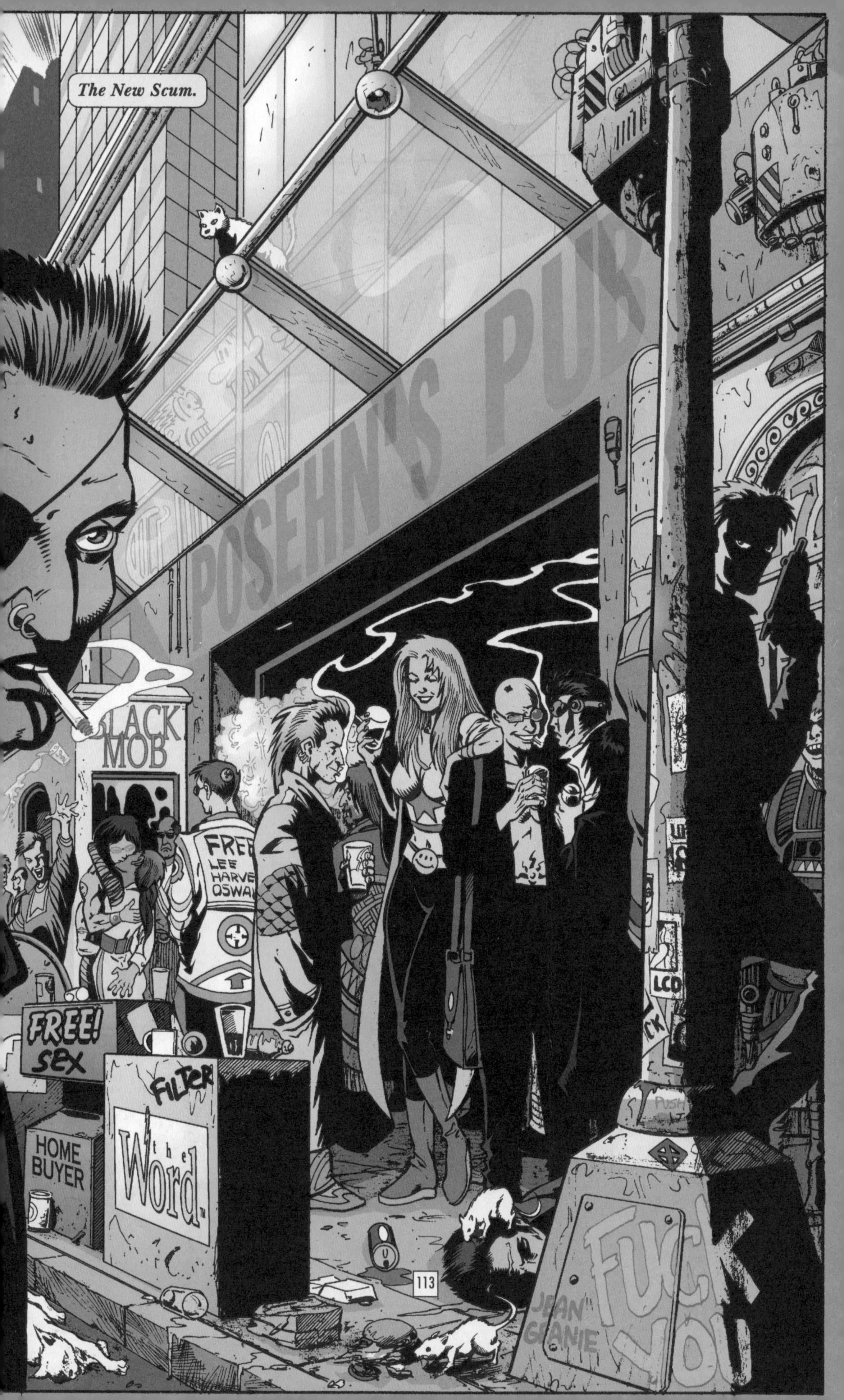
The New Scum.
POSEHN'S PUB
BLACK MOB
FREE LEE HARVEY OSWALD
FREE! SEX
FILTER
the Word
HOME BUYER
LCD
PUSH
JEAN GENIE
FUCK YOU

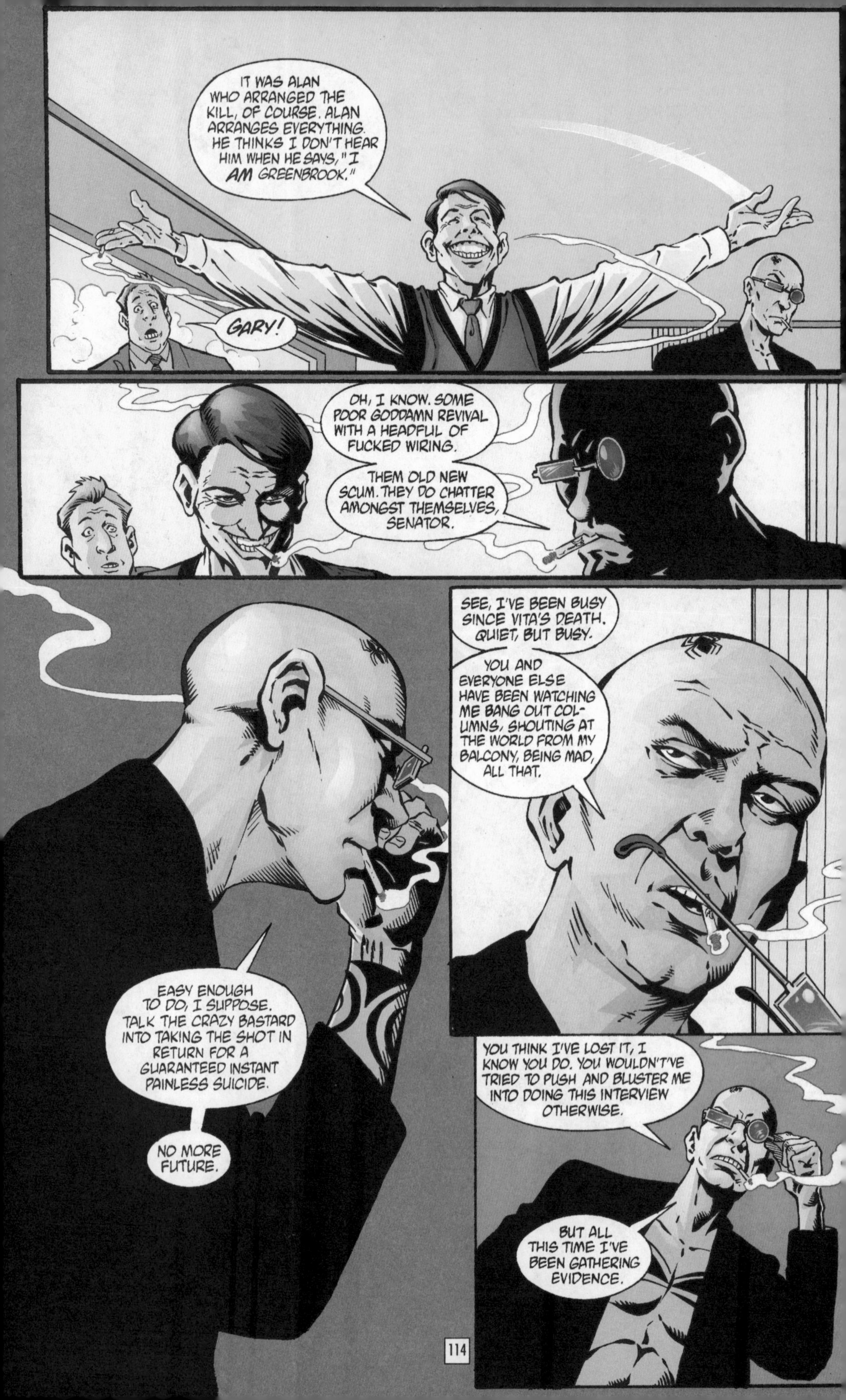
IT WAS ALAN WHO ARRANGED THE KILL, OF COURSE. ALAN ARRANGES EVERYTHING. HE THINKS I DON'T HEAR HIM WHEN HE SAYS, "I AM GREENBROOK."
GARY!
OH, I KNOW. SOME POOR GODDAMN REVIVAL WITH A HEADFUL OF FUCKED WIRING.
THEM OLD NEW SCUM. THEY DO CHATTER AMONGST THEMSELVES, SENATOR.
EASY ENOUGH TO DO, I SUPPOSE. TALK THE CRAZY BASTARD INTO TAKING THE SHOT IN RETURN FOR A GUARANTEED INSTANT PAINLESS SUICIDE.
NO MORE FUTURE.
SEE, I'VE BEEN BUSY SINCE VITA'S DEATH. QUIET, BUT BUSY.
YOU AND EVERYONE ELSE HAVE BEEN WATCHING ME BANG OUT COL-UMNS, SHOUTING AT THE WORLD FROM MY BALCONY, BEING MAD, ALL THAT.
YOU THINK I'VE LOST IT, I KNOW YOU DO. YOU WOULDN'T'VE TRIED TO PUSH AND BLUSTER ME INTO DOING THIS INTERVIEW OTHERWISE.
BUT ALL THIS TIME I'VE BEEN GATHERING EVIDENCE.

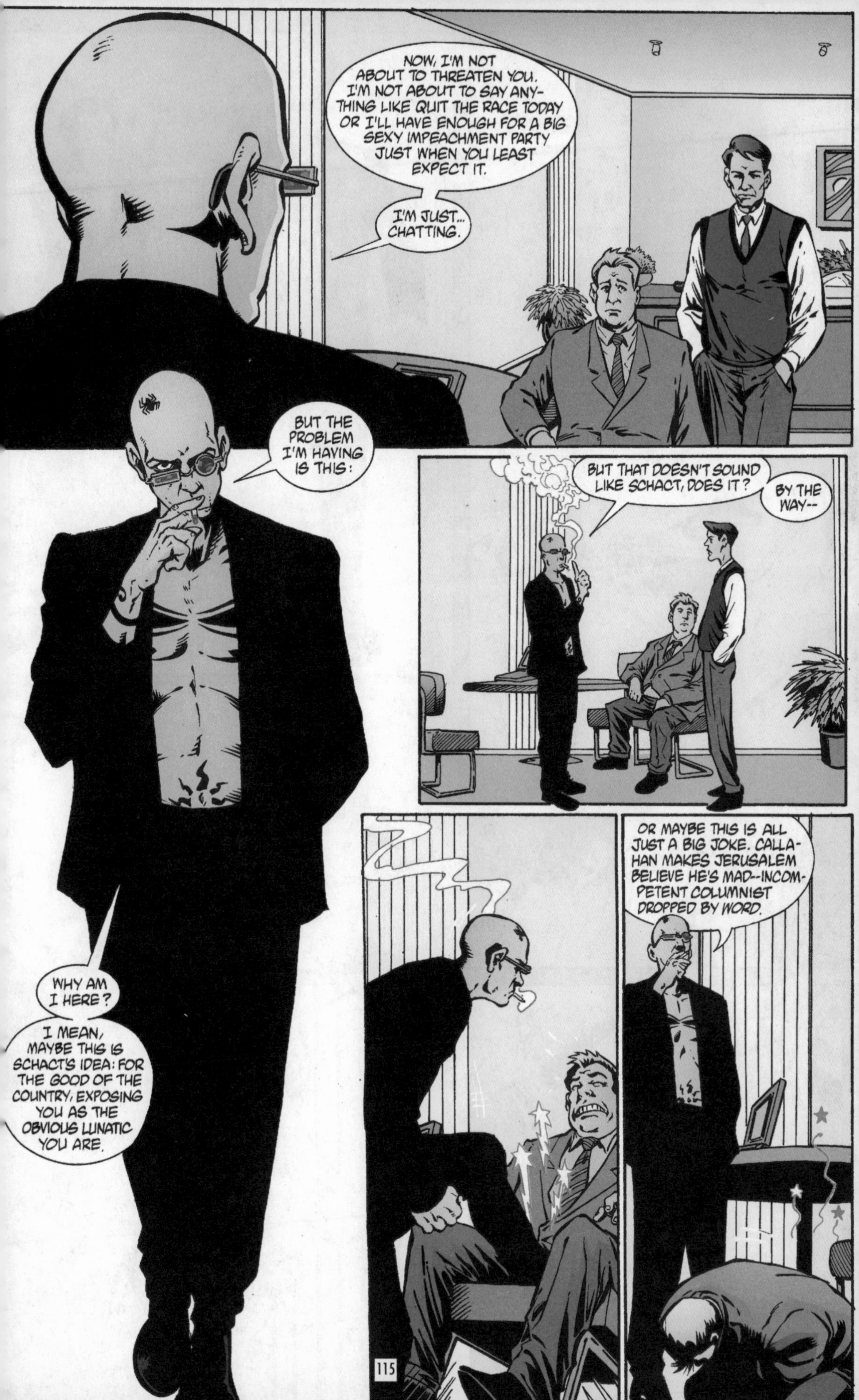
NOW, I'M NOT ABOUT TO THREATEN YOU. I'M NOT ABOUT TO SAY ANYTHING LIKE QUIT THE RACE TODAY OR I'LL HAVE ENOUGH FOR A BIG SEXY IMPEACHMENT PARTY JUST WHEN YOU LEAST EXPECT IT.
I'M JUST... CHATTING.
BUT THE PROBLEM I'M HAVING IS THIS:
WHY AM I HERE?
I MEAN, MAYBE THIS IS SCHACT'S IDEA: FOR THE GOOD OF THE COUNTRY, EXPOSING YOU AS THE OBVIOUS LUNATIC YOU ARE.
BUT THAT DOESN'T SOUND LIKE SCHACT, DOES IT?
BY THE WAY--
OR MAYBE THIS IS ALL JUST A BIG JOKE. CALLAHAN MAKES JERUSALEM BELIEVE HE'S MAD--INCOMPETENT COLUMNIST DROPPED BY WORD.

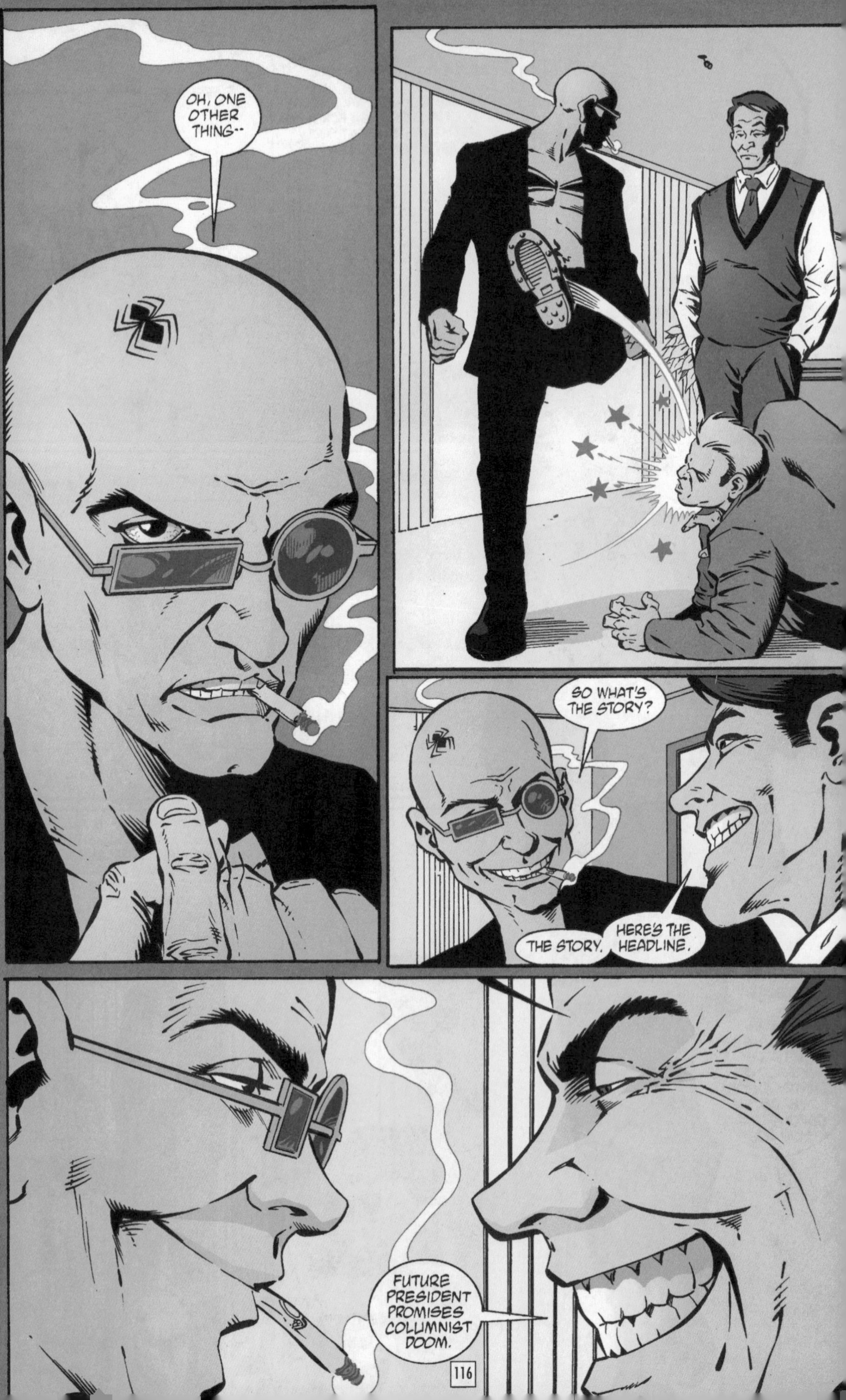
OH, ONE OTHER THING--
SO WHAT'S THE STORY?
HERE'S THE HEADLINE.
THE STORY.
FUTURE PRESIDENT PROMISES COLUMNIST DOOM.

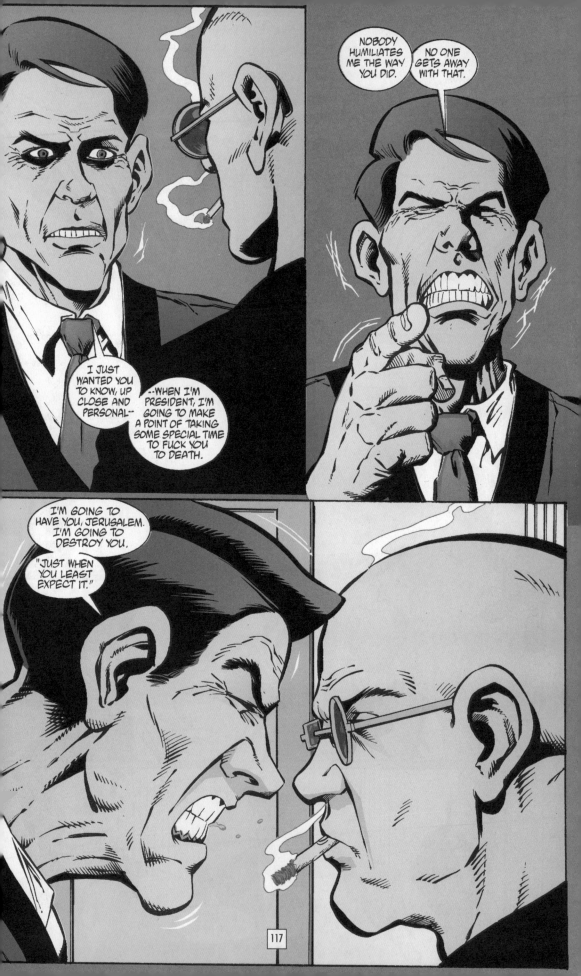

NOBODY HUMILIATES ME THE WAY YOU DID.

NO ONE GETS AWAY WITH THAT.

I JUST WANTED YOU TO KNOW, UP CLOSE AND PERSONAL--

--WHEN I'M PRESIDENT, I'M GOING TO MAKE A POINT OF TAKING SOME SPECIAL TIME TO FUCK YOU TO DEATH.

I'M GOING TO HAVE YOU, JERUSALEM. I'M GOING TO DESTROY YOU.

"JUST WHEN YOU LEAST EXPECT IT."

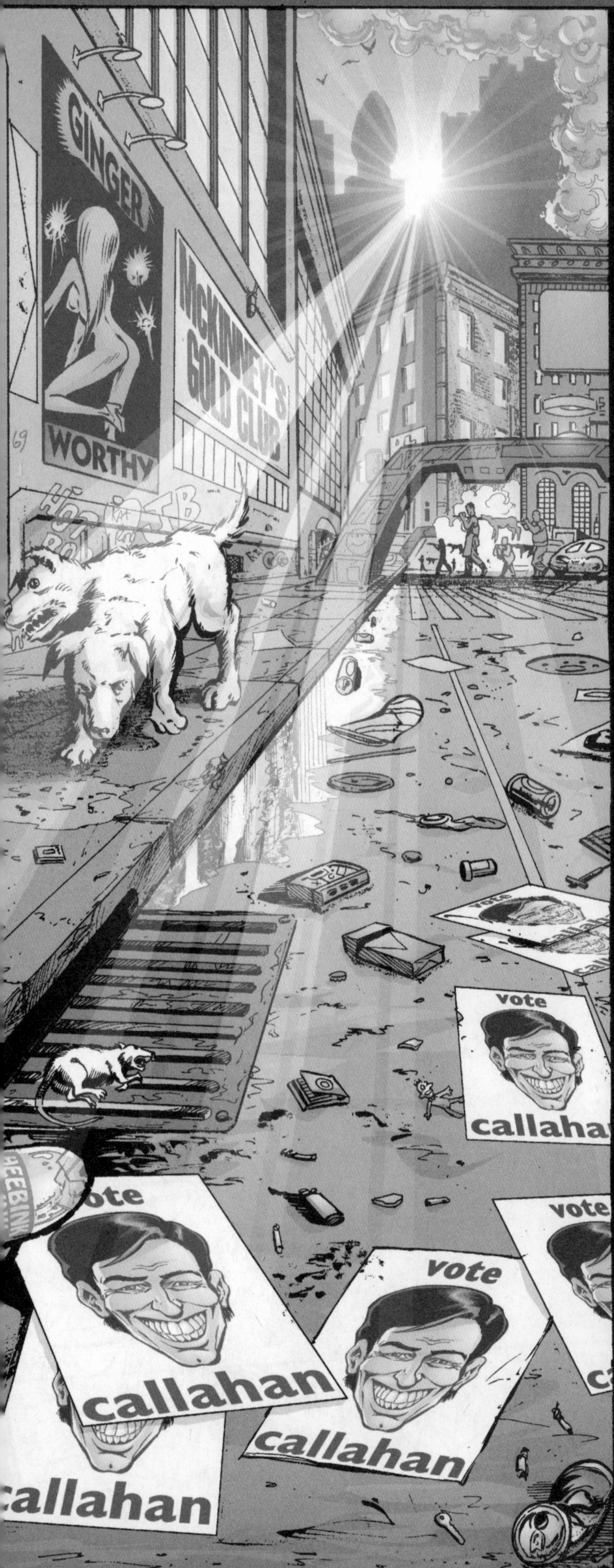
GINGER
WORTHY
McKINNEY'S GOLD CLUB
vote
callahan
vote
callahan
vote
callahan
callahan
vote
callahan

The Presidential Election is tomorrow.

Lots to do.

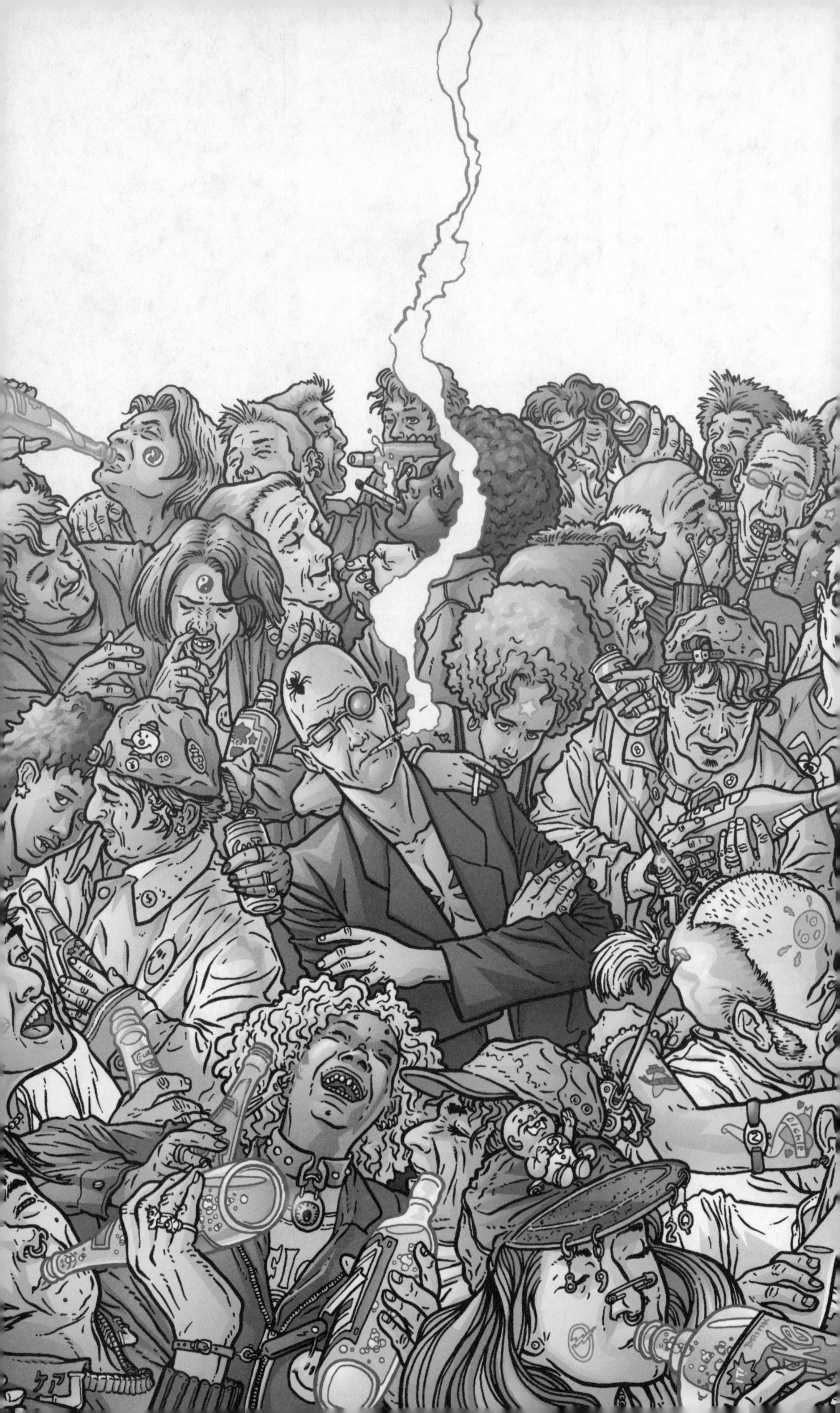

WARREN ELLIS writes and DARICK ROBERTSON pencils

THE NEW SCUM
6: new scum

RODNEY RAMOS, inker   CLEM ROBINS, letterer   NATHAN EYRING, color & separations

GEOF DARROW, cover artist   CLIFF CHIANG, assistant editor   STUART MOORE, editor

TRANSMETROPOLITAN created by WARREN ELLIS & DARICK ROBERTSON

AM I EARLY?

NO, YOU'RE FINE. COME ON IN...

IS SPIDER HERE YET?

KIND OF.

YOU SEE, WE WERE ABLE TO ARRANGE THE WHOLE ELECTION NIGHT PARTY THROUGH ONE SIMPLE ACT.

THE ACT OF NOT TELLING SPIDER WE WERE DOING IT.

AND NOW THAT WE'VE FILLED THE PLACE WITH PEOPLE, AND HIDDEN ALL HIS WEAPONS, HE'S KIND OF STUCK WITH IT.

SPLUCK

I WOULDN'T GET TOO CLOSE TO HIM.

LUSCIOUS

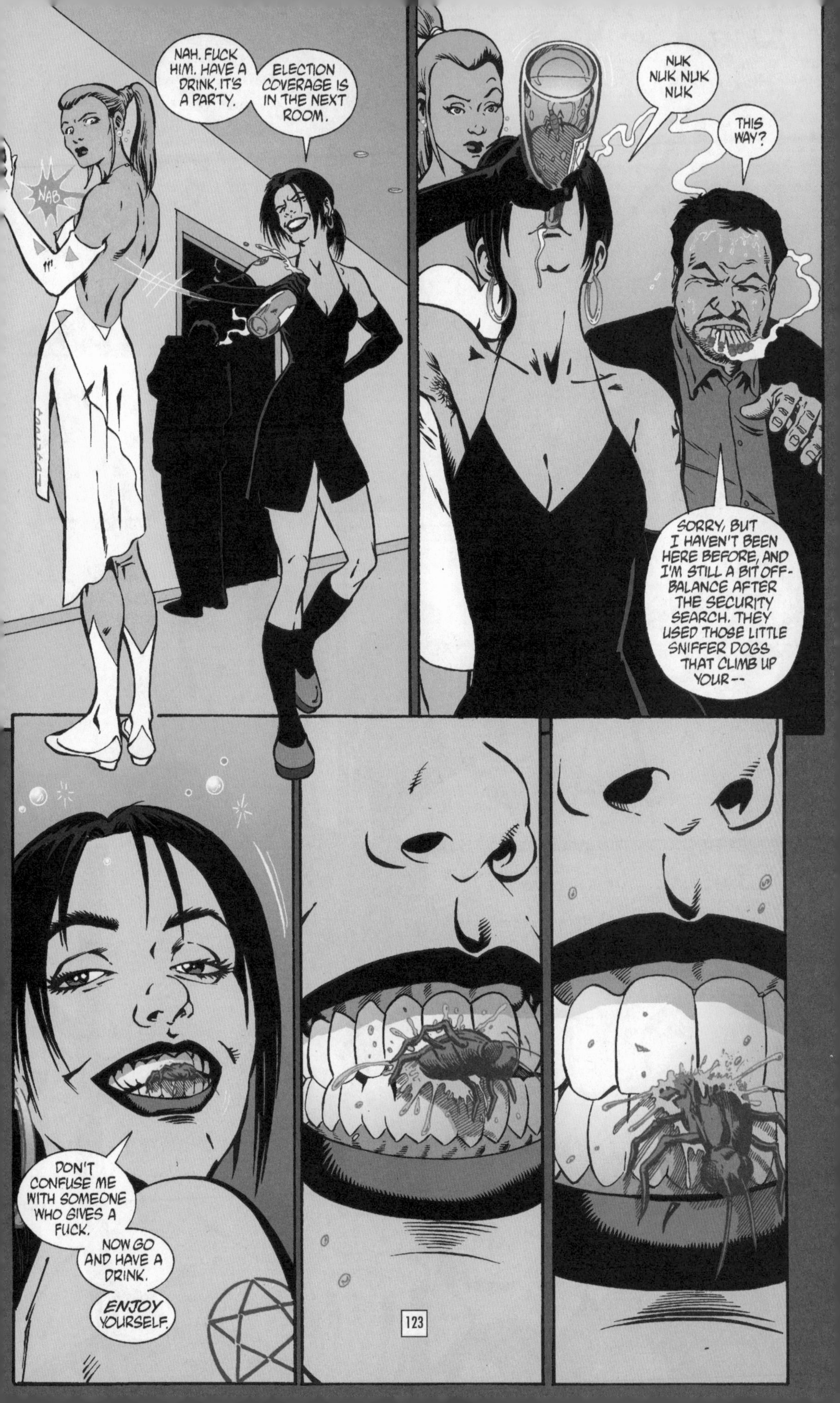
NAH. FUCK HIM. HAVE A DRINK. IT'S A PARTY.
ELECTION COVERAGE IS IN THE NEXT ROOM.
NAB
NUK NUK NUK NUK
THIS WAY?
SORRY, BUT I HAVEN'T BEEN HERE BEFORE, AND I'M STILL A BIT OFF-BALANCE AFTER THE SECURITY SEARCH. THEY USED THOSE LITTLE SNIFFER DOGS THAT CLIMB UP YOUR--
DON'T CONFUSE ME WITH SOMEONE WHO GIVES A FUCK.
NOW GO AND HAVE A DRINK.
ENJOY YOURSELF.

SLOW DOWN.

WHAT'RE YOU, MY FUCKING BOSS?

NO, I'M YOUR FUCKING FRIEND.

YOU HAVEN'T BEEN THE SAME SINCE I FOUND OUT--

I'M ALSO THE ONE WHO'S GOING TO KICK THE EGGS OUT OF YOU IF YOU GIVE ME ANY SHIT OVER THIS, YELENA.

NOTHING.

HAPPENED.

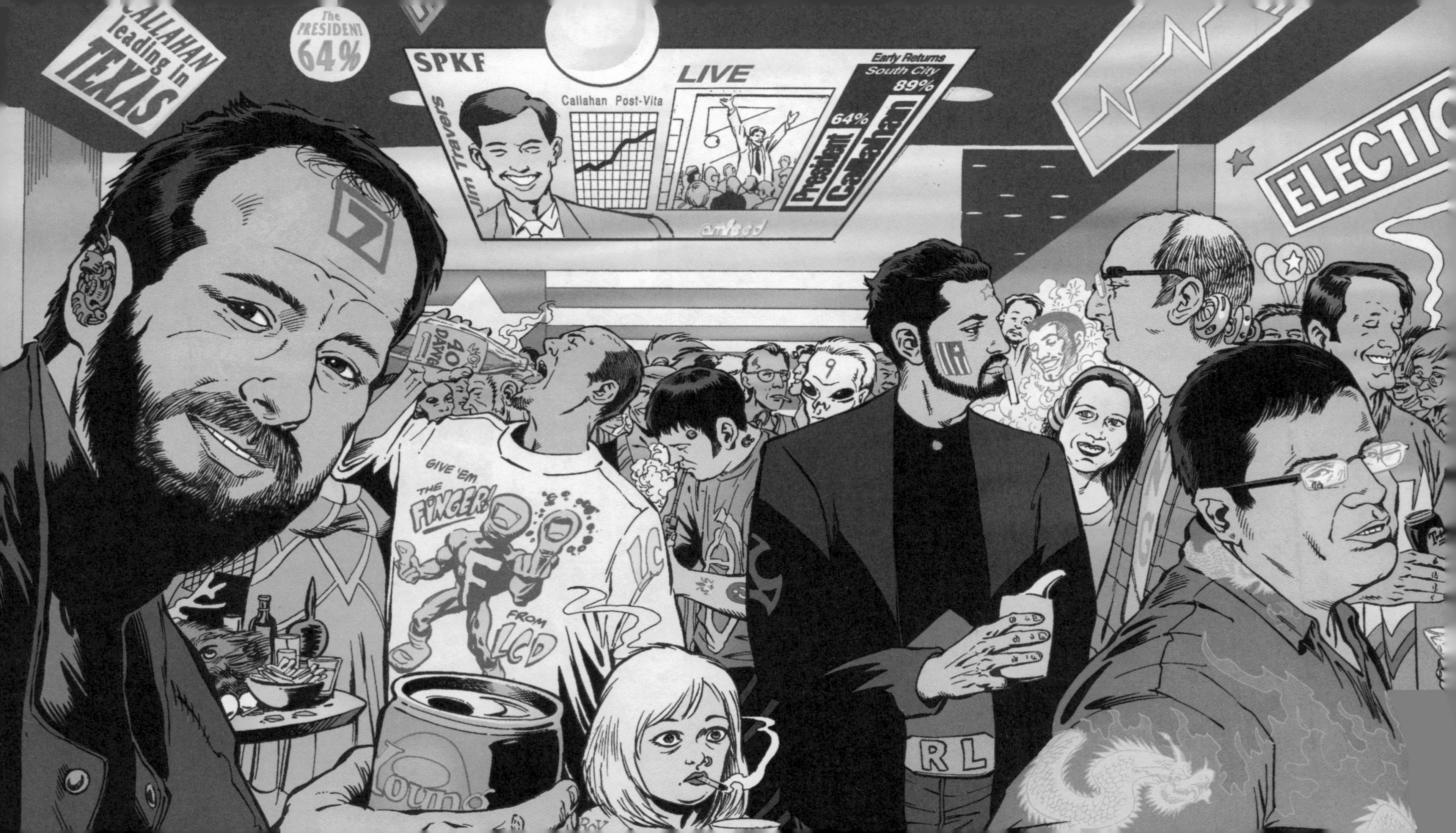
CALLAHAN leading in TEXAS
The PRESIDENT 64%
SPKF
Jim Travers
Callahan Post-Vita
LIVE
Early Returns
South City
89%
64%
President Callahan
ELECTIO
40 DAWG
GIVE 'EM THE FINGER!
FROM LCD
R L

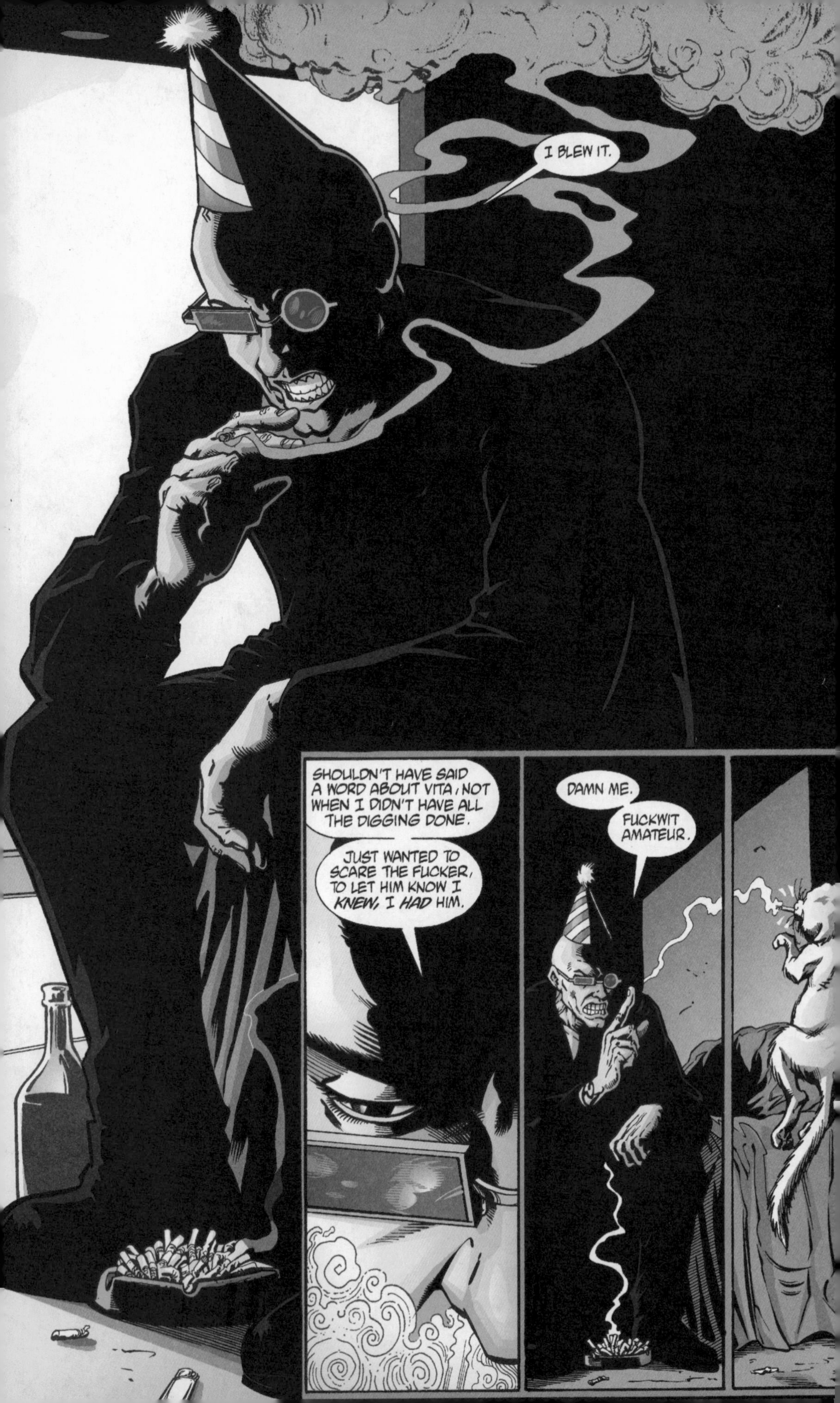
I BLEW IT.
SHOULDN'T HAVE SAID A WORD ABOUT VITA, NOT WHEN I DIDN'T HAVE ALL THE DIGGING DONE.
JUST WANTED TO SCARE THE FUCKER, TO LET HIM KNOW I *KNEW*, I *HAD* HIM.
DAMN ME.
FUCKWIT AMATEUR.

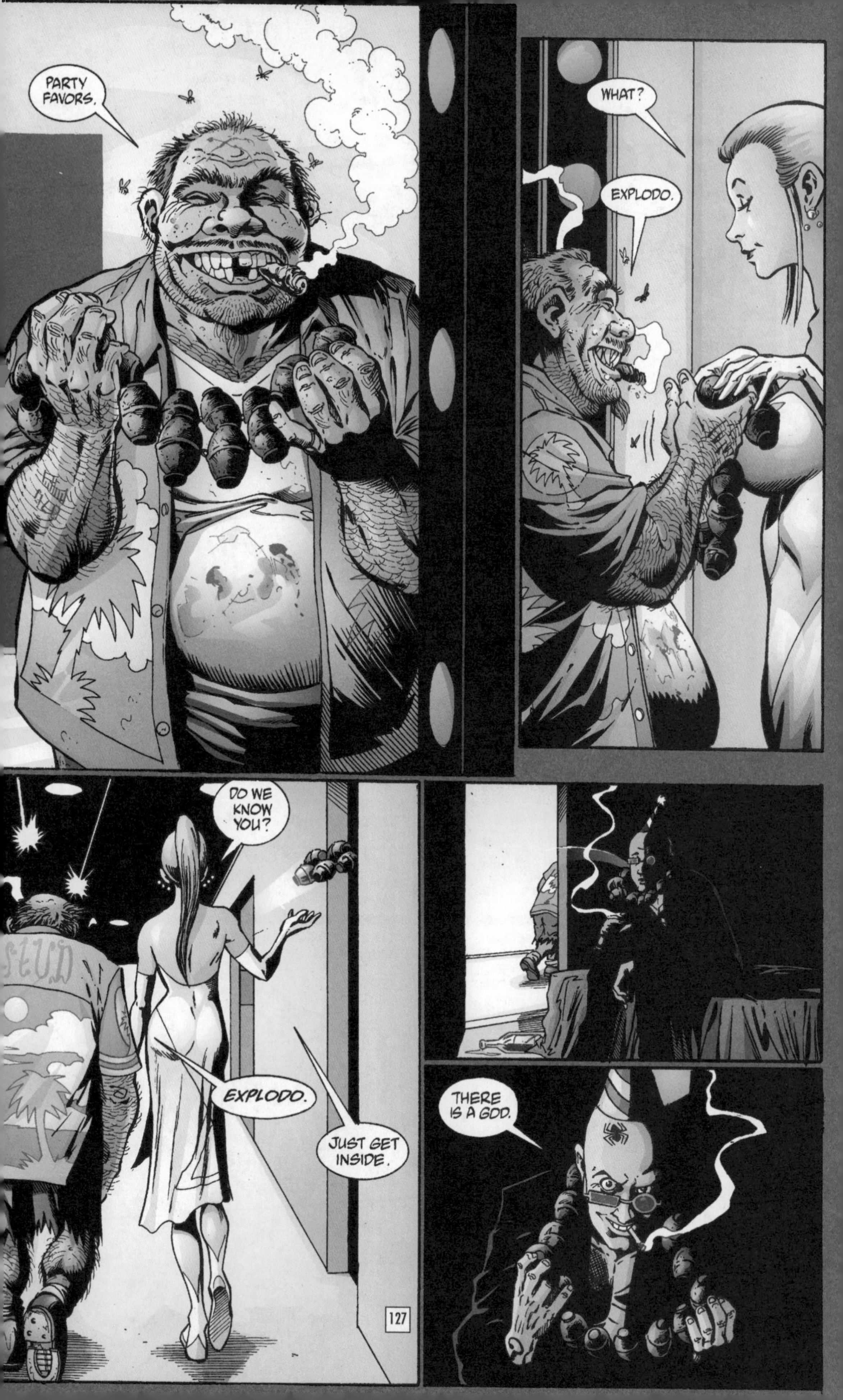
PARTY FAVORS.
WHAT?
EXPLODO.
DO WE KNOW YOU?
EXPLODO.
JUST GET INSIDE.
THERE IS A GOD.

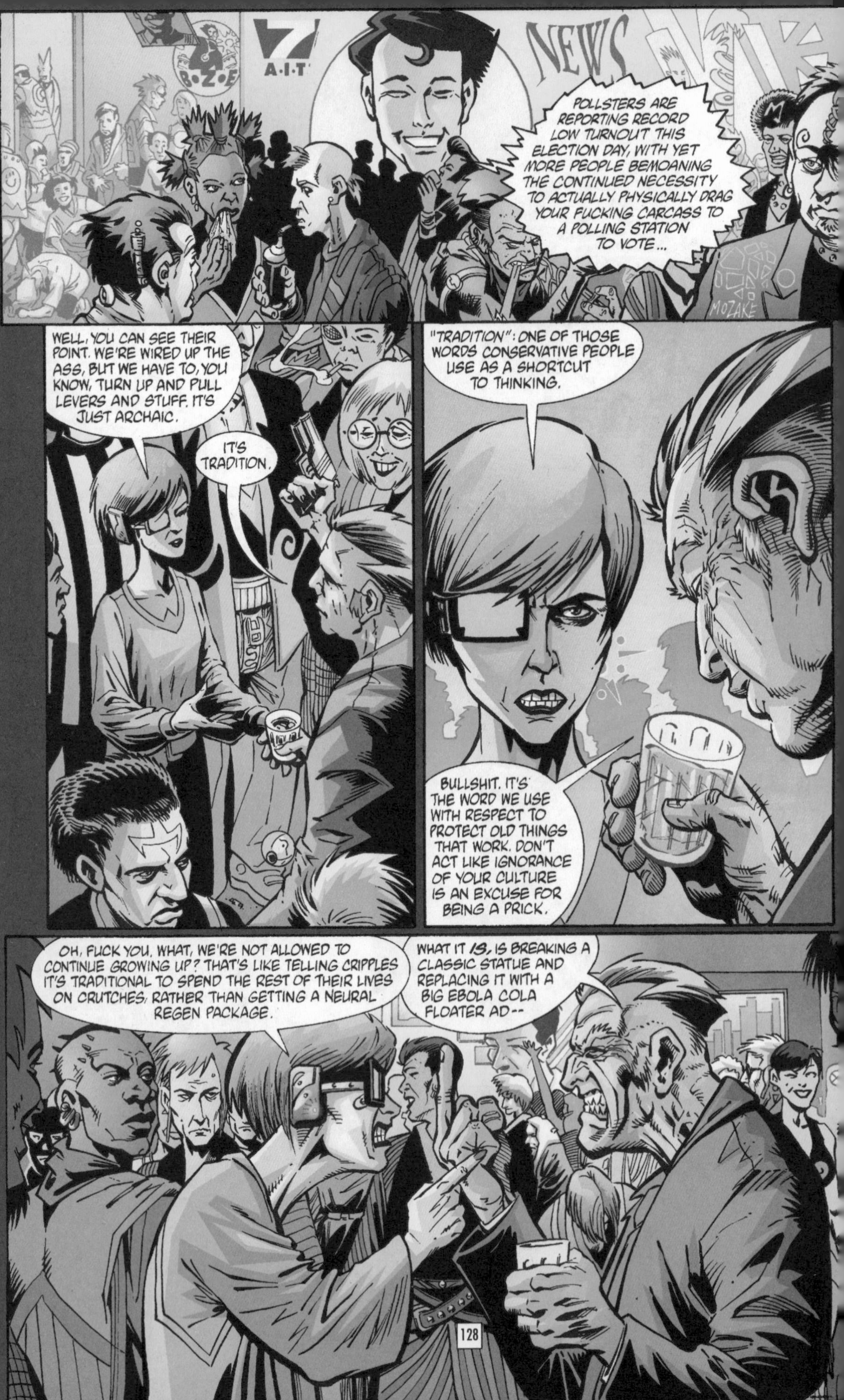

7 A·I·T
NEWS
POLLSTERS ARE REPORTING RECORD LOW TURNOUT THIS ELECTION DAY, WITH YET MORE PEOPLE BEMOANING THE CONTINUED NECESSITY TO ACTUALLY PHYSICALLY DRAG YOUR FUCKING CARCASS TO A POLLING STATION TO VOTE...
MOZAKE
WELL, YOU CAN SEE THEIR POINT. WE'RE WIRED UP THE ASS, BUT WE HAVE TO, YOU KNOW, TURN UP AND PULL LEVERS AND STUFF. IT'S JUST ARCHAIC.
IT'S TRADITION.
"TRADITION": ONE OF THOSE WORDS CONSERVATIVE PEOPLE USE AS A SHORTCUT TO THINKING.
BULLSHIT. IT'S THE WORD WE USE WITH RESPECT TO PROTECT OLD THINGS THAT WORK. DON'T ACT LIKE IGNORANCE OF YOUR CULTURE IS AN EXCUSE FOR BEING A PRICK.
OH, FUCK YOU. WHAT, WE'RE NOT ALLOWED TO CONTINUE GROWING UP? THAT'S LIKE TELLING CRIPPLES IT'S TRADITIONAL TO SPEND THE REST OF THEIR LIVES ON CRUTCHES, RATHER THAN GETTING A NEURAL REGEN PACKAGE.
WHAT IT IS, IS BREAKING A CLASSIC STATUE AND REPLACING IT WITH A BIG EBOLA COLA FLOATER AD--

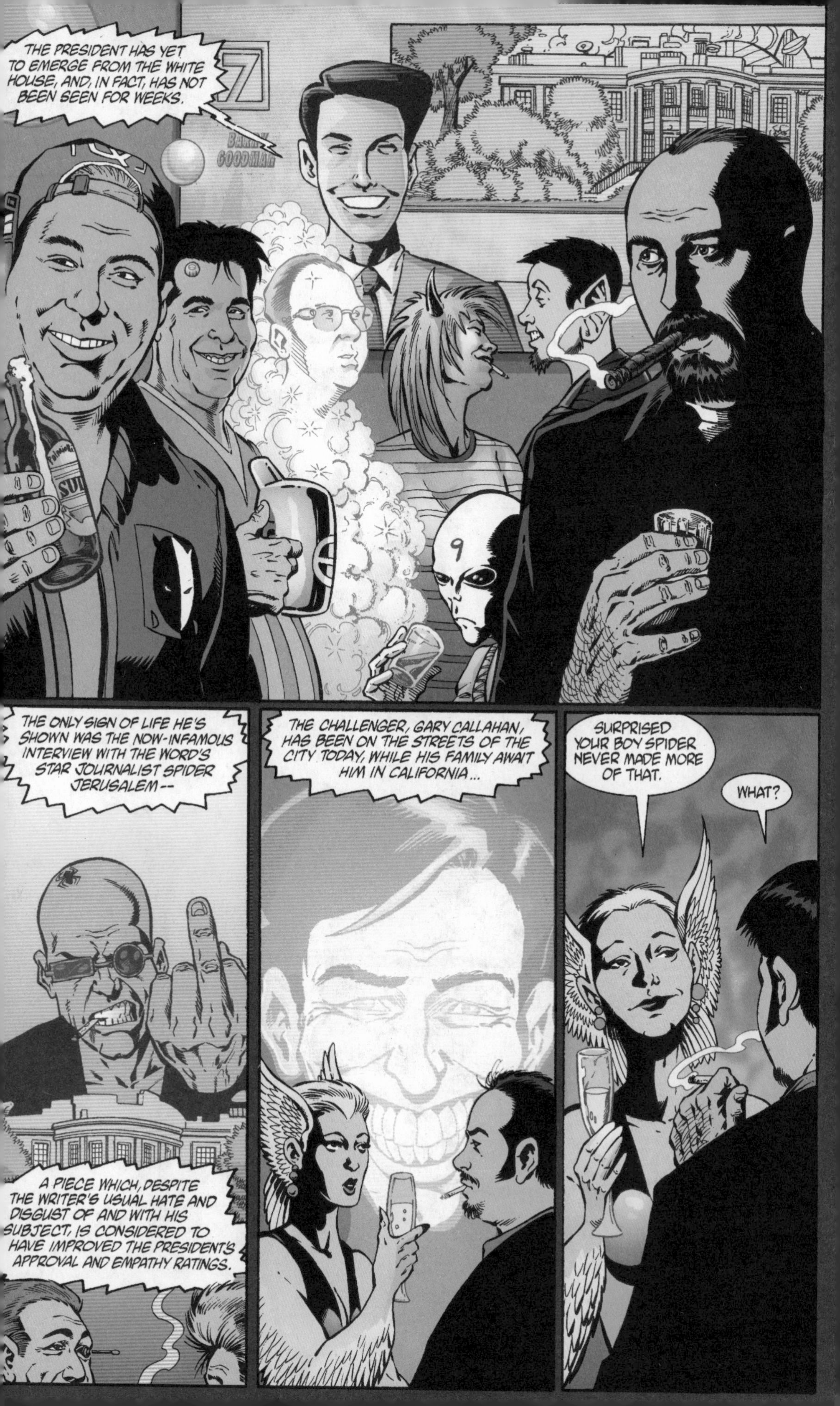

THE PRESIDENT HAS YET TO EMERGE FROM THE WHITE HOUSE, AND, IN FACT, HAS NOT BEEN SEEN FOR WEEKS.
7
BARRY GOODMAN
THE ONLY SIGN OF LIFE HE'S SHOWN WAS THE NOW-INFAMOUS INTERVIEW WITH THE WORD'S STAR JOURNALIST SPIDER JERUSALEM--
A PIECE WHICH, DESPITE THE WRITER'S USUAL HATE AND DISGUST OF AND WITH HIS SUBJECT, IS CONSIDERED TO HAVE IMPROVED THE PRESIDENT'S APPROVAL AND EMPATHY RATINGS.
THE CHALLENGER, GARY CALLAHAN, HAS BEEN ON THE STREETS OF THE CITY TODAY, WHILE HIS FAMILY AWAIT HIM IN CALIFORNIA...
SURPRISED YOUR BOY SPIDER NEVER MADE MORE OF THAT.
WHAT?

CALLAHAN'S FAMILY PERMANENTLY "IN CALIFORNIA" WHILE THE MAN HIMSELF RUNS LOOSE ALL OVER THE COUNTRY.

IT'S NOT THEM HE WANTS. IT'S US.

HE CAN FUCK HER EVERY NIGHT OF THE WEEK, AFTER ALL.

BUT WE ONLY COME FOR A POLITICIAN ONCE EVERY FOUR YEARS.

I'LL BE GLAD WHEN IT'S ALL OVER. BACK TO REAL LIFE.

YOU DON'T THINK THIS IS REAL LIFE?

AT THE VERY LEAST IT PROBABLY CONSTITUTES CONSTRUCTIVE ABANDONMENT IN A DIVORCE HEARING.

GOOD GOD, NO. THEY'VE ONLY JUST PUT IT ON TELEVISION, FOR CHRIST'S SAKE.

THE EVENT: CYCLE COVERAGE OF THE ELECTION IS SPONSORED BY--

GLADIATOR DOOM ARENA

--TOP-RATED 7pm-SLOT FAMILY SHOW GLADIATOR DOOM ARENA! AMERICA'S HARDEST MEN IN TV'S MOST ELABORATE ARENA, IN COMPETITION, NOT AGAINST EACH OTHER --

--BUT AGAINST AN AUDIENCE ARMED WITH OVER SEVEN HUNDRED HANDGUNS!

BIG BEN

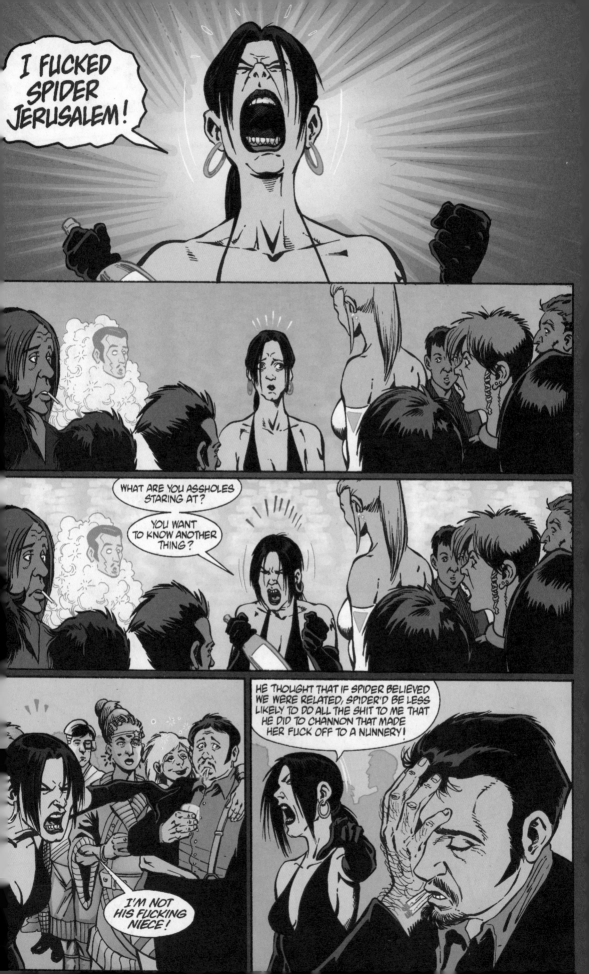

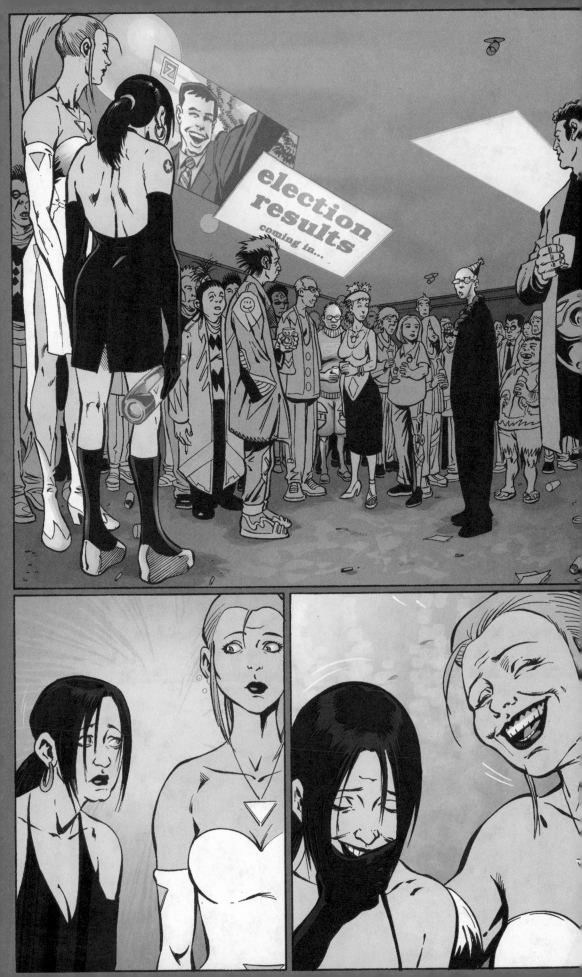

election
results
coming in...

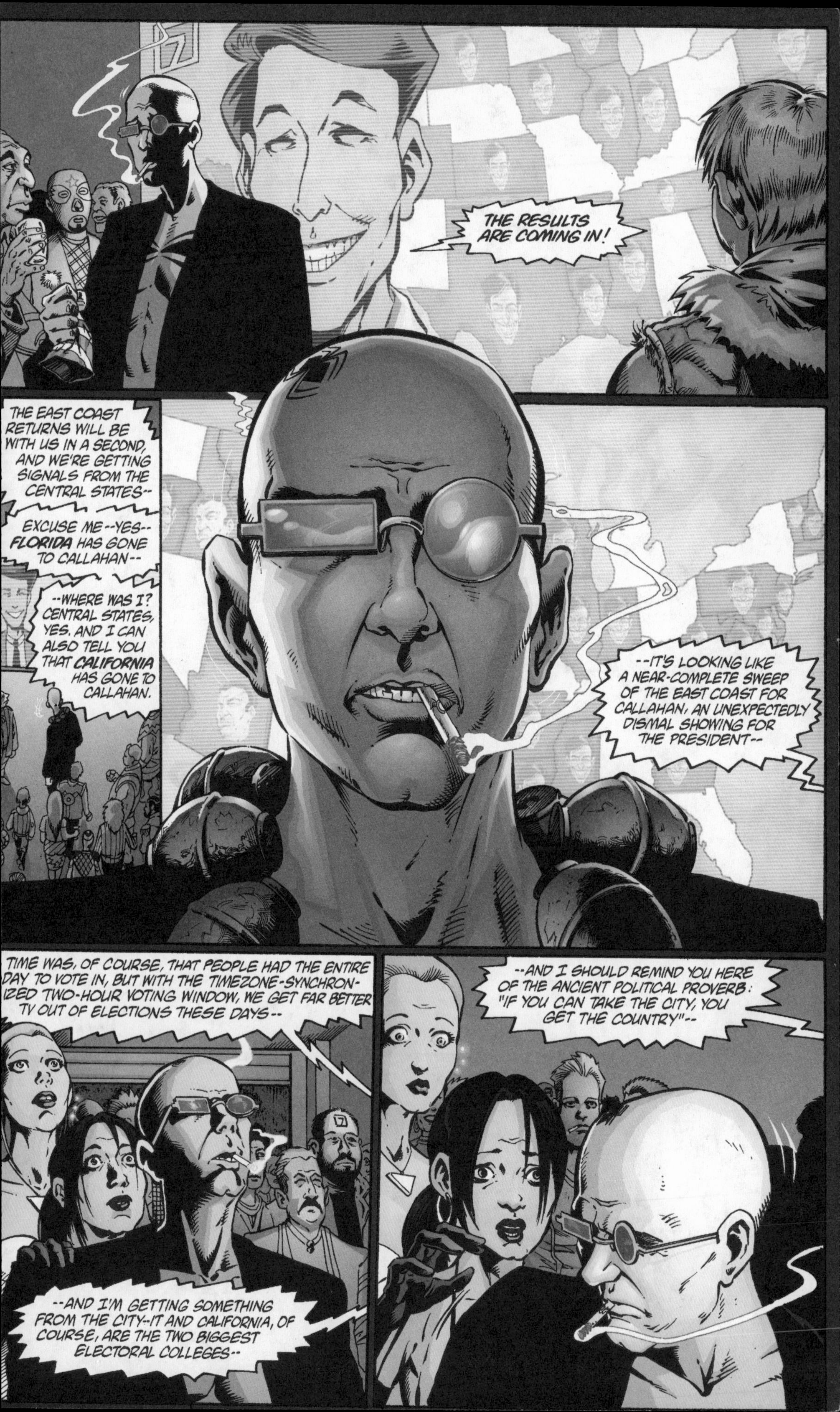
THE RESULTS ARE COMING IN!
THE EAST COAST RETURNS WILL BE WITH US IN A SECOND, AND WE'RE GETTING SIGNALS FROM THE CENTRAL STATES--
EXCUSE ME--YES-- FLORIDA HAS GONE TO CALLAHAN--
--WHERE WAS I? CENTRAL STATES, YES. AND I CAN ALSO TELL YOU THAT CALIFORNIA HAS GONE TO CALLAHAN.
--IT'S LOOKING LIKE A NEAR-COMPLETE SWEEP OF THE EAST COAST FOR CALLAHAN, AN UNEXPECTEDLY DISMAL SHOWING FOR THE PRESIDENT--
TIME WAS, OF COURSE, THAT PEOPLE HAD THE ENTIRE DAY TO VOTE IN, BUT WITH THE TIMEZONE-SYNCHRONIZED TWO-HOUR VOTING WINDOW, WE GET FAR BETTER TV OUT OF ELECTIONS THESE DAYS--
--AND I'M GETTING SOMETHING FROM THE CITY--IT AND CALIFORNIA, OF COURSE, ARE THE TWO BIGGEST ELECTORAL COLLEGES--
--AND I SHOULD REMIND YOU HERE OF THE ANCIENT POLITICAL PROVERB: "IF YOU CAN TAKE THE CITY, YOU GET THE COUNTRY"--

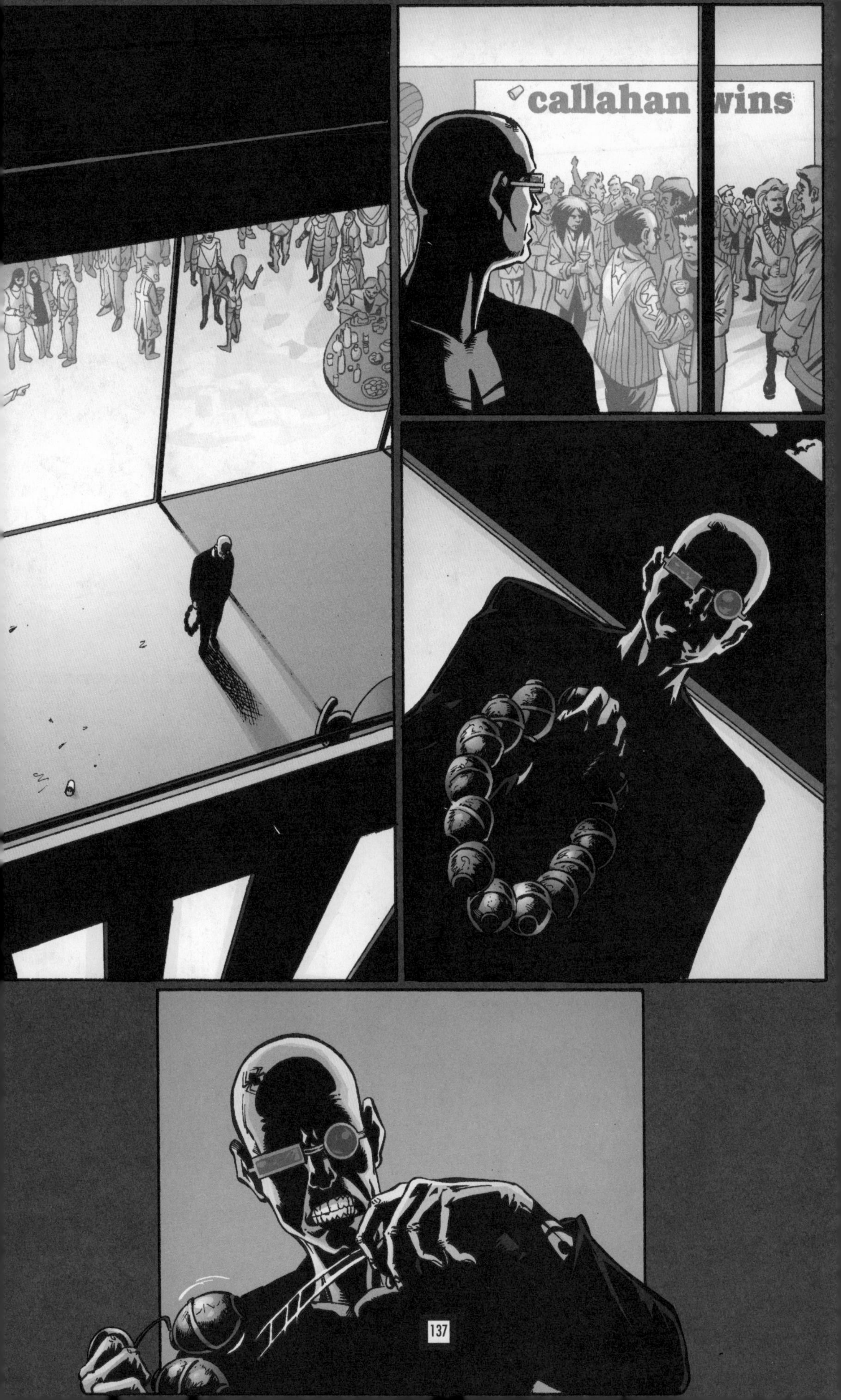
callahan wins

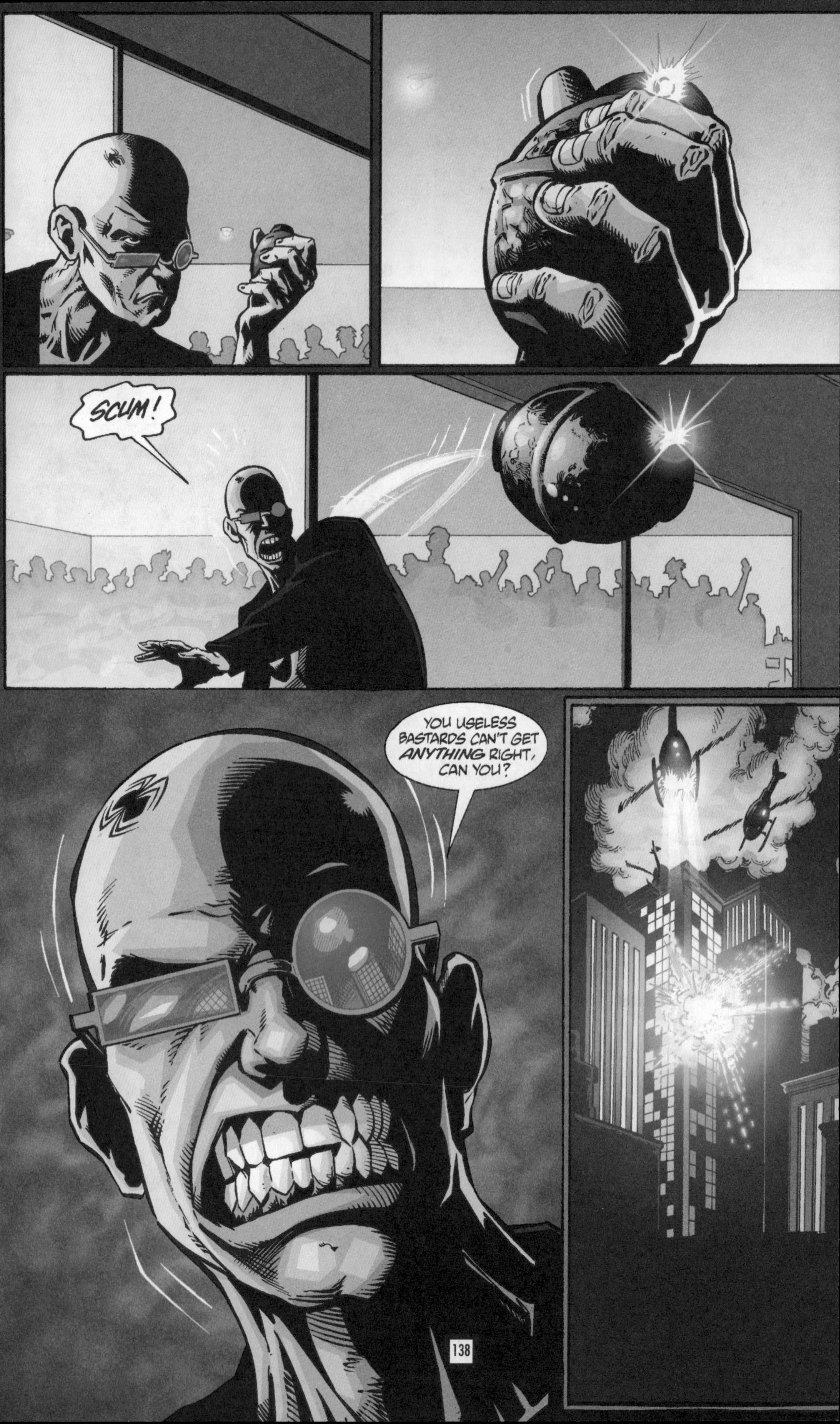
SCUM!
YOU USELESS BASTARDS CAN'T GET *ANYTHING* RIGHT, CAN YOU?

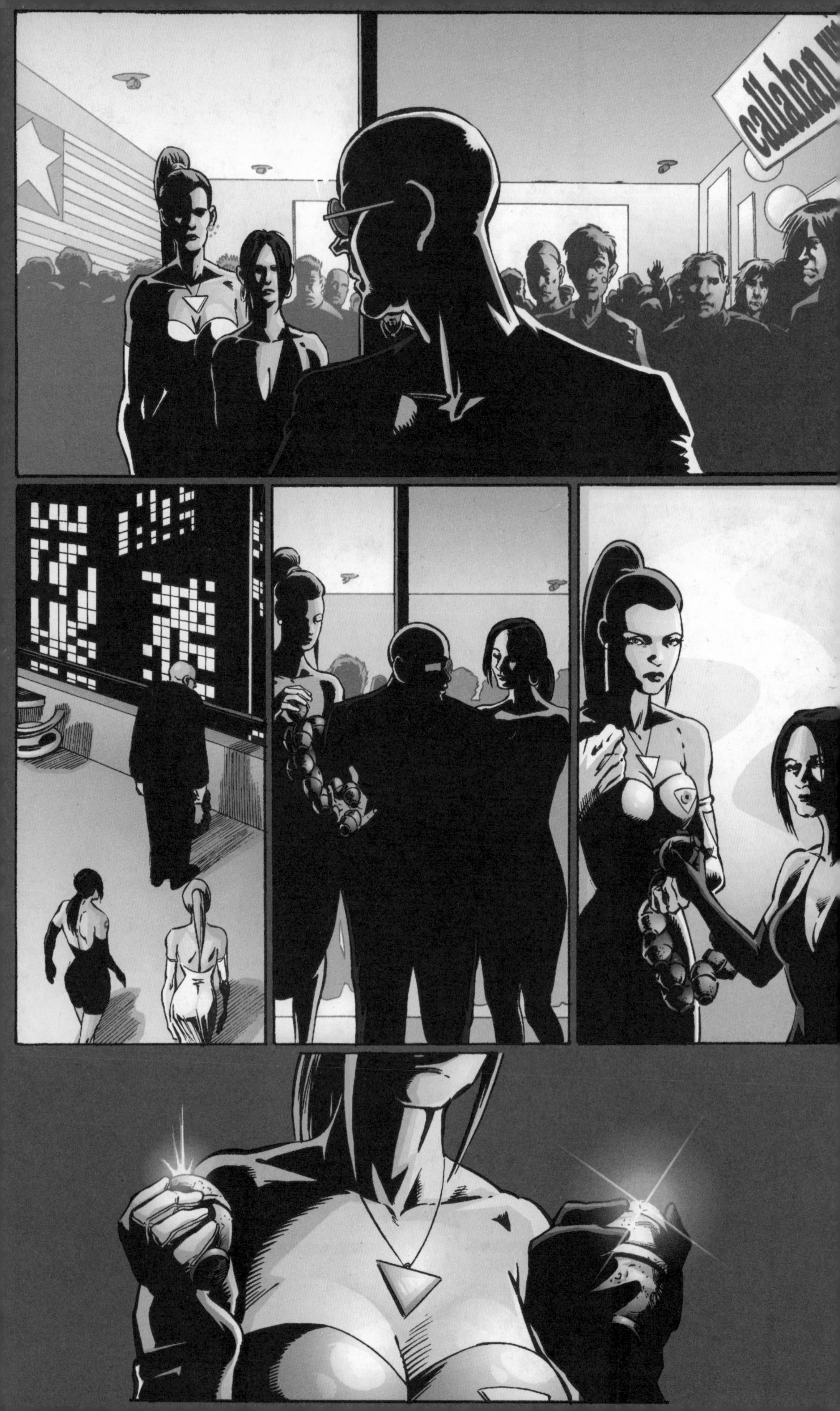
callahan

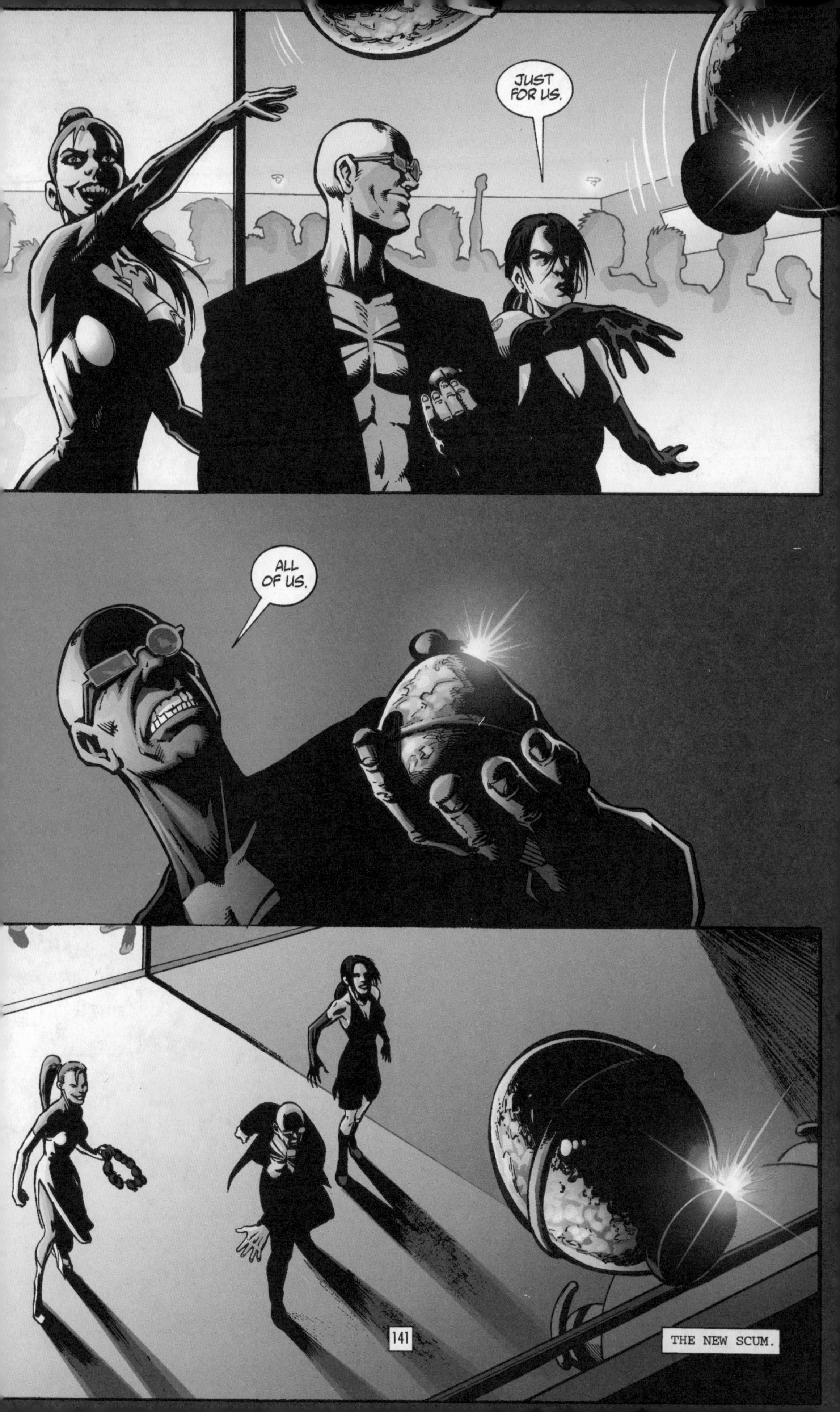
JUST FOR US.
ALL OF US.
THE NEW SCUM.

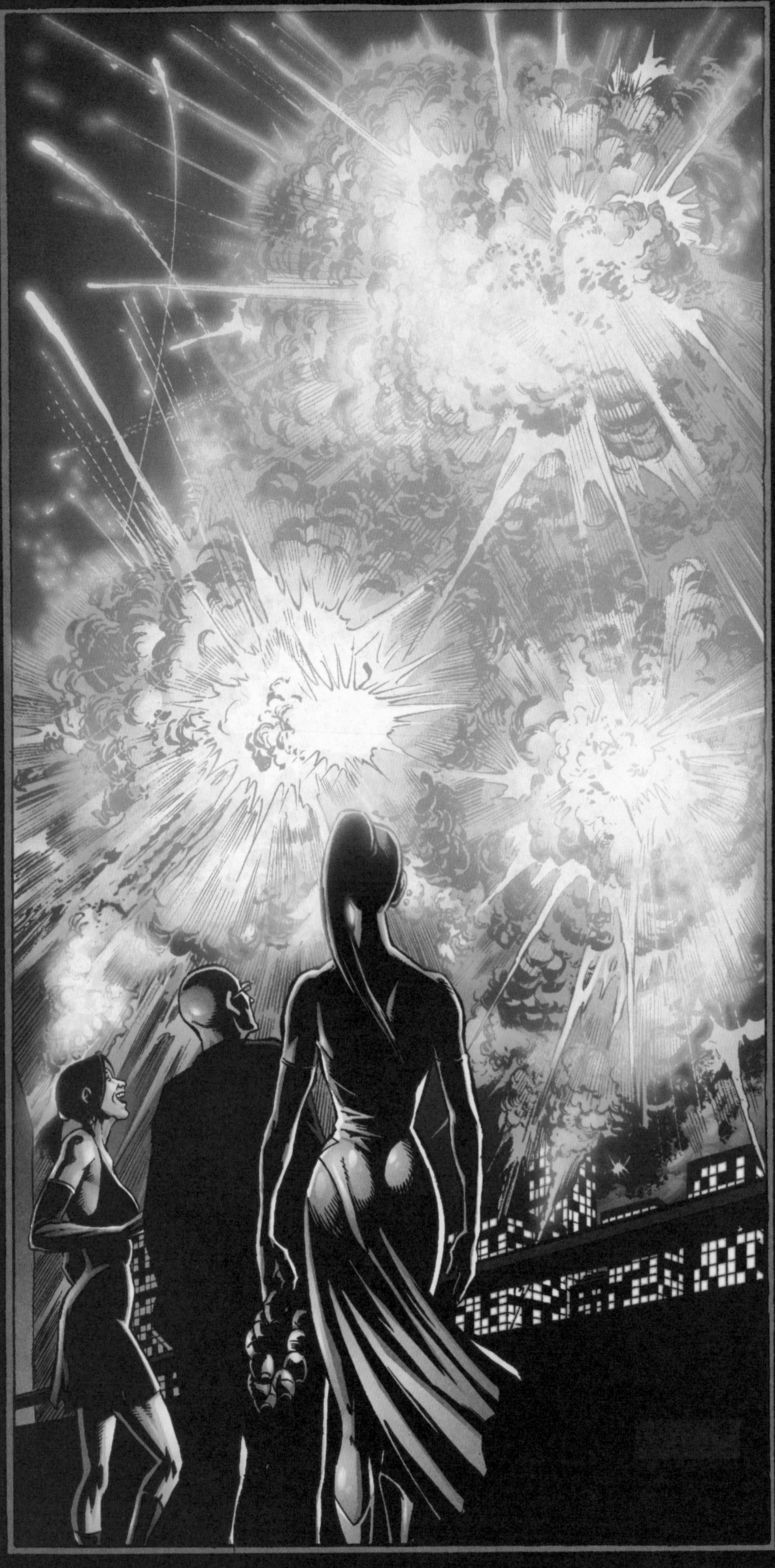

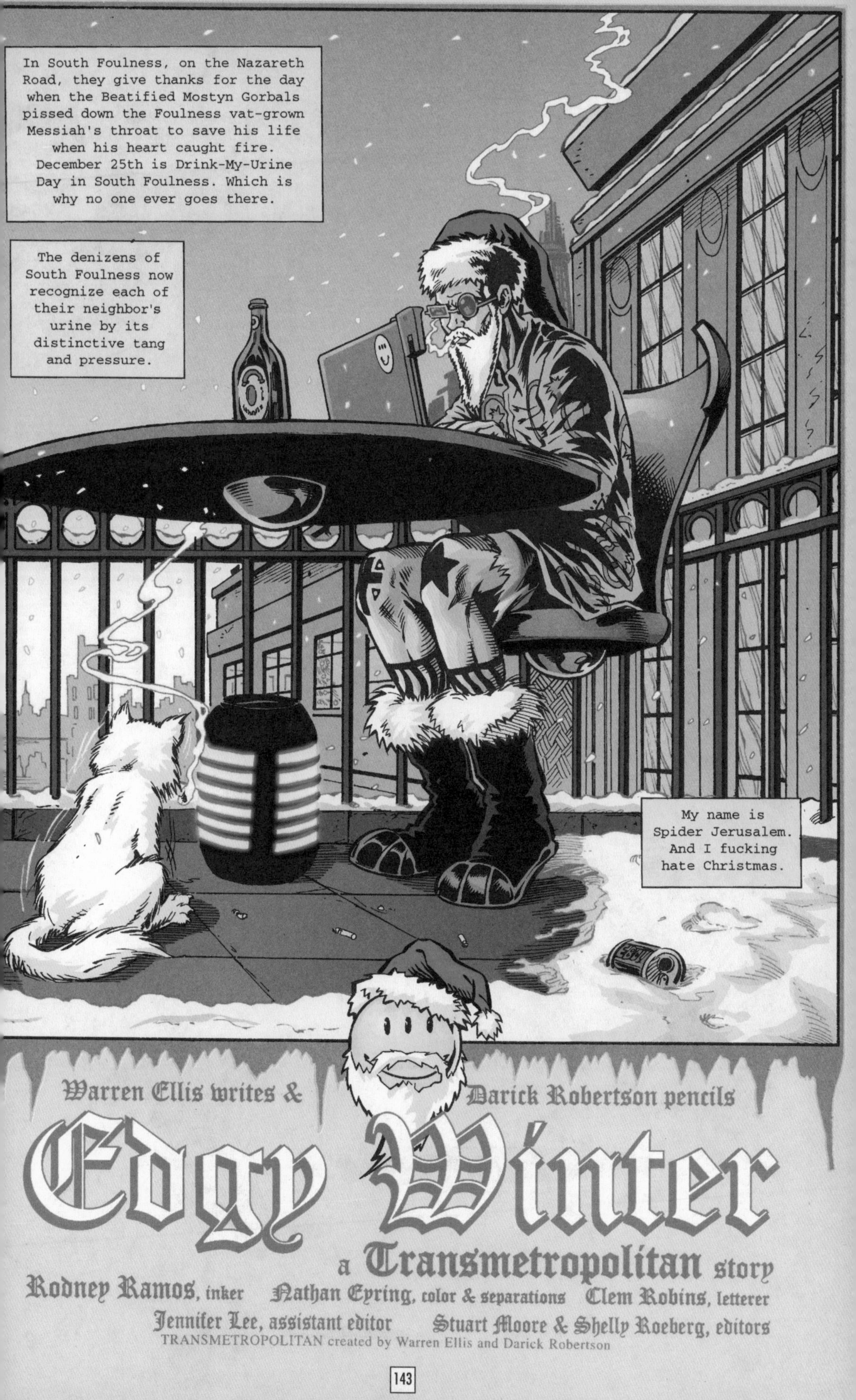
In South Foulness, on the Nazareth Road, they give thanks for the day when the Beatified Mostyn Gorbals pissed down the Foulness vat-grown Messiah's throat to save his life when his heart caught fire. December 25th is Drink-My-Urine Day in South Foulness. Which is why no one ever goes there.
The denizens of South Foulness now recognize each of their neighbor's urine by its distinctive tang and pressure.
My name is Spider Jerusalem. And I fucking hate Christmas.

Warren Ellis writes & Darick Robertson pencils

Edgy Winter

a Transmetropolitan story

Rodney Ramos, inker Nathan Eyring, color & separations Clem Robins, letterer
Jennifer Lee, assistant editor Stuart Moore & Shelly Roeberg, editors
TRANSMETROPOLITAN created by Warren Ellis and Darick Robertson

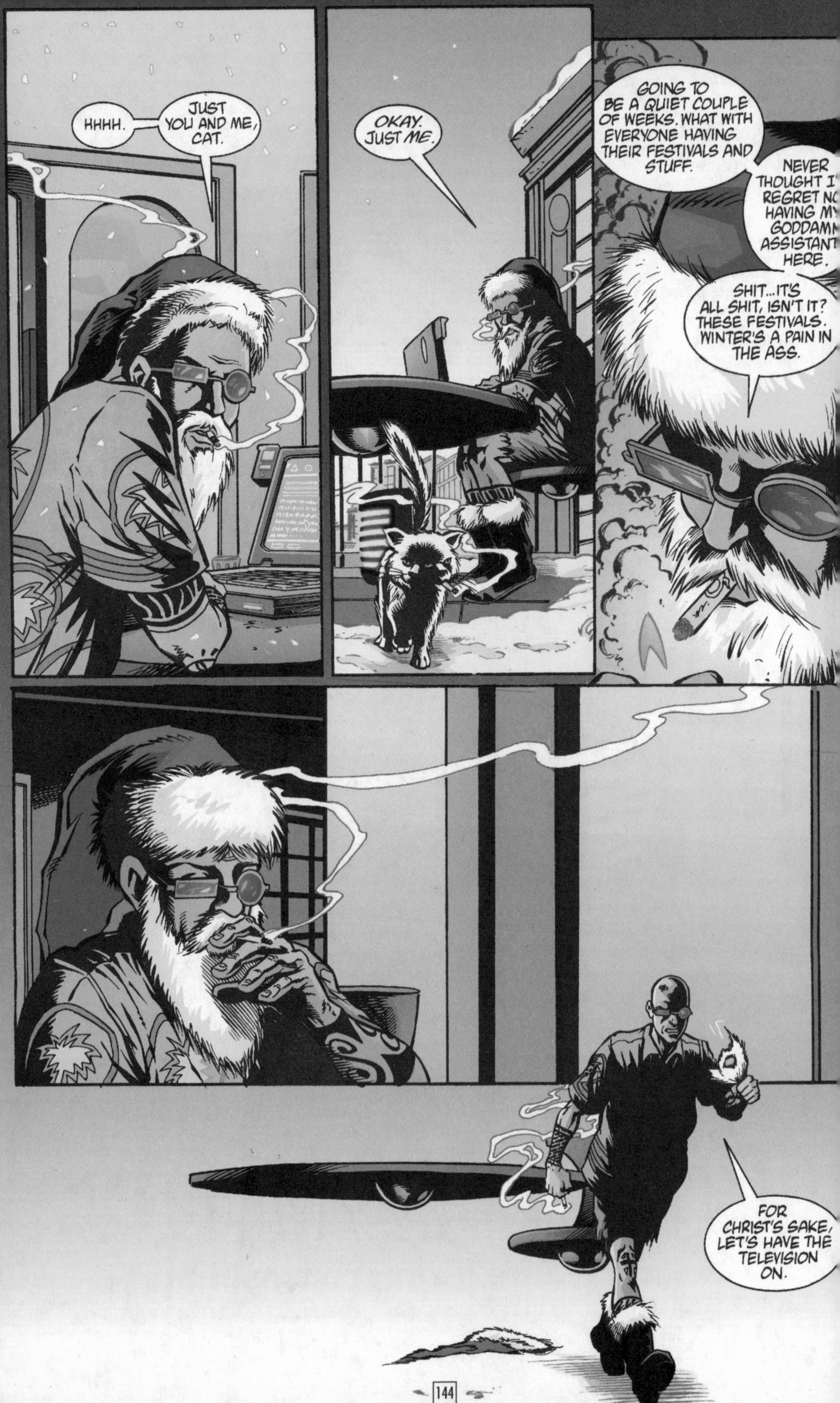
HHHH.
JUST YOU AND ME, CAT.
OKAY. JUST ME.
GOING TO BE A QUIET COUPLE OF WEEKS. WHAT WITH EVERYONE HAVING THEIR FESTIVALS AND STUFF.
NEVER THOUGHT I' REGRET NO HAVING MY GODDAM ASSISTANT HERE.
SHIT...IT'S ALL SHIT, ISN'T IT? THESE FESTIVALS. WINTER'S A PAIN IN THE ASS.
FOR CHRIST'S SAKE, LET'S HAVE THE TELEVISION ON.

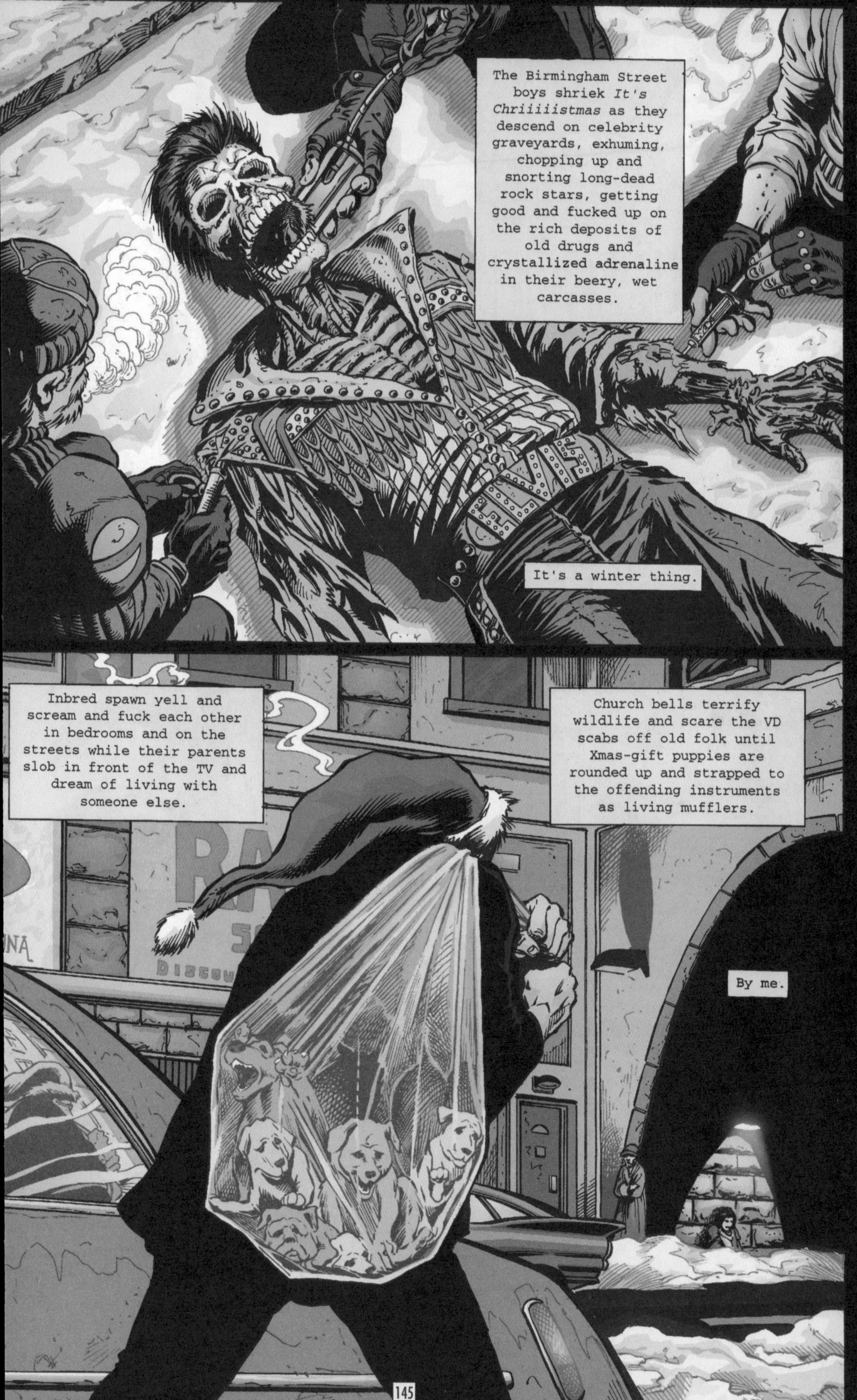

The Birmingham Street boys shriek *It's Chriiiiistmas* as they descend on celebrity graveyards, exhuming, chopping up and snorting long-dead rock stars, getting good and fucked up on the rich deposits of old drugs and crystallized adrenaline in their beery, wet carcasses.
It's a winter thing.
Inbred spawn yell and scream and fuck each other in bedrooms and on the streets while their parents slob in front of the TV and dream of living with someone else.
Church bells terrify wildlife and scare the VD scabs off old folk until Xmas-gift puppies are rounded up and strapped to the offending instruments as living mufflers.
By me.

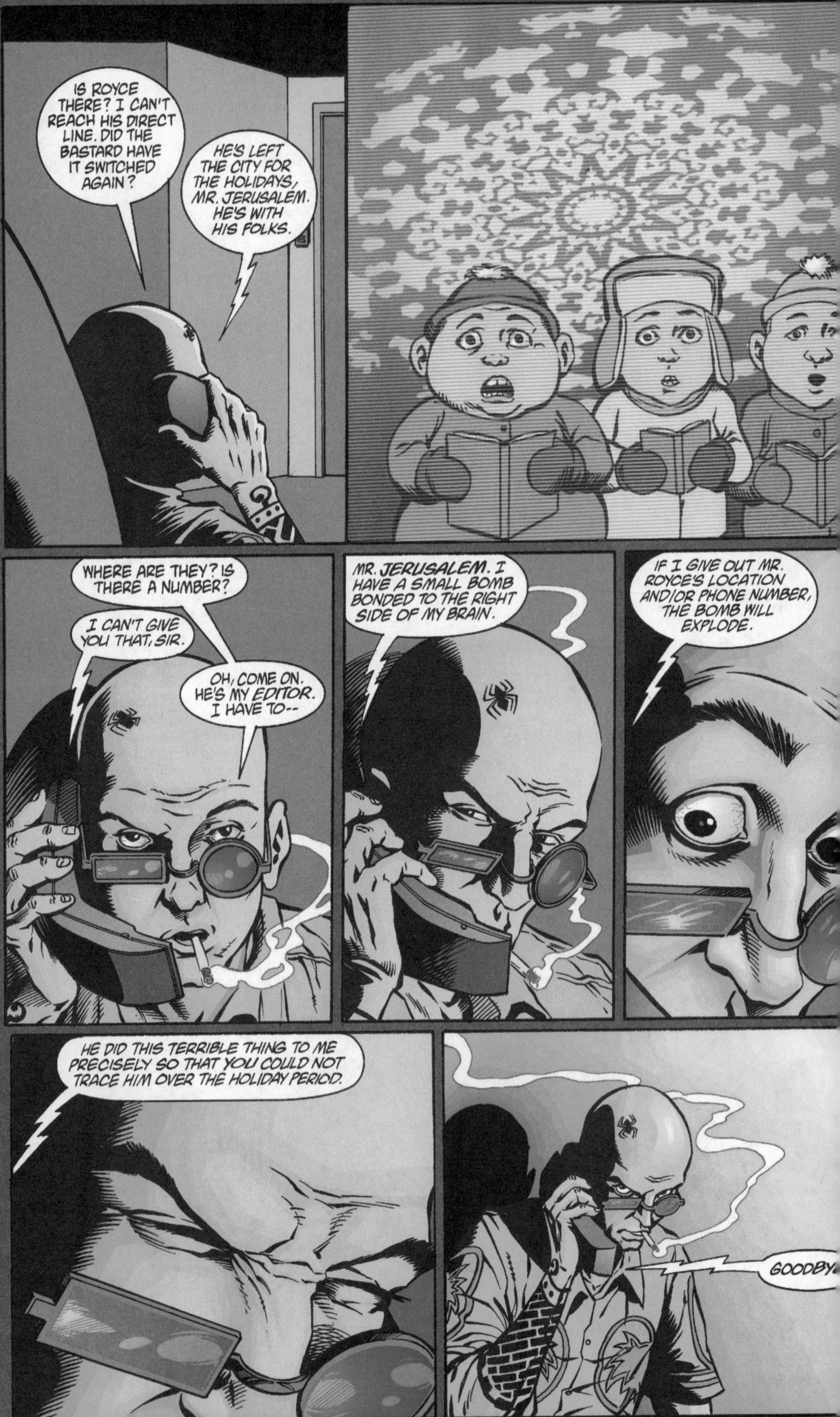
IS ROYCE THERE? I CAN'T REACH HIS DIRECT LINE. DID THE BASTARD HAVE IT SWITCHED AGAIN?
HE'S LEFT THE CITY FOR THE HOLIDAYS, MR. JERUSALEM. HE'S WITH HIS FOLKS.
WHERE ARE THEY? IS THERE A NUMBER?
I CAN'T GIVE YOU THAT, SIR.
OH, COME ON. HE'S MY EDITOR. I HAVE TO--
MR. JERUSALEM. I HAVE A SMALL BOMB BONDED TO THE RIGHT SIDE OF MY BRAIN.
IF I GIVE OUT MR. ROYCE'S LOCATION AND/OR PHONE NUMBER, THE BOMB WILL EXPLODE.
HE DID THIS TERRIBLE THING TO ME PRECISELY SO THAT YOU COULD NOT TRACE HIM OVER THE HOLIDAY PERIOD.
GOODBY

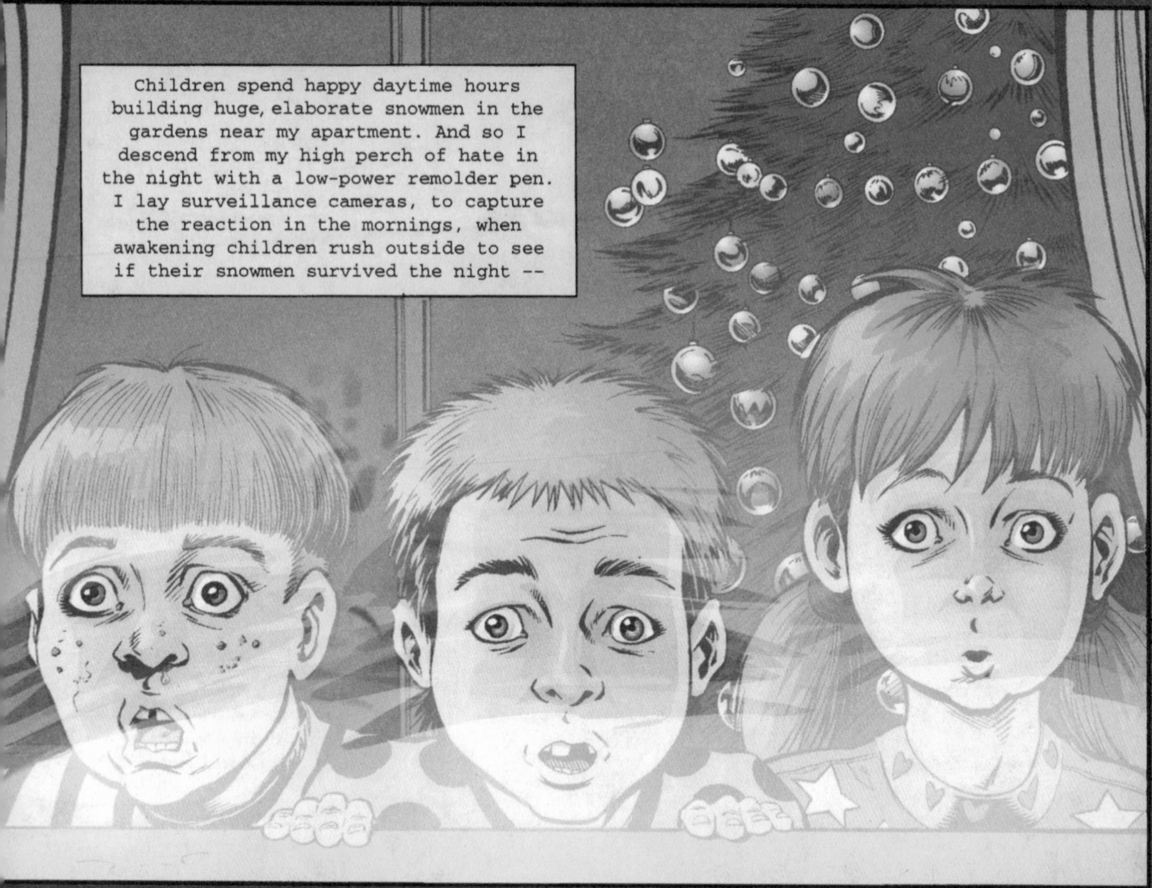
Children spend happy daytime hours building huge, elaborate snowmen in the gardens near my apartment. And so I descend from my high perch of hate in the night with a low-power remolder pen. I lay surveillance cameras, to capture the reaction in the mornings, when awakening children rush outside to see if their snowmen survived the night --

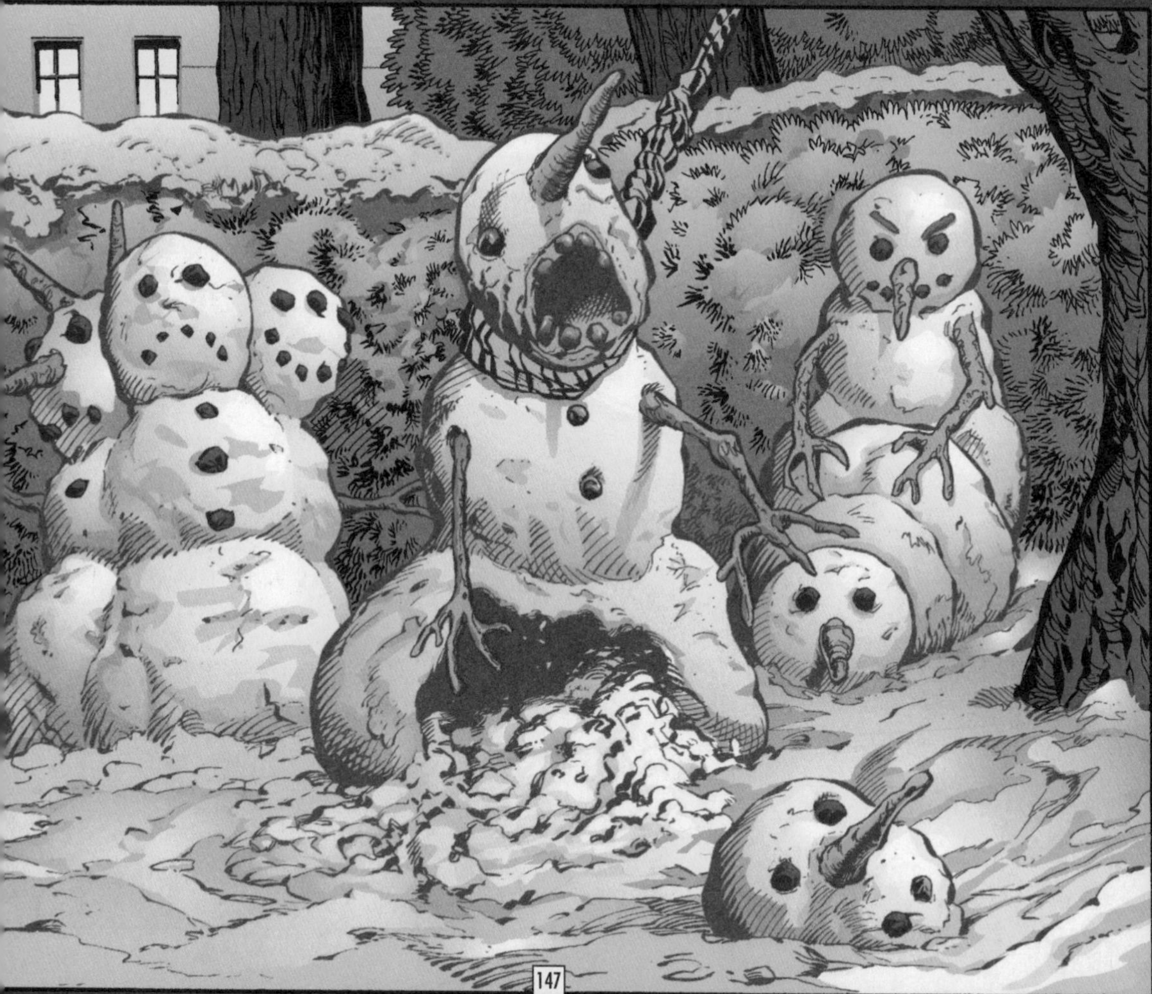

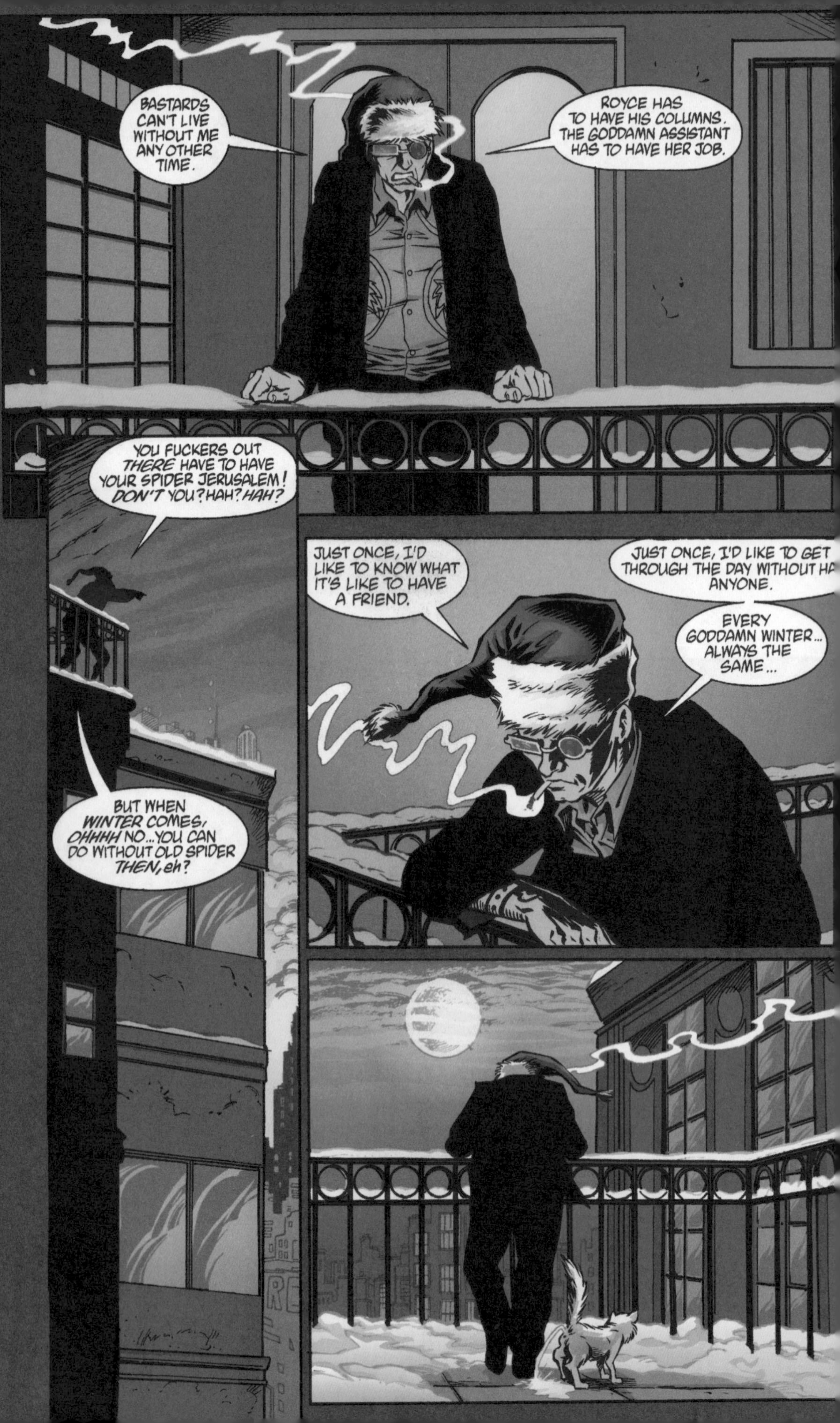
BASTARDS CAN'T LIVE WITHOUT ME ANY OTHER TIME.
ROYCE HAS TO HAVE HIS COLUMNS. THE GODDAMN ASSISTANT HAS TO HAVE HER JOB.
YOU FUCKERS OUT *THERE* HAVE TO HAVE YOUR SPIDER JERUSALEM! *DON'T* YOU? HAH? *HAH?*
BUT WHEN *WINTER COMES,* *OHHHH* NO...YOU CAN DO WITHOUT OLD SPIDER *THEN,* eh?
JUST ONCE, I'D LIKE TO KNOW WHAT IT'S LIKE TO HAVE A FRIEND.
JUST ONCE, I'D LIKE TO GET THROUGH THE DAY WITHOUT HA ANYONE.
EVERY GODDAMN WINTER... ALWAYS THE SAME...

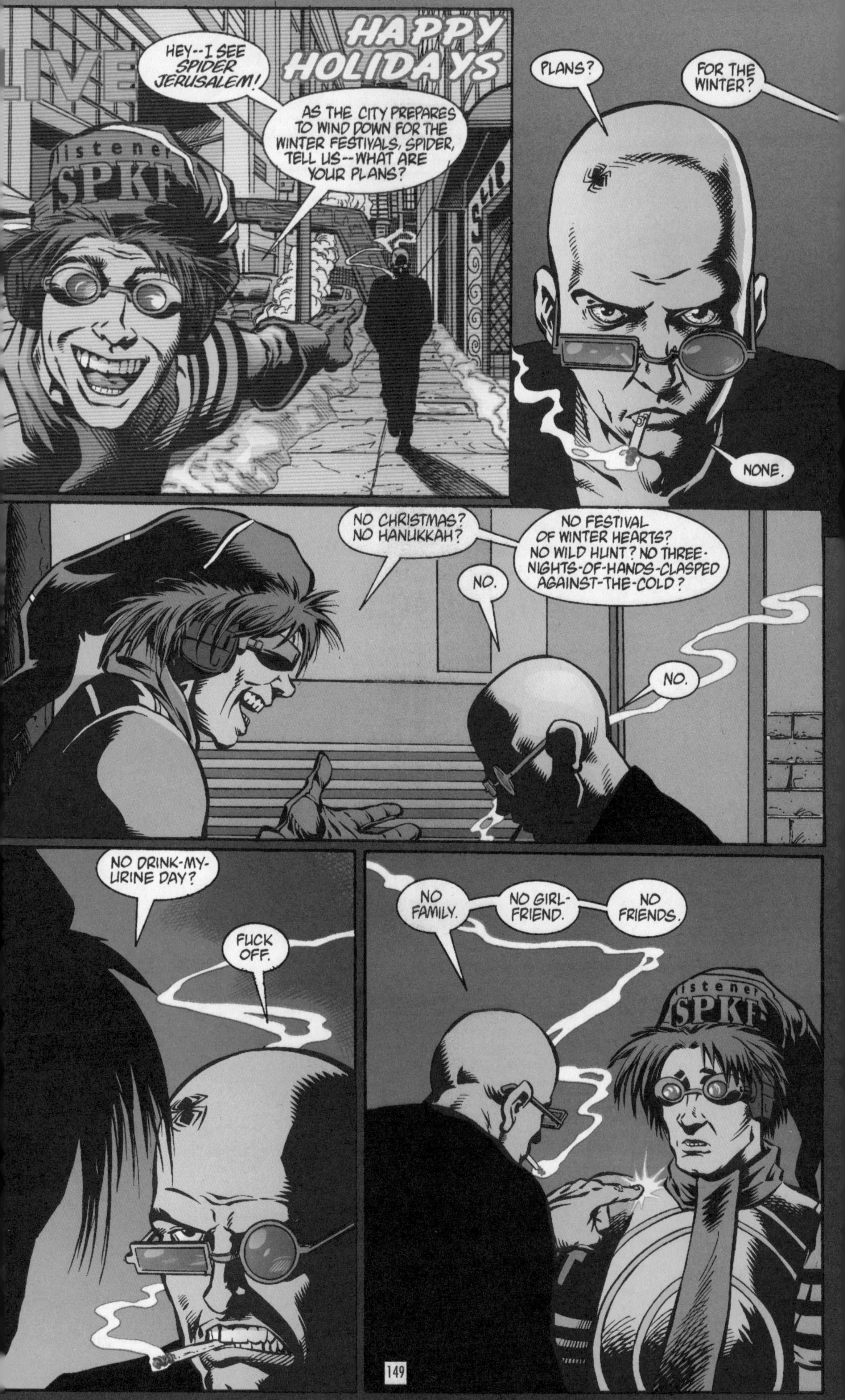
LIVE
HAPPY HOLIDAYS
HEY--I SEE SPIDER JERUSALEM!
AS THE CITY PREPARES TO WIND DOWN FOR THE WINTER FESTIVALS, SPIDER, TELL US--WHAT ARE YOUR PLANS?
listener SPKF
SLIP
PLANS?
FOR THE WINTER?
NONE.
NO CHRISTMAS? NO HANUKKAH?
NO.
NO FESTIVAL OF WINTER HEARTS? NO WILD HUNT? NO THREE-NIGHTS-OF-HANDS-CLASPED AGAINST-THE-COLD?
NO.
NO DRINK-MY-URINE DAY?
FUCK OFF.
NO FAMILY.
NO GIRL-FRIEND.
NO FRIENDS.
listener SPKF

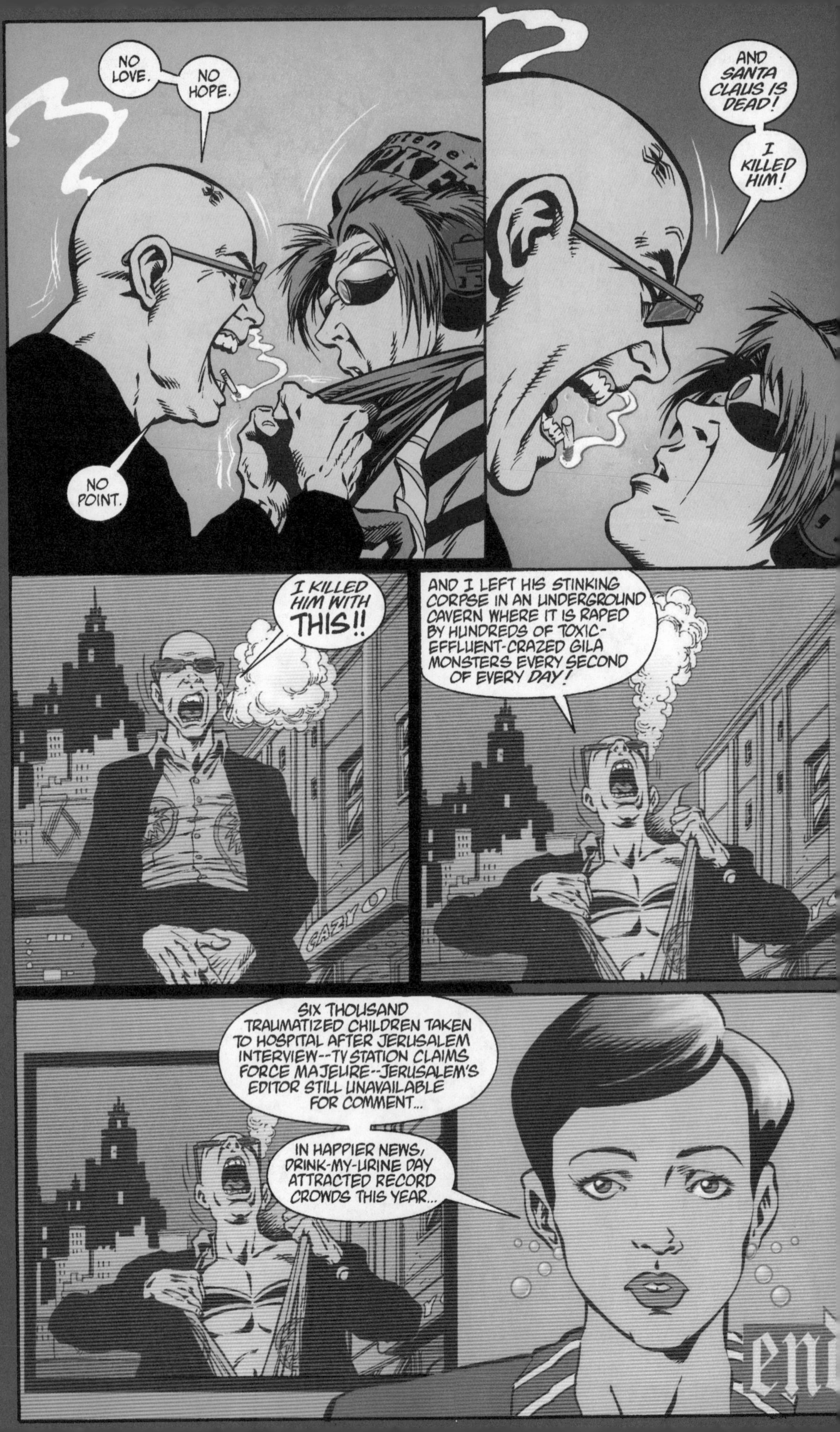
NO LOVE.
NO HOPE.
NO POINT.
AND SANTA CLAUS IS DEAD!
I KILLED HIM!
I KILLED HIM WITH THIS!!
AND I LEFT HIS STINKING CORPSE IN AN UNDERGROUND CAVERN WHERE IT IS RAPED BY HUNDREDS OF TOXIC-EFFLUENT-CRAZED GILA MONSTERS EVERY SECOND OF EVERY DAY!
SIX THOUSAND TRAUMATIZED CHILDREN TAKEN TO HOSPITAL AFTER JERUSALEM INTERVIEW--TV STATION CLAIMS FORCE MAJEURE--JERUSALEM'S EDITOR STILL UNAVAILABLE FOR COMMENT...
IN HAPPIER NEWS, DRINK-MY-URINE DAY ATTRACTED RECORD CROWDS THIS YEAR...

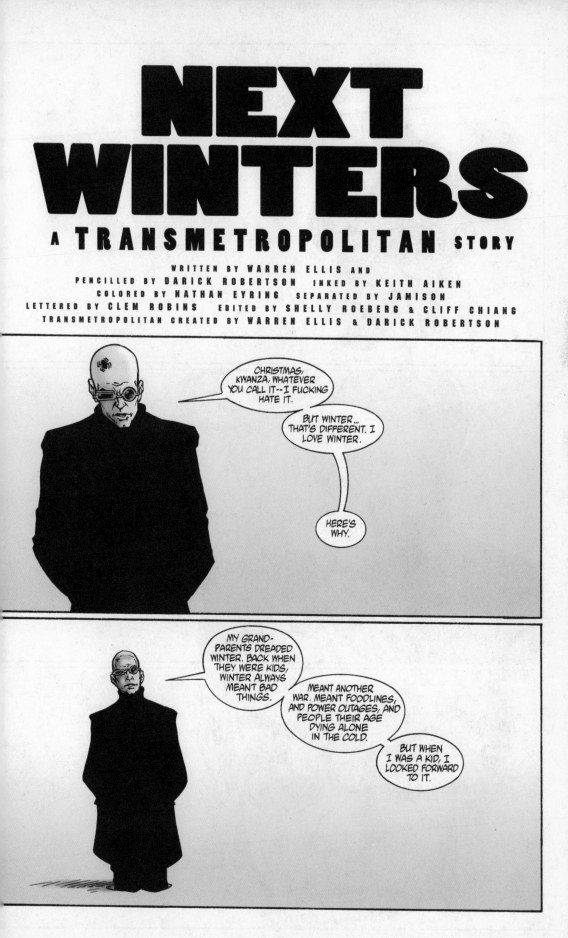

PLANETARY
1

PLANETARY
2

PLANETARY
3

PLANETARY
CROSSING WORLDS

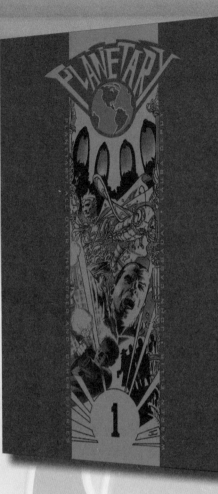

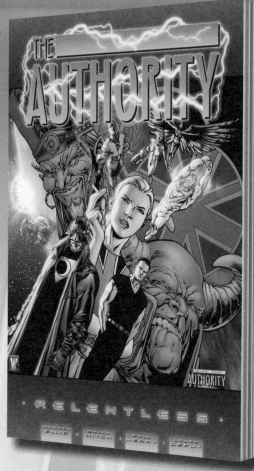

FROM INDIE COMICS SENSATION

BRIAN WOOD

DMZ
BRIAN WOOD RICCARDO BURCHIELLI
INTRODUCTION BY BRIAN AZZARELLO
"Gut-wrenchingly portrays the chaotic reality of life in a war zone." —WASHINGTON POST
ON THE GROUND
VERTIGO

"If residents of Manhattan often feel at odds with the rest of the country, the comic book series DMZ magnifies that anxiety with its radical premise."
–THE NEW YORK TIMES

"Measures up to any summer blockbuster."
–TIME OUT NEW YORK

"The dramatic images recall the nightly news, and stories of warzone life ring true. **GRADE: A-"**
– ENTERTAINMENT WEEKLY

"One of the strongest ongoing series to come out of DC's Vertigo line in some time. **GRADE: A-"**
–THE ONION

"Looking for the next FABLES or Y:THE LAST MAN? Look no further than... DMZ."
–WIZARD MAGAZINE

"Look out Willingham and Vaughan, Brian Wood has made DMZ one of the top three best Vertigo books."
– IGN.COM

DMZ VOL. 2:
BODY OF A JOURNALIST

DMZ
BRIAN WOOD RICCARDO BURCHIELLI KRISTIAN DONALDSON
BODY OF A JOURNALIST
VERTIGO

DMZ VOL. 3:
PUBLIC WORKS

DMZ
BRIAN WOOD RICCARDO BURCHIELLI
PUBLIC WORKS
INTRODUCTION BY CORY DOCTOROW
VERTIGO

DMZ VOL. 4:
FRIENDLY FIRE

DMZ
BRIAN WOOD / RICCARDO BURCHIELLI / NATHAN FOX
FRIENDLY FIRE
VERTIGO

GO TO
VERTIGOBOOKS.COM
FOR FREE SAMPLES OF THE FIRST ISSUES OF OUR GRAPHIC NOVELS

Suggested for Mature Readers

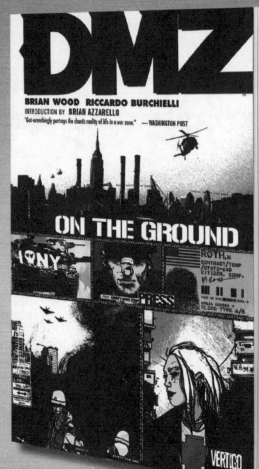

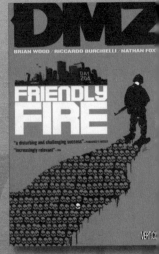